How to use your Connected Casebook

Step 1: Go to **www.CasebookConnect.com** and redeem your access code to get started.

Access Code:

Step 2: Go to your **BOOKSHELF** and select your Connected Casebook to start reading, highlighting, and taking notes in the margins of your e-book.

Step 3: Select the **STUDY** tab in your toolbar to access a variety of practice materials designed to help you master the course material. These materials may include explanations, videos, multiple-choice questions, flashcards, short answer, essays, and issue spotting.

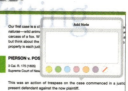

Step 4: Select the **OUTLINE** tab in your toolbar to access chapter outlines that automatically incorporate your highlights and annotations from the e-book. Use the My Notes area for copying, pasting, and editing your book notes or creating new notes.

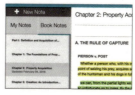

Step 5: If your professor has enrolled your class, you can select the **CLASS INSIGHTS** tab and compare your own study center results against the average of your classmates.

Is this a used casebook? Access code already scratched off?

You can purchase the Digital Version and still access all of the powerful tools listed above.
Please visit CasebookConnect.com and select Catalog to learn more.

PLEASE NOTE: Each access code can only be used once. This access code will expire one year after the discontinuation of the corresponding print title and must be redeemed before then. CCH reserves the right to discontinue this program at any time for any business reason. For further details, please see the Casebook Connect End User Agreement.

PIN: 9111149540

57217

Aspen Coursebook Series

Just Writing

Grammar, Punctuation, and Style for the Legal Writer

Fifth Edition

Anne Enquist
Professor Emerita
Seattle University School of Law

Laurel Currie Oates
Professor of Law
Seattle University School of Law

Jeremy Francis
Associate Clinical Professor of Law
Writing Specialist
Michigan State University College of Law

Wolters Kluwer

Published by Wolters Kluwer in New York.

Wolters Kluwer Legal & Regulatory U.S. serves customers worldwide with CCH, Aspen Publishers, and Kluwer Law International products. (www.WKLegaledu .com)

To contact Customer Service, e-mail customer.service@wolterskluwer.com, call 1-800-234-1660, fax 1-800-901-9075, or mail correspondence to:

Wolters Kluwer
Attn: Order Department
PO Box 990
Frederick, MD 21705

Printed in the United States of America.

3 4 5 6 7 8 9 0

ISBN 978-1-4548-8080-6

Library of Congress Cataloging-in-Publication Data
Names: Enquist, Anne, 1950- author. | Oates, Laurel Currie, 1951- author. |
   Francis, Jeremy, (Law teacher) author.
Title: Just writing : grammar, punctuation, and style for the legal writer /
   Anne Enquist, Professor Emerita Seattle University School of Law, Laurel
   Currie Oates, Professor of Law Seattle University School of Law, Jeremy
   Francis, Associate Clinical Professor of Law, Writing Specialist, Michigan
   State University College of Law.
Description: Fifth Edition | New York : Wolters Kluwer Law & Business, [2017]
Identifiers: LCCN 2016059826 | ISBN 9781454880806
Subjects: LCSH: Legal composition. | Legal correspondence--United States.
Classification: LCC KF250 .E57 2017 | DDC 808.06/634--dc23
LC record available at https://lccn.loc.gov/2016059826

About Wolters Kluwer Legal & Regulatory U.S.

Wolters Kluwer Legal & Regulatory U.S. delivers expert content and solutions in the areas of law, corporate compliance, health compliance, reimbursement, and legal education. Its practical solutions help customers successfully navigate the demands of a changing environment to drive their daily activities, enhance decision quality and inspire confident outcomes.

Serving customers worldwide, its legal and regulatory portfolio includes products under the Aspen Publishers, CCH Incorporated, Kluwer Law International, ftwilliam.com and MediRegs names. They are regarded as exceptional and trusted resources for general legal and practice-specific knowledge, compliance and risk management, dynamic workflow solutions, and expert commentary.

To our students,
who have inspired us by
their commitment to becoming excellent writers

Summary of Contents

Contents

Acknowledgments

Writing and publishing this book would not have been possible without the support of our law schools and our deans. Our deepest thanks to Seattle University School of Law and especially Dean Annette Clark for her years of support, encouragement, and friendship. This edition would not have been possible without the guidance and support of Michigan State University College of Law Deans Lawrence Ponoroff and Joan Howarth.

We would like to acknowledge two groups of people for their contributions to this book: our legal writing colleagues and our legal writing students. Chief among the legal writing colleagues that we would like to thank are Jessie Grearson, Susan McClellan, and Lorraine Bannai. Their insights about writing and how to teach writing were invaluable.

The examples throughout the book are primarily taken from the work of our former students. We are particularly grateful to Annette Clark, Luanne Coachman, Mary Lobdell, Eileen Peterson, Lance Palmer, Edwina Martin-Arnold, Vonda Sargent, Melissa May, Kevin Dougherty, Cindy Burdue, Amy Blume, Chris Fredrikson, Nancy Bradburn-Johnson, Susan McClellan, James Harlan Corning, and J. Spencer Thorson for allowing us to use their student writing as examples.

In addition, the chapter on "Legal Writing for English-as-a-Second-Language Writers" would not have been possible without the help of several colleagues and students. Thanks to Donn R. Callaway for his guidance as we first began to explore this topic, to Dana Yaffee, Linda Chu, and Ekaterina Markova for their excellent research, and to Jessie Grearson and Jeffrey Gore for their comments and suggestions on early drafts. Thanks too to our many ESL law students who inspired us with their dedication and hard work. We are particularly grateful to Stephanie Ko, NeliEspe, Nicolay Kvasnyuk, Masha Fartoutchnaia, Linda Chu, Meihuei Hu, and Julian Lin for allowing us to use their writing as examples and for reading early drafts of the chapter and suggesting changes. Thanks to Erin Shea, Mary Shea, and Professor Teri Mcmurtry-Chubb for their assistance with the bias-free language section; to Kelly Dalcin for her work updating many examples; to Regina Henenlotter, Brianna Venturo, and Natalie Schultz for their excellent organizational support; and to Carmen Butler for her research on procrastination. Cynthia Chu and Brent Domann were instrumental in helping us update many examples.

The diagnostic test that is available with this edition has also been a collaborative effort. Special thanks to Connie Krontz and Judi Maier for their help with early versions of the test, to all the Seattle University School of Law legal writing faculty in 2001-02 for helping us iron out the kinks, and to Professor Nancy Wanderer and her students at the University of Maine School of Law for "testing the test" in the fall of 2001.

Just Writing

Introduction

Writing in the law—people who are new to the field always want to know whether it will be similar to the writing they have done before or totally different. The good news for novice legal writers is that it has more similarities than differences from other kinds of writing. Legal writing relies on organizational patterns and traditional ways of connecting ideas that, for the most part, resemble the organizational patterns and connections of many other kinds of writing. Like most other writing, correct grammar and punctuation are assumed. More important, just as in any other kind of writing, the decisions a legal writer must make always depend on the reader, the purpose of the writing, the author's role in the larger context in which the piece of writing exists, and the conventions for the type of document being written.

The differences from other types of writing are perhaps most obvious in legal writing's conventions. Aside from the dramatic differences in citation format, legal writing differs from many other types of writing because it is more formal. Lawyers tend to avoid first-person pronouns, contractions, abbreviations in text, idiomatic phrases and slang (unless these occur in a quotation), and punctuation marks such as dashes or exclamation points that may suggest informality.

Because of the complexity of much of the material they write about, lawyers adhere to the convention of using explicit organizational references. Roadmaps (e.g., "the person trying to establish title must prove five elements of adverse possession . . .") and signposts ("the first element . . .")

may initially feel obvious and heavy-handed to novice legal writers, but legal readers seem to want, expect, and even demand them. Complexity also prompts legal writers to sum up frequently; closure after each section in the discussion of a legal issue is highly valued. The effect of numerous mini-conclusions, combined with an overall conclusion, is that legal readers often feel led by the hand to the position the writer wants those readers to adopt.

A more subtle challenge for new legal writers is distinguishing which writing virtues are highly prized and which are not. Highest on the list are what one judge[1] has dubbed the ABC's of legal writing: accuracy, brevity, and clarity. Accurate representation of the facts, law, and cases is crucial. Misstatements, even small ones, can have severe consequences, both for clients and for the reputations, credibility, and careers of the lawyers who make them.

Brevity is a legal writing virtue that seems to get the most attention. The public shakes its head about the flood of paper that some lawsuits generate, and many in the profession love to say things such as "briefs should be brief." Virtually all legal readers, particularly judges, rail about verbosity because they quickly realize that wordy writers consume more than their share of time and energy. The brevity bandwagon is an easy one to jump on; it seems that long-winded, rambling writing is a waste of everyone's time.

The issue of brevity in legal writing is more nuanced, however, than it first appears. While it is true that being concise is highly valued, skillful legal writers often use selective repetition to emphasize a point. In advocacy writing, favorable facts get more airtime, while unfavorable facts get the briefest mention possible. A key advocacy notion, having a theory of the case, means that the writer has a theme that must be skillfully repeated and reinforced throughout a persuasive piece of writing. Brevity, then, is an important virtue, but one must know how and *when* to be brief.

Clarity is another legal writing virtue that may seem straightforward but in fact deserves closer examination. At first it may seem that everyone agrees on the importance of clarity in legal writing. From many states' legislation requiring clear, easy-to-understand consumer contracts to former Chief Justice William H. Rehnquist's published statement that "an ability to write clearly has become the most important prerequisite for an American appellate lawyer,"[2] one could easily surmise that clarity is a bedrock principle of good legal writing. In most cases it is. Nevertheless, there are instances when a certain amount of deliberate vagueness is in the client's best interests. This is not to suggest that lawyers should misuse language to hide culpability or deceive readers. Rather, deliberate vagueness can be appropriate when all parties want to retain some flexibility, when crystal clear language would misrepresent a truly fuzzy reality. Intentional vagueness is certainly appropriate in drafting some legislation.

---

[1] Chief Judge Emeritus Edward D. Re, the Court of International Trade, in his remarks to the Legal Writing Institute National Conference (1988).

[2] From Webster to Word-Processing: the Ascendance of the Appellate Brief, 1 J. App. Prac. & Process 1, 3 (1999).

Also at the top of the list of legal writing virtues are the paired traits, "well researched" and "well supported." Whether in a brief or a law review article, points are not persuasive to legal readers unless they are supported by statutes, case law, the record, or other recognized authority. Interjecting personal opinion or other editorial asides may be well received or simply tolerated in other types of writing, but in legal writing they are treated as a novice's mistakes.

In contrast, variety in writing, particularly variety in vocabulary, is not the typical virtue in legal writing that it is in many other types of writing. Indeed, when it comes to key terms, using the same term over and over again is expected. The conventional wisdom about this expectation is that using synonyms may create confusion; a different term for the same idea suggests to legal readers that the writer intended a difference in meaning. Such consistency may seem boring at first, but legal readers prefer clarity, even if it is boring, over variety that may be confusing.

Finally, because legal writing occurs in the context of the adversarial legal system, legal writers have to be more careful than most other writers. All of one's readers in the law are not friendly readers who are willing to fill in the blanks or overlook small and not so small errors. Mistakes are chinks in the armor, weak links that an adversary may use to his or her advantage.

The preceding discussion may make legal writing seem like a minefield. It isn't. Rather, it is a specific genre of writing, as distinct as poetry writing or screenwriting or writing repair manuals for automobiles. It has some things in common with all good writing, and it has its own unique features. The trick is to pay attention: Learn what you can apply from what you knew before about writing and learn what is new and different. *Just Writing* will help you do just that.

By purchasing a copy of this book, you have access to practice exercises that are designed to reinforce the advice about writing style and the rules of grammar and punctuation. This edition also includes "Quick Tips" about writing. The "Quick Tips" are interspersed through the chapters and are identified in the margin by the ⊕ icon. These tips will help you learn applied solutions to common problems that emerge in legal writing. Refer to the sticker on the inside front cover of your book for instructions on accessing the website where the exercises and Quick Tips are available. Visit www.CasebookConnect .com/Resources for more information.

The chapters in *Just Writing* are excerpted from *The Legal Writing Handbook*. They have been renumbered and condensed. Part I, "A Guide to Effective Writing," focuses on how general principles of good writing manifest themselves in legal writing. Part II, "A Guide to Correct Writing," focuses on correct grammar and punctuation as they apply to legal writing. Part III, "A Guide to Legal Writing for English-as-a-Second-Language Writers," which is specially designed for legal writers who speak and write English as a second language, focuses on special ESL grammar issues and on the rhetorical differences that writers from other cultures face in legal writing. The Glossary of Usage that follows Part III gives helpful hints on troublesome pairs such as "affect/effect" and "who/whom."

Just Writing, then, tries to live up to all three interpretations of its title. It is "just the writing" sections of *The Legal Writing Handbook.* It is "just writing" in the sense that it covers only the writing aspects of legal writing, not the research and legal analysis. And it is "just" writing in the sense that it is not a generic writing book; it is a book that focuses on writing about the law in an ongoing effort to do justice.

A Guide to Effective Writing

This part of the book gives legal writers general recommendations and rules of thumb about what makes some legal writing effective. We believe what follows is good advice, but we also want to alert readers to three caveats about the notion of "effective legal writing."

First, effectiveness in legal writing is a relative thing. The same level of effectiveness is not needed in every situation. The trick, of course, is to make the writing effective enough so that it accomplishes its goal without laboring over it to the point that it consumes all of the working day and night. In short, some balance is appropriate.

Second, effectiveness in legal writing, and in all writing for that matter, always depends on the context. What will please and even delight one reader may irritate or anger another. An organizational scheme that is effective in one instance may be dead wrong in another. Even precision and conciseness, those most sought-after characteristics of effective legal writing, can be ineffective in some instances in which vagueness and verbosity accomplish the desired objective. In other words, writing that most readers would consider competent, stylistically pleasing, and even eloquent in the abstract but that does not work in a given context is, in that context, ineffective.

Finally, effectiveness is a fairly subjective notion. Again, we can give you the standard advice and some insights of our own about what is and is not effective legal writing, but ultimately you must determine whether you think something works. If, as you are writing a given piece, your instincts tell you it is working (or it is not working) and all the theory and advice tell you the opposite, we suggest that you look at it again. If your instincts and common sense still insist that the conventional wisdom about effective legal writing is not working here, trust your instincts.

1

Effective Writing—The Whole Paper

§ 1.1 The Psychology of Writing

Legal writing is not for the faint-hearted. It takes courage, perseverance, creativity, and flexibility, not to mention intelligence and a solid foundation of writing skills. A fair number of lawyers and judges profess to like writing and even say that they find the process satisfying. If you are in this fortunate group, this section is not addressed to you.

If you are among the less fortunate—those who have felt overwhelmed by the prospect of writing, who have struggled with writer's block, or who have found writing to be a difficult, perhaps even painful, process—there is hope. Writing, like most other skills, becomes more pleasurable with each successful experience. It also helps to know where the usual stumbling blocks are in the process and how to get past them.

Few legal writers have trouble getting started on the research phase of a writing project. Many encounter their first stumbling block when it is time to move from research to writing. A typical avoidance mechanism is to keep researching long past the point of need. Writers who have developed this pattern of approaching writing tasks usually postpone putting fingers to keyboard until the last possible moment. Then they write, almost out of desperation, and end up turning in as a final product something that is really a rough draft. By getting stuck at the research phase of the writing

See Quick Tip:
Defeating
Procrastination

process, they make it virtually impossible to do any quality drafting, revising, editing, and proofreading. The result is yet another unsatisfying writing experience.

If this describes your typical writing process, you may be able to break this habit by developing a schedule for the completion of the entire document. In this schedule, allot a reasonable amount of time to complete the research but be firm about when you will begin writing. Give yourself mini-deadlines for completing an outline, producing a first draft, revising, editing, and proofreading. Allow breathing room in this timetable for problems such as a printer malfunction or a flat tire. If at all possible, plan as though your deadline is sooner than the real deadline. To do this, you may find it easier to write the schedule backwards, starting with the final deadline and allowing time for proofreading, then editing, all the way back to research.

Chart 1.1   Sample Schedule for a Two-Week Writing Project

Week 1   Research and organize research
Week 2   Day 1 brainstorm, create plan, outline
          Day 2 drafting
          Day 3 drafting
          Day 4 revising
          Day 5 editing, last-minute citation checks
          Day 6 proofreading
          Day 7 final product (ready a day early!)

For shorter time frames and quick turnarounds, a writing schedule is even more critical. In such cases, you will probably be working with half-day, quarter-day, or even hour units, but the principles are still the same. Figure out how much of the total time should be spent researching and how much should be spent writing. Create mini-deadlines for yourself. Start with your final deadline and work backwards as you plan.

Chart 1.2   Sample Schedule for a Two-Day Writing Project

Day 1   Research and organize research
Day 2   By 10:00 a.m. brainstorm, plan outline
         By 2:00 p.m. drafting
         By 3:00 p.m. revising
         By 4:00 p.m. editing
         By 4:30 p.m. proofreading
         By 5:00 p.m. final product completed (and in the partner's hands!)

With practice, you may find that you don't need as much time for research and that you can begin to allow a larger percentage of your time for writing.

Schedules are invaluable, but many writers need more than a schedule to get them started writing. It is an enormous help if your research notes are organized in a way that will facilitate the writing process. Instead of organizing your research around cases, organize it around the law or the points you want to make. For example, once you have identified the steps in the analysis, create a template for your document and, as you research, place the information that you find under the appropriate heading or headings. In the alternative, you can color code either the electronic copies of the authorities or any photocopies you made of those authorities. Color coding helps during the drafting phase because it gives you a quick way to gather up all the information you have collected on a given point (grab all the yellow) and then physically order those sheets. The same sheets may have other colors on them, but while you are writing about the "yellow point" you can stay focused on the part of the notes and photocopied cases that concern that point. When it comes time to do the "blue point," the blue sheets get picked up and ordered into the information about that point.

If color coding does not appeal to you, you may find that having separate file folders or a tabbed notebook works for you. The key is to develop files or sections of the notebook for the points you want to make in the whole document, not separate files or notebook sections for each analogous case. This means you may need two or more photocopies of the same page of a case so that it may be filed under each of the appropriate points.

§ 1.2 Outlines, Writing Plans, and Ordered Lists

For professional writers (and lawyers are professional writers) who must organize extensive and complex material, spending time creating an outline or writing plan or even just an ordered list almost always saves time in the end. Done properly, an outline or plan will keep you from backtracking, repeating yourself, missing a key point, or only discovering what it is you want to say after you have written the whole thing the wrong way.

But creating order in extensive and complex material is not easy; it takes the writer's complete attention. Consequently, this task deserves a distinct block of time. Don't fall into the trap of trying to create order at the same time you are drafting sentences and paragraphs. That approach is needlessly stressful because it forces you to keep track of several big tasks all at once.

Writing a good outline or plan may also mean that you have to change some of your preconceived ideas about outlines. First of all, the outline or plan is for you, the writer, not for a teacher or future reader. Roman numerals and capital A's and B's are not important. Use them if they help; discard them if they hinder. If you discard the roman numerals, letters, and numbers, keep the indentations. They will help you distinguish among main points, subpoints, sub-subpoints, and supporting details.

There are as many ways to go about creating an outline or writing plan as there are writers. The rest of this section describes some time-tested techniques that you may find helpful.

§ 1.2.1 Read It All; Mull It Over

Before beginning to write the outline or plan, read through all of your research. Let your mind mull it over while you do some mindless task such as mowing the lawn, swimming laps, or taking a bath. While you are engaged in the mindless task, your mind will almost certainly begin organizing the ideas.

§ 1.2.2 Don't Overlook Obvious Ways to Organize

One obvious way of beginning to organize is to determine how the court will approach the problem. Are there any threshold questions the court will consider first? If so, place them first in your outline. What will the court look at and decide second, third, and so on? Your organizational scheme should mirror the process the court will follow.

Furthermore, in creating an organization for your document, do not assume that you always have to create a brand-new, never-seen-before organizational scheme. Most documents fit comfortably in one of the common organizational plans. Borrow freely from the bank of common knowledge about how to organize an elements analysis, a balancing test, or a discussion of the development of a trend, to name but a few. Many discussion sections follow an IRAC (issue, rule, analysis, conclusion) plan or use mini-IRACs in some of the sections.

§ 1.2.3 Find Order Using a Three-Column Chart

The three-column chart can be an effective way to find order in a document, particularly when the document does not immediately appear to fall into any of the typical organizational patterns. In the first column, make one giant list of everything you think the final document should include. Be as comprehensive as possible. Dump everything you have in your brain about the problem into this list. Do not worry about the order of the items.

Once Column One is complete, use Column Two to begin doing some preliminary ordering of the list in Column One. Column One will probably already contain some natural groupings of ideas. If so, place them together in Column Two at roughly the point in the document where you guess they will go.

Use Column Three to further refine the order of the list. This is the time to test out various places where the stray items may fit. Also check to see if you forgot anything. Look for all the standard features of legal analysis (burden of proof, plain language arguments, policy arguments, and so on) and all the standard "moves" a lawyer makes (argument, counterargument, rebuttal, countervailing policy argument, and so on).

Working in this way, you will find that the secret to the three-column chart is that you focus on one main task with each column, and as you move through the columns, you get more and more control over the material until voilà! You have an outline.

§ 1.2.4 Talk to a Colleague

Whenever you are having trouble getting a large amount of material organized in your mind, try talking it over with a colleague. Use the approach that you are going to explain the issues to your listener. As you are talking, notice how you naturally organize the material. Jot down key words and phrases that come to mind as you are speaking. Don't be afraid to talk through the parts with which you are having the most difficulty. It may free you to address these areas if you begin by saying something like, "this is the part I'm having trouble with" or "this is the part that is still rough in my mind." Let your listener question you and provide his or her own insights.

If talking out the issues seemed helpful, sit down immediately afterwards and write out the organization you discovered as you were speaking. Then, if talking-before-writing becomes a valuable organizing technique for you, you may even want to record the talking-before-writing sessions.

§ 1.2.5 Try a New Analogy or Format

If you have a phobia about outlines, rename what it is you are doing when you develop the organization for a document. Some writers are more comfortable developing a "writing plan." Others like to think in terms of an "ordered list." You may need an entirely new analogy for what you are doing. Think instead of an architect creating a blueprint for a building or an engineer designing an aircraft.

Some people prefer horizontal flow charts to vertical outlines. There is nothing magical about organizing ideas from top to bottom in an outline. If working from left to right in a flow chart feels more comfortable to you, do it.

Others can find and better visualize an organizational scheme by using a technique called "clustering." To use clustering, simply begin by putting one main idea in a circle and then attach related nodes. Exhibit 1.1 is an example of a basic cluster.

Once you have a basic cluster, begin a new circle for each main idea, each time attaching related subpoints. See Exhibit 1.2 for an expanded but not yet complete cluster for the same case. By continuing to expand the cluster diagram, you will end up with a map of how your mind is thinking about a legal problem.

Now look for clusters of ideas; these will usually become sections in the final document. You may even find that after doing the clustering diagram

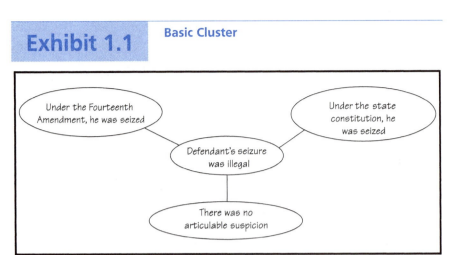

Exhibit 1.1   **Basic Cluster**

you can see that the material fits into one of the standard organizational plans. The final step is to translate the clustering diagram into a traditional outline.

§ 1.2.6 Create a Dining Room Table, Bedroom Floor, or Multiple Monitor Outline

Many writers have difficulty developing a big picture perspective about the document they are trying to write. One way to get a big picture perspective is to create a "dining room table" (or "bedroom floor") outline. The process is simple: just jot each key point or idea that should appear in the document on a separate index card or Post-it Note®. Then start laying out the index cards or Post-it Notes® on a big table or counter or floor. Put related points together and put them roughly in the spot where they will appear in the document. For example, you might have two rules that you know will go together and need to be discussed near the beginning of the document; you might have three cases that work together to make one argument that will appear somewhere in the middle of the document. Because each point is on an index card or Post-it Note®, you can maneuver the pieces and try them out in several locations. You can also begin to see where there might be holes. The key to the dining room table or bedroom floor outline is that it allows you to step back, get the big picture, and imagine how the various ways the pieces might fit together.

An electronic method to create an effective dining room table or bedroom floor outline is to use multiple computer monitors, multiple computer windows, or a note-taking application on a tablet. In lieu of writing your key points and ideas on index cards, type your key points and ideas in one word processing document; the key points and ideas do not have to be in any specific order. After you are finished recording your key points and ideas, create a new blank word processing document.

Exhibit 1.2 **Expanded Cluster**

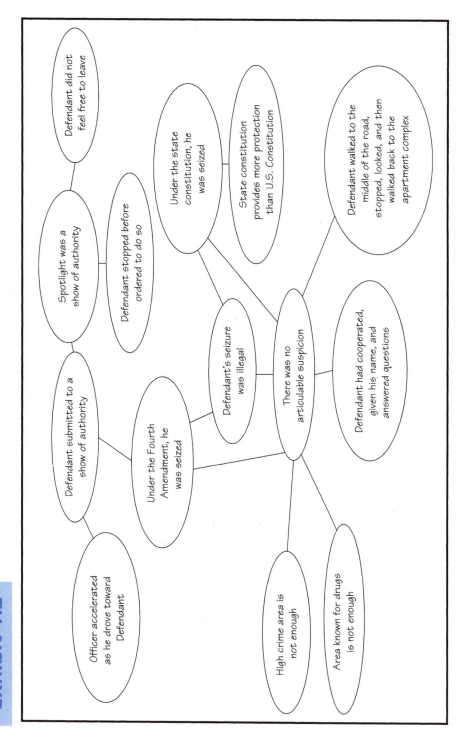

If you are using two monitors, arrange the two documents so that one document is on one monitor, and the other document is on the other monitor. This can be done by clicking and dragging the title bar of the document into position. At this point, the documents should be side by side.

If you only have one monitor, you can arrange the documents to appear side by side on one screen. Simply minimize the window for each document, sizing the windows so that each document takes up half the monitor. Then click and drag the title bar of one document to one side of your monitor, and click and drag the title bar for the other document to the other side of the monitor. If you are using a tablet, install an application that creates digital sticky notes. You can use your tablet to move and organize notes on the screen.

As you review your key points and ideas in one document, copy and paste each point or idea into the new blank document where you anticipate it will appear in the document. Just as if you were using index cards, you will want to put related points and ideas together. Sometimes, it helps to create a structural outline of headings in the blank document before copying and pasting your key points or ideas. For example, your new document might have headings for each element of a claim and you might copy and paste key points or ideas related to each element under those headings.

§ 1.2.7 Consider Your Reader and Purpose and How You View the Case

After spending hours doing research in the library or online—in the trenches, so to speak—it is a good idea to review the basics before composing a battle plan. For either a memo or a brief, ask yourself, for whom am I writing this document? What are that reader's purposes? What are my purposes? Above all, do not forget what legal question someone asked you to answer. Make sure your document answers that question.

For briefs, ask yourself, what is my overall theme? Is this a case about mistaken identity, inappropriate police procedures, self-defense, or freedom to assemble? The theme, or what some lawyers call "the theory of the case" in persuasive writing, should be evident in every section of the outline, from the statement of facts or statement of the case to the rule, discussion, or argument sections.

One final note before leaving the subject of outlines: Like the blueprint for a building or the design for an aircraft, outlines should be aids and not straitjackets for the writer. Don't be afraid to change an outline when it isn't working or when you get a better idea.

§ 1.3 Drafting the Document

If creating an outline is the first stumbling block for most writers, the second comes when it is time to start drafting. Some people develop "writer's block." Faced with what seems to be an overwhelming task, they freeze. Nothing seems like the perfect beginning, so nothing gets written.

If you tend to freeze when you must start writing, try some of the following techniques.

§ 1.3.1 Give Yourself Optimal Writing Conditions

Make writing as pleasant as possible. Start drafting at the time of day and in the place where you do your best thinking and writing. If you are a morning person, don't start drafting at 5:00 p.m. unless you absolutely must. If you prefer a legal pad to a computer, by all means use a legal pad. Treat yourself to a new fancy pen if that will make you feel better about writing. If you are new to legal writing, try multiple environments and methods until you find the one that "clicks" best with you.

§ 1.3.2 Trick Yourself into Getting Started

For many writers, the key to getting started drafting goes all the way back to the research phase. If, for example, as you read each case you stop afterwards and summarize in your own words the key point of the case and what it contributes to the analysis of the issue you are addressing, you will have started drafting. Keeping research notes in your own words or writing an outline will get you started before you even realize you are now writing a draft. By expanding outline labels into phrases, then clauses, then sentences, you begin developing the language that will appear in your draft. You can also type fragments of ideas in a "working" space at the bottom of your document where you won't forget them. For some writers, this gradual "drift" into drafting helps them avoid writer's block.

§ 1.3.3 Write What You Know Best First

For some reason, many writers seem to think that they must write a document in order—the first sentence first, then the second sentence; the first paragraph before the second paragraph; and so on. This notion about writing is not a problem as long as the writer knows how to begin.

However, when you are not quite sure how to begin, it's often a good idea to start writing a draft at the point in the material where you are the most confident. Get the writing rolling and let your instincts guide you through how to begin the document.

The same is true when you are hopelessly stuck in the middle of a document. Try skipping over the problem area for a time and write another section. Leave yourself a note in bold of the problem you skipped so you can revisit it later. With a bit of luck, you may figure out what to do about the problem area without letting it bring the project to a halt.

One caution, though: If you start in the middle of a document or if you skip over a problem area for the time being, you will have to come back and make sure the sections are logically and stylistically connected.

§ 1.3.4 "Get the Juices Flowing"

Athletes who are preparing to perform do warm-up and stretching exercises. Some writers find that freewriting has similar benefits when done before drafting. Others find that they can "get the writing juices flowing" by reading similar documents or rereading other documents that they have written. Experiment with what works for you.

§ 1.3.5 Take It One Step at a Time

Many writers are overwhelmed by the prospect of drafting 20 pages or more. Writing a page or even just a paragraph, however, seems relatively easy. The trick then is to give yourself only small parts of the whole document to do at any one time. Scheduling your time into discrete tasks in 20-, 30-, or 60-minute blocks will make the entire project more manageable.

Your goal for the next hour, for example, may be to write the rule section. Before lunch you may want to complete a paragraph about the plaintiff's policy argument on the last element. By breaking the large task into several smaller tasks, you allow yourself to focus on one part at a time and direct all your energy toward writing that part well.

§ 1.3.6 Stay Focused

One of the biggest drafting challenges is staying focused on the writing project and not allowing yourself to get distracted. Avoiding distractions may mean shutting the office door, muting the phone, and, above all, turning off the internet and email. Disciplined writers know that their computer, which is the very tool they need for writing, can also be their biggest source of interruptions and distractions. For some, it is the temptation to surf the internet. For others, it is the little box that appears at the bottom corner of the screen indicating new emails from family, friends, and co-workers. Remember that Facebook and Twitter will still be there for you to check *after* your writing session. Rather than allow social networking sites to interrupt you, use checking them as a reward after you have completed a section or your writing goal for a set time period. The key to achieving focus is to manage distractions. It bears saying again: to stay focused you will probably have to log off the internet.

§ 1.3.7 Reward Yourself

As you complete small parts of the larger writing task and as you see yourself meeting deadlines in your personal timetable, reward yourself. Rewards can be something small like a coffee break or checking Facebook or something big like an evening off for a movie or a Saturday afternoon hike. What matters is that writing becomes a pleasurable task at which you feel successful.

§ 1.3.8 Organize Your Drafts

On extended writing projects, you will likely save the document dozens of times. By creating an organized electronic file system to track drafts across time, you can avoid the pitfalls of wishing you hadn't deleted a paragraph or accidentally changing a well-phrased argument. Keep a dedicated file folder on your computer for each assignment. Assigning each draft filename a sequence-based identifier will allow you to revisit older versions of the same document. For example, each file can include the date (year, month, day works the best); an alpha-numeric combination (A1, A2, A3, B1); or a numeric sequence similar to what is used in software development (1.1, 1.2, 1.3, 2.0).

§ 1.4 Revising

Revision, or re-vision, means "to see again." When you revise, you step back from the project and try to see it with fresh eyes. This is not an easy thing to do. Many writers have difficulty adopting a revisionist perspective. Most avoid rethinking the whole document and prefer the safety of tinkering with smaller editing issues such as sentence structure or word choice. To help make the shift from drafter to reviser, you may find one of the following techniques helpful.

See Quick Tip: Myths about Writing ⊕

§ 1.4.1 Develop a Revision Checklist

A revision checklist should focus on the large issues in writing. Below is a sample revision checklist that can be used for most documents.

Revision Checklist

- Have I answered the question I was asked?
- Will this document meet the reader's needs?
- Is the tone right for this document and this reader?
- Is the document well organized?
- Are the ideas well developed?
- Is the analysis conclusory or superficial? What would make it more sophisticated?
- What else should be included?
  - A plain language argument?
  - An argument based on an analogous case?
  - A policy argument?
  - A countervailing policy argument?
  - A rebuttal to an argument?
- What can be omitted?
- Is the theme, or theory of the case, evident in all sections of the document?

On your own revision checklist, add any other habitual writing problems that have been pointed out to you by your legal writing professor, classmates, colleagues, or other readers.

§ 1.4.2 Write an After-the-Fact Outline

Of all the areas to rethink when you are revising, the most challenging is often the organization. One simple way to check the paper's organization is to create an after-the-fact outline. An after-the-fact outline is an outline describing what you actually wrote, not a plan that precedes the writing.

To create an after-the-fact outline, read each of your paragraphs and try to sum up the point in that paragraph in a phrase, clause, or, at most, a sentence. (If you can't do this summarizing, that alone suggests that the paragraph needs revision.) Record the summarizing phrase, clause, or sentence on the outline, using indentations to distinguish main points, subpoints, and sub-subpoints.

Use after-the-fact outlines the way you would an aerial photograph of ground you just covered on a hike. Seen from this perspective, is the way you traveled through the material the most efficient one? Do you have any needless backtracking? Repetition? Did you miss anything along the way? If so, where can you easily add it? Is this the way you want your reader to move through the material?

Now that you have the "big picture" in mind, are there ways you can prepare your reader for the twists and turns your path will take? For example, are there insights you should add to your roadmap paragraph that will help your reader? What kinds of signposts will help the reader stay on track? (See section 2.2.2.)

§ 1.4.3 Do a Self-Critique

Leave the role of the writer and become a critical reader. Play the devil's advocate. Where can you punch holes in this thing? Where are its weaknesses? Where are its strengths? Using what you find, you can return to the role of the writer and improve the draft.

§ 1.4.4 Check for Unity and Coherence

For a draft to be well written, the entire document, as well as each paragraph and section, must have unity and coherence. Unity at the document level means that every part of the document contributes to the overall thesis. In a memo, the thesis is essentially the same as your conclusion.

Many writers, though, do not have a clear idea of what their thesis is until they have completed a draft. While drafting, however, they discover what it is they are trying to say. This way of arriving at a thesis, or controlling idea, is perfectly fine. What it means, though, is that now that the writer has discovered the thesis, he or she must go back through the draft with that thesis in mind, making sure that all parts are working toward that goal.

The same process may be true at the paragraph level. The writer may begin drafting a paragraph without a clear idea of what point he or she is trying to make. After drafting the paragraph, however, the writer discovers what the point is and how it contributes to the larger whole. At this point, then, the writer should first add or revise the topic sentence and then go back through the paragraph making sure all the parts contribute to the paragraph's point. See section 3.3.1 for more about unity.

Like unity, coherence is also important at both the document and the paragraph level. Consequently, a good revision strategy is to check (at both the document and the paragraph level) to see if you are using the following common devices for creating coherence:

- Logical organization
  - Chronological, spatial, topical
  - General to specific, specific to general
  - IRAC: issues, rules, analysis, conclusion
- Roadmap paragraphs
- Topic sentences
- Signposts, dovetailing, and transitions
- Repetition of key terms
- Parallelism
- Pronouns

See section 3.3.2 for more about how these devices create coherence.

Two final points about revising: First, drafting and revising are not always distinct stages in the writing process; some revising occurs even as you write the first draft. Second, if possible, do some revising on hard copy. Seeing your writing on just a computer screen can be misleading. Because you can see only a small portion of a whole document at a time, you may overlook problems with some of the larger issues in writing.

§ 1.5 Editing

Editing is an examination of the smaller issues in writing. As with revising, you must once again step out of the role of the drafter and look at the writing with a critical eye. This time, the critical eye is focused on smaller issues such as sentence structure and word choice.

When editing for sentence structure, writers should pay particular attention to the subjects and verbs of their sentences. If the subject-verb combination is effective, many other writing problems will clear up automatically. See Chapter 5.

Legal writers should also make an extra effort to edit for precision and conciseness. See sections 6.1 and 6.2. Sloppy word choice and added verbiage may be overlooked in other types of writing, but they are unforgivable in legal writing. In addition to editing for sentence structure and word choice, you should become aware of and edit for your habitual problem areas.

If this seems like a lot to think about all at once, you are right. For this reason, many writers find it easier to edit for just one or two writing problems at a time. If, for example, your habitual problem is wordiness, do one reading with the single goal of editing out all unnecessary words.

A Few Editing Tips

1. Read your writing aloud or, better yet, have a colleague read it aloud to you while you follow along on another copy. Mark any part that the reader misreads or stumbles over, or anything that just doesn't sound right. This technique may not tell you how to fix something, but it will give you a good idea of what needs to be fixed.

2. As with revising, if at all possible, do some of your editing on hard copy. The same language looks slightly different on a page than it does on a computer screen. For some reason, that small change from screen to page allows you to see the writing with different, fresh eyes.

3. Spend the majority of your editing time on the section(s) of the document that you found hardest to write. No need to keep massaging the opening sentence long after you know it reads smoothly. Force yourself to focus your editing energy on the rockiest parts of the document.

4. Don't let yourself fall in love with a particular phrase or sentence. No matter how well crafted it might be, if it doesn't work with the whole paragraph, indeed the whole document, it is not an effective phrase or sentence.

5. Be selective about whom you ask for editing advice. Although you can sometimes get excellent editing advice from others, there are far too many instances of the blind leading the mildly nearsighted. What often works better is to notice the parts of the document your reader/editor pointed out as problems and figure out with that reader what threw him or her off track. This procedure is much less risky than the unquestioning use of an inexperienced editor's rewrites.

§ 1.6 Proofreading

Whether you or your secretary types your writing, you will be the one who is responsible for the final product. Any missed words, format problems, or typos are ultimately your missed words, format problems, or typos. Consequently, every lawyer, no matter how competent his or her support staff, needs to know a few simple proofreading strategies.

First of all, proofreading is a distinct skill. It is not the same as normal reading or revising or editing. It is reading for errors. Consequently, to proofread properly, you need to remember a few important things.

- Slow down. Speed-reading and proofreading are mutually exclusive terms. Proofreading should be done at your slowest reading rate. One technique for slowing yourself down is to cover up with another sheet of paper all but the line you are proofreading. This technique also helps you to focus on the individual words on the page, so you will see transposed letters in the middle of words and notice missing words rather than mistakenly reading them in where they *should* be.

- Consider proofreading the last third of your document first. Chances are there are more errors in the last sections simply because you and your typist were probably more tired and rushed when these final sections were done. If that's true, then it makes sense to use the time when you are freshest on the part of the document that needs it most.

- If at all possible, do your proofreading at a completely separate time—ideally, a day or more after you have completed drafting and revising. Even a small break in time allows you to see the document anew and bring fresh eyes to the pages.

- Proofread all parts of the document, including headings, charts, appendices, captions, and page numbers. Double-check all dates and monetary figures and the spelling of every name.

- Finally, do not be lulled into complacence by your word processor's spell-checking tool. Even the best computer software does not know a "trail" from a "trial."

See Quick Tip: Proofreading—A Few Ideas ⊕

CHAPTER 2

Connections Between Paragraphs

§ 2.1 Headings

Headings serve two purposes for the reader: They signal the overall organization, and they help the reader locate where he or she is in a document.

As indicators of organization, headings work a bit like a table of contents. They give the reader the framework within which to fit the ideas.

As locating devices, headings are invaluable to readers. A reader who does not have the time to read the whole document can use the headings to find the exact section he or she must read. For readers who have already read the whole document and later need to refer to a point, headings are a quick way to locate that point.[1]

For headings to be helpful, they must be written in parallel form (see section 8.7) and in a consistent format. If the document has headings and subheadings, the reader will be able to identify the different levels of headings if they use compatible but different formats. For example, the main

---

[1] Like all other headings, argumentative headings in briefs must be both indicators of overall organization and locating devices. In addition, they must persuade.

Even though headings in objective memos are somewhat less important to the overall document than argumentative headings are to a brief, they still must be well written. The best headings in memos are fairly short, not more than one typed line and usually less than half a line, and they capture the content in a nutshell.

headings may use Roman numerals and boldface while the subheadings may use capital letters and underlining.

I.   **Main Heading**
   A.   <u>Subheading</u>
   B.   <u>Subheading</u>

II. **Main Heading**
   A.   <u>Subheading</u>
   B.   <u>Subheading</u>

When creating headings, remember the time-honored advice that "You can't have a 1 without a 2, and you can't have an A without a B." In other words, do not create a heading or a subheading unless there is at least one more heading or subheading at that same level.

Developing a good and consistent format for headings is simple. The bigger challenge is composing their content. To be useful finding devices, headings must capture the essence of the section with enough specificity to be meaningful and enough generality to encompass the entire section.

Often the law itself will suggest the content of various sections of the document and hence the headings. An elements analysis or a list of factors, for example, naturally suggests a document with the elements or factors as the headings.

But don't automatically assume that each element or factor deserves its own heading. Because undisputed elements will probably require minimal discussion, the document will appear chopped up if the writer uses a separate heading for each one. More importantly, the reader is not likely to need a heading for each undisputed element.

To compose good headings, find the key words and phrases that sum up the section. Sometimes the easiest way to write a heading is to reread the section and ask yourself, "In a nutshell, what is this section about?" The answer should be close to what would make a good heading. For example, if the answer is "the court's lack of jurisdiction in this matter," then the heading becomes "Lack of Jurisdiction."

But suppose you were writing an office memo for a case and your answer to the question "What is this section about?" was something like "whether the court will admit the eyewitnesses' line-up identifications." Although this clause may accurately sum up the section, consider how it will look as a heading.

Weak Heading

**Whether the Court Will Admit the Eyewitnesses'
Line-up Identifications**

The example heading exceeds the one-line limit and includes some information that the reader can easily infer. Now consider the following four substitute headings for the same section.

EXAMPLE   **Substitute Headings**

1. The Line-up
2. Line-up Identifications
3. Admissibility of Line-up Identifications
4. Admissibility of Eyewitnesses' Line-up Identifications

Option 1 is probably too general. The following section will not likely include everything about the line-up. Option 2 is better. Even so, if the focus of the following section is on the *admissibility* of the identifications, that key word in the heading will be helpful to the reader. Option 4 is also acceptable, but the word "eyewitnesses" can probably be inferred. Option 3 is the best. It sums up the section, it includes the key words and phrases, and it is short enough to be read at a glance.

One last thought about headings: Headings are for the reader, not the writer. The most common mistake legal writers make regarding headings is to use them as crutches for the writer. Headings should not be used as artificial bridges between two sections of the document. The connection between the sections should be made without the heading.

§ 2.2 Roadmaps and Signposts

§ 2.2.1 Roadmaps

Roadmaps are introductory paragraphs that give readers an overview of the entire document. They give readers the "big picture" perspective.

Like real roadmaps, roadmap paragraphs orient readers in several ways: They establish the overall structure of the discussion; they suggest what will be important and hence what deserves the readers' particular attention; and they create expectations for how the discussion will unfold and conclude.

Although not every objective memo needs a roadmap paragraph, those with several steps in the analysis are easier to read if the writer uses a road-map to set the stage for what follows. For example, an attorney writing a memo on whether electromagnetic fields are a nuisance used the following roadmap to show the two steps in the court's analysis.

EXAMPLE

In deciding whether New Mexico will allow a cause of action in nuisance, the New Mexico courts will look first at whether EMFs constitute a public nuisance and then at whether they constitute a private nuisance.

A roadmap paragraph like the one that follows provides a helpful overview of how the court will analyze a particular issue.

EXAMPLE

The McKibbins' claim is that, because there was no written contract, the oral contract is unenforceable under this state's version of the UCC Statute of Frauds. The first thing the court will have to determine, then, is whether the UCC applies at all. If the court finds that the UCC does govern the contract, the court will then have to decide whether the Statute of Frauds bars BCC's claim. Because BCC did not comply with the formal requirements of the Statute of Frauds, the court will find that the contract is unenforceable unless one of the exceptions included in the Statute applies. The only exception likely to apply is the specially manufactured goods exception.

A good roadmap paragraph also tells readers where to focus their attention. For example, if the applicable law includes several elements or factors, the reader will find it helpful to be told in the roadmap paragraph which elements or factors are critical to a case.

EXAMPLE

To claim a prescriptive easement, the Oregon Wilderness Watchers (OWW) will have to satisfy four elements by clear and convincing evidence: (1) that its use was open and notorious; (2) that its use was continuous and uninterrupted; (3) that its use was adverse to the right of the owner; and (4) that its use of the property met each of the other requirements for over ten years. *See Thompson v. Scott*, 528 P.2d 509, 510 (Or. 1974). Although OWW should have no difficulty satisfying the first and fourth elements, the second element and especially the third element will be difficult to satisfy.

Roadmap paragraphs that use the "first, we will look at _____; then we will look at _____; and finally we will look at _____" approach tend to sound unsophisticated. Substituting "I" or "this memorandum" is no better. A better approach is to use the court as the actor.

Compare the following roadmap paragraphs. Notice how much more sophisticated the last two examples sound.

EXAMPLE

Unsophisticated Roadmap Paragraph

In this memorandum, we will examine three issues. First, we will look at whether the statute applies. If we find that it does not, then we will look at whether the Oregon Wilderness Watchers had an easement. If we find that an easement was created, then we will examine the scope of the easement.

Better Roadmap

Our client would like to prevent or limit the use of a path across his property by the Oregon Wilderness Watchers (OWW). An Oregon statute exists that provides for public recreational use, while protecting the owner's interest in his land, and we will argue that it applies to this case. OWW will contend that the statute does not apply and that a prescriptive easement exists. If a prescriptive easement does exist, our client wants to limit the scope of its use.

Better Roadmap

In deciding this case, a court will consider three issues. First, a court will determine whether the statute applies. If it does not, the court will then determine whether the Oregon Wilderness Watchers had an easement. If the court determines that an easement had been created, the court will then decide the scope of the easement.

§ 2.2.2 Signposts

Signposts are those words and phrases that keep readers oriented as they progress through a piece of writing. Signposts can be used as a connecting thread throughout a whole document or through a smaller section.

To be the most effective, a series of signposts needs to be signaled in advance. For example, a writer may signal a series of signposts by saying, "The court examines four exceptions to the Statute of Frauds." In the subsequent discussion, the writer can then use the words "first," "second," "third," "fourth" (or "final" or "last"), and "exception" to signal shifts to each new exception.

The following example is an excerpt from a memo about whether a contract is enforceable under the UCC Statute of Frauds. The setup for the signpost series and the signposts are in boldface type.

EXAMPLE

The court examines four exceptions to the Statute of Frauds, but three of them are not applicable. The first of these inapplicable exceptions, § 4-2-201(2), applies only to transactions "between merchants." In an earlier section, § 42201(1), a merchant is defined as "a person who deals in goods of the kind or otherwise holds himself out as having knowledge or skill peculiar to the practices or goods involved in the transaction or to whom such knowledge or skill may be attributed by his employment of an agent or broker or other intermediary who by his occupation holds himself out as having such knowledge or skill." Because the McKibbins presumably had little or no experience in the carpeting business and because they hired no intermediary to negotiate the transaction for them, the court will probably not find that they are merchants. This exception, then, does not apply.

The second inapplicable exception, § 4-2-201(3)(b), provides that a contract that does not satisfy the requirements of subsection (1) is still enforceable if the party against whom enforcement is sought admits in his or her pleading, testimony, or otherwise in court that a contract for sale was made. Because we are not at the litigation stage of this case yet, this exception does not apply.

The third inapplicable exception, § 4-2-201(3)(c), provides that a contract is enforceable with respect to goods for which payment has been made and accepted or which have been received and accepted. The McKibbins made no payment for the rugs, and they never received the rugs, so this exception also does not apply.

The exception that may be applicable is the exception for specially manufactured goods . . . .

Notice that most signpost series use the ordinal numbers (first, second, third, and so on) before a noun such as "element," "exception," "factor," "issue," "part," "prong," "reason," "requirement," "question," or "section."

EXAMPLE

three issues
the first issue, the second issue, the third issue

a two-part test
the first part of the test, the second part of the test

Once a signpost series is set up, do not change terminology. If there were "three questions" in the introduction to the series, it may confuse readers if the second question is suddenly re-labeled "the second issue."

CHAPTER 3

Effective Paragraphs

§ 3.1 The Function of a Paragraph

Paragraphs exist for many reasons. First, they help writers organize what they are writing. Second, they help readers see and understand that organization. Third, they give readers a psychological, as well as a logical, break.

Writers need paragraphs to help them stay organized and in control of what they are writing. For writers, paragraphs are like tidy boxes in which to sort information. They make writing a manageable task.

Readers need paragraphs so that they can absorb information in manageable bits. If the typical legal reader must comprehend twenty hours' worth of research in the roughly twenty minutes it takes to study an eight-page memo, he or she will need some way to see significant groupings of ideas. That way is the paragraph.

But paragraphing is more than a matter of logic and organization. It is also a matter of reader comfort and aesthetics. After all, those "boxes" into which the writer is fitting ideas can be huge containers that are too heavy to lift or small cartons with barely enough room for half of an idea.

When paragraphs are too long, readers tend to become bewildered, even lost, or worse, lulled into inattention. Paragraphs that are too short, on the other hand, can make the writing and the thinking seem skimpy and inconsequential. Readers need paragraphs that are the right size to comfortably follow what the writer is saying.

Paragraphs also change the look of a page. They create more white space, which can be a welcome relief. Anyone who has opened a book to see a solid mass of type on page one knows how intimidating overly long paragraphs can be. In contrast, the visual break at the beginning of a paragraph signals a brief mental breather.

As the first significant grouping of sentences, a paragraph becomes a kind of mini-composition all its own. It has a beginning, a middle, and an end.

The following paragraph, which is taken from the middle of an argument section of a brief in opposition to a motion to disclose the identity of a state informant, illustrates how a paragraph is a mini-composition.

EXAMPLE

Beginning   The fact that the informant is present at the alleged drug transaction is not determinative of whether the testimony of that informant is relevant or necessary. *Lewandowski v. State*, 389 N.E.2d 706 (Ind. 1979). In *Lewandowski*, the Indiana Supreme Court held that "[m]ere presence of the informer when marijuana was sold to a police officer has been held to be insufficient
Middle   to overcome the privilege of nondisclosure." *Id.* at 710. The court made the same ruling on nearly identical facts in *Craig v. State*, 404 N.E.2d 580 (Ind. 1980) (informant introduced officer to defendant and was present during purchase of illegal drugs). In the present case, the state's informant served mainly as a line of introduction and
Ending   as such her testimony does not automatically become relevant or necessary to the defendant's case simply because she was present at the scene.

---

§ 3.2 Paragraph Patterns

Every paragraph needs a focus, a topic, a point to make. In addition, every paragraph needs a shape, a way of moving through sentences to make that point. The example paragraph in section 3.1 about the relevance of the informant's testimony has one of the most common shapes or patterns: that of a stout hourglass.

An hourglass paragraph begins with a general statement about the topic. This statement may take up one or more sentences. The paragraph then narrows to the specific support or elaboration or explanation the writer has for that general statement. The paragraph concludes with a more general sentence or two about the topic.

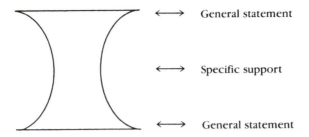

More common in legal writing is a variation of this pattern, the V-shaped paragraph. Like the hourglass paragraph, the V-shaped paragraph begins with a general discussion of the topic and then narrows to the specific support. The V-shaped paragraph does not return to a general statement.

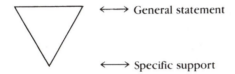

EXAMPLE   **V-Shaped Paragraph**

    Kraft Savings, one of three savings and loans represented on   General
Kraft Island, does a significant amount of the banking business on   statement
Kraft Island. As of 2009, Kraft Savings had $3.2 million in deposits,
$11.6 million in outstanding loans, and a large volume of busi-   Specific
ness with the Kraft City Council. In 2009, Kraft Savings handled   support
$50 million in transactions for almost 1,900 customers in about
2,400 accounts.

Both the hourglass and the V-shaped paragraph patterns work well in legal writing. Both use the opening sentence or sentences as an overview of what is to come and then proceed to support that generalization with specifics.

§ 3.3 Unity and Coherence in Paragraphs

§ 3.3.1 Paragraph Unity

To be a mini-composition, a paragraph must have its own topic, that is, its own point to make, and all elements in the paragraph must work together to make that point. When they do, the paragraph has unity.

    Look again at the example in section 3.1 about the state informant. All of the information is about one topic: The informant's testimony is not necessarily relevant or necessary simply because the informant was present at the drug transaction. This topic is introduced at the beginning of the paragraph by a topic sentence, developed and supported by two sentences in the middle of the paragraph, and then concluded by the last sentence.

What the paragraph does not do is stray from this topic. Even though the writer will need to refer to both *Lewandowski* and *Craig* later in the memo to support other points, the writer did not get sidetracked and try to do it here. The paragraph stays on course and makes its point. It has a clear focus; it has unity.

§ 3.3.2 Paragraph Coherence

When a paragraph is coherent, the various elements of the paragraph are connected in such a way that the reader can easily follow the writer's development of ideas. Coherence can be achieved in a number of ways: by using familiar organizational patterns, particularly those that are established patterns for legal writing; by establishing and then using key terms; and by using sentence structure and other coherence devices to reinforce the connections between ideas.

a. Using Familiar Organizational Patterns

All readers expect certain patterns—cause/effect, problem/solution, chronological order—and when writers meet those expectations, the ideas are easy to follow. Legal readers have some additional patterns that they expect in legal writing. For example, once a rule, standard, or definition has been laid out, legal readers expect it to be applied. They expect a court's holding to be followed by its rationale. In office memos, arguments are almost always followed by counterarguments. In both office memos and briefs, the IRAC pattern (issue, rule, analysis/application, and conclusion) and all its variations are commonplace and expected.

Writers can also achieve coherence in paragraphs by creating reader expectations and then fulfilling them. For example, when a writer sets up a list of factors, elements, reasons, or issues, the reader expects the writing to follow up on that list, typically in the order in which the list was first set out. In the following paragraph, the writer uses this technique to create a coherent discussion of how the statutory term "ways of the state" will be construed in a case in which an intoxicated driver was on the shoulder of the road.

EXAMPLE

A narrow construction of the term "ways" is unlikely. In fact, there are two strong indications that Montana will favor a broad construction: (1) a broad statutory definition of "highway"; and (2) an interpretation of "ways" given in a Montana Supreme Court decision. By statutory definition, "[h]ighway includes rights-of-way or other interests in land, embankments, retaining walls, culverts, sluices, drainage structures, bridges, railroad-highway crossings, tunnels, signs, guardrails, and protective structures." Mont. Code Ann. § 60-1-103 (2015). By including all facets of the highway like the retaining walls and embankments, it follows that the legislature intended to broaden, not narrow, the term. In addition, the Montana Supreme Court stipulated that "ways" encompasses state and county right-of-ways, including borrow pits, which road maintenance crews use as sources of dirt and gravel. *State v. Taylor*, 661 P.2d 33, 35 (Mont. 1983). It is highly unlikely that the court would include borrow pits but exempt shoulders from the term "ways." Therefore, the court will probably conclude that Mr. Renko's truck was on the ways of the state open to the public.

b. Using Key Terms

Of the various methods writers have for creating coherence, repetition of key terms is the easiest and one of the most important. In the following example paragraph, we have used different typefaces for each of the key terms—informant or informer, **present** or **presence**, testimony, and RELEVANT OR NECESSARY—so you can see how the repetition of key terms gives the paragraph coherence. Together the key terms are part of a network of connecting threads that create a coherent theme for the paragraph.

See Quick Tip: Principle vs. Principal

See Quick Tip: Counsel vs. Council

> **EXAMPLE**   **With Key Terms Highlighted**
>
> The fact that the informant is present at the alleged drug transaction is not determinative of whether the testimony of that informant is RELEVANT OR NECESSARY. *Lewandowski v. State*, 389 N.E.2d 706 (Ind. 1979). In *Lewandowski*, the Indiana Supreme Court held that "[m]ere **presence** of the informer when marijuana was sold to a police officer has been held to be insufficient to overcome the privilege of nondisclosure." *Id.* at 710. The court made the same ruling on nearly identical facts in *Craig v. State*, 404 N.E.2d 580 (Ind. 1980) (informant introduced officer to defendant and was **present** during purchase of illegal drugs). In the present case, the state's informant served mainly as a line of introduction and as such her testimony does not automatically become RELEVANT OR NECESSARY to the defendant's case simply because she was **present** at the scene.

c. Using Sentence Structure and Other Coherence Devices

Writers can also create coherence through sentence structure and through a number of other common coherence devices. "Dovetailing" (beginning a sentence with a reference to the preceding sentence) and other transitions create connections by establishing links between sentences. See section 4.3. Parallelism within a sentence or between sentences shows the reader which ideas should be considered together and which should be compared and contrasted. See section 8.7. Even pronouns in their own small way provide subtle links within the writing because they are a connection to the noun they replace.

In the following example, notice how the parallel phrases "on the defendant's ability to operate the vehicle" and "on the vehicle's condition" in the opening topic sentence set up the organizational pattern. The writer then signals the beginning of each half of the discussion by using the parallel sentence openers "in focusing on the defendant's condition" and "in focusing on the vehicle's condition." Note too the dovetailing between sentences 2 and 3 ("he would have been able to operate the vehicle" → "not only is it possible that he could have operated the truck") and between sentences 4 and 5 ("defined" → "by that definition"). Once again, pronouns also subtly provide coherence ("defendant" → "he," "truck" → "it," "court" → "it").

EXAMPLE

If some form of operability is required, then the court must decide whether to focus **on the defendant's ability to operate the vehicle** or **on the vehicle's condition**. *See State v. Smelter*, 674 P.2d 690, 693 (Wash. Ct. App. 1983). **In focusing on the defendant's condition**, the court could find that because the defendant had the key and was in the cab of the truck, **he would have been able to operate the vehicle** had he been awakened. **Not only is it possible that he could have operated the truck**, it is evident that he did drive the truck from the tavern to the freeway before parking it on the shoulder. **In focusing on the vehicle's condition**, the Washington court used the trial court's "reasonably operable" standard and **defined** that term as any malfunction short of a cracked block or a similar problem that would render the vehicle totally inoperable. *Id.* at 693. **By that definition**, Mr. Renko's **truck** was reasonably operable regardless of whether **it** would start. Therefore, if the Montana **court** considers operability an issue, **it** would probably find that Mr. Renko was capable of operating the vehicle and that the vehicle was in reasonably operable condition.

---

§ 3.4 Paragraph Length

First, the truth: Not all paragraphs are three to five sentences long. In fact, quite a few well-written paragraphs are as short as two sentences, and, yes, some well-written paragraphs contain only one sentence. One-sentence paragraphs are neither a goal to strive for nor a taboo to be feared. Writers simply need to know when they have finished what they set out to do in the paragraph.

Similarly, good paragraphs may run many sentences longer than five. It is not outrageous for a paragraph in legal writing to include seven or even eight sentences, as long as the writer needs that many to make the point. However, writers should keep in mind the reader's comfort and avoid seven- and eight-sentence paragraphs about complicated discussions of law.

Remember too that an eight-sentence paragraph is likely to create a solid page of type, which has a negative psychological impact on readers.

The paragraphs in the following example are from a section in an appellate brief. Notice the number of sentences in and the length of each paragraph. (Citation sentences are not counted as substantive sentences.)

EXAMPLE

I. The Trial Court Erred in Holding That the Plaintiff Is a Public Figure as a Matter of Law

The states have a legitimate interest in compensating plaintiffs for damage to reputation inflicted through defamatory publications. *Gertz v. Robert Welch, Inc.*, 418 U.S. 323, 341 (1974). While recognizing that "[s]ome tension necessarily exists between the need for a vigorous and uninhibited press and the legitimate interest in redressing wrongful injury," the U.S. Supreme Court has stressed that the plaintiff's right to the protection of his reputation must not be sacrificed when the court balances these two competing interests. *Id.*

Two-sentence paragraph

In an attempt to balance the interests of the media against the interests of plaintiffs injured by defamatory statements, the Court developed three classes of plaintiffs: public officials, public figures, and private figures. *Gertz*, 418 U.S. at 343; *Curtis Publ'g Co. v. Butts*, 388 U.S. 130 (1966); *New York Times Co. v. Sullivan*, 376 U.S. 254, 279 (1964). Because public figure plaintiffs are held to a higher standard of proof in defamation suits, the Court has made it clear that the public figure standard is to be construed narrowly. *Gertz*, 418 U.S. at 352. The Court will not lightly find a plaintiff to be a public figure. *Id.*

Three-sentence paragraph

The first class of public figure defined by the Court in *Gertz* is the limited purpose public figure. To become a limited purpose public figure, a plaintiff must voluntarily inject himself or herself into a particular public controversy and attempt to influence its outcome. *Id.* at 351, 352. By doing so, the plaintiff invites public attention and comment on a limited range of issues relating to his or her involvement in the controversy. *Id.* at 351.

Three-sentence paragraph

The Court described the second class of public figure, the all-purpose public figure, as having "assumed roles of especial prominence in the affairs of society," or as occupying "positions of such persuasive power and influence," or as "achieving such pervasive fame or notoriety that he becomes a public figure for all purposes and in all contexts." *Id.* at 345, 351.

One-sentence paragraph

Six-sentence paragraph

Under these narrow definitions laid down by the U.S. Supreme Court, Kraft Savings and Loan is neither a limited purpose public figure nor an all-purpose public figure. Therefore, the trial court erred in granting defendants' motion for partial summary judgment on the public figure issue. Furthermore, this error was prejudicial because it resulted in the plaintiffs being held to a higher standard of proof at trial. But because the standard of review is *de novo* when a partial summary judgment order is appealed, this court is not bound by the erroneous trial court decision below. *Herron v. Tribune Publ'g Co.*, 108 Wash. 2d 162, 169, 736 P.2d 249, 255 (1987); *Noel v. King Cnty.*, 48 Wash. App. 227, 231, 738 P.2d 692, 695 (1987). Rather, the court should apply the *Gertz* public figure standard to the facts of this case and reach its own independent determination. Correct application of the standard will result in a holding that Kraft Savings and Loan is a private figure for purposes of this defamation suit.

First, a few comments about the preceding example: Notice that the length of each paragraph is primarily determined by content. The writer wrote as few or as many sentences as she needed to make each point. The length of each paragraph is further determined by reader comfort and interest. Some variety in paragraph length helps keep the writing interesting. Short, one- or two-sentence paragraphs tend to work in places where the reader needs a bit of a break before or after an unusually long paragraph. Too many short paragraphs, though, and the writing begins to seem choppy and undeveloped.

Short paragraphs can also be effective when the writer is making a major shift, change, or connection between ideas. Consequently, short paragraphs frequently serve as transitions between major sections and as introductions or conclusions to major sections.

An occasional long paragraph allows the writer to go into depth on a point. Too many long paragraphs, though, and the writing slows down to a plod and seems heavy and ponderous. No single paragraph should exceed a single page in length.

§ 3.5 Topic and Concluding Sentences

Again, the truth: Not all paragraphs have topic and concluding sentences. In fact, many well-written paragraphs have neither.

However, and this is a big "however," most well-written paragraphs do have topic sentences, and those that don't have an implied topic sentence that governs the paragraph as firmly as any written topic sentence. The truth about concluding sentences is that sometimes they are useful to the reader and sometimes they are not. You have to use your common sense about when to include one and when to leave one out. Readers are most likely to find concluding sentences helpful after longer, more complicated points. If, on the other hand, you are confident that the information in the concluding sentence would be painfully obvious, then leave it out.

The point then is to know what topic and concluding sentences do for a paragraph. Then you can decide whether a stated or an implied topic or concluding sentence works in a given situation.

§ 3.5.1 Stated Topic Sentences

The following examples demonstrate how the standard topic sentence works. Notice that the topic sentence has two functions: It introduces or names the topic, and it asserts something about the topic.

EXAMPLE 1

In determining whether service is proper under Fed. R. Civ. P. 4, courts consider several factors. First, the courts recognize that "each decision proceeds on its own facts." *Karlsson*, 318 F.2d at 668. Second, the courts consider whether the defendant will return to the place where service was left. *Id.* Third, the courts look at whether service was reasonably calculated to provide actual notice to the defendant. *Minnesota Mining & Mfg. Co. v. Kirkevold*, 87 F.R.D. 317, 323 (D. Minn. 1980).

EXAMPLE 2

Defendants have successfully used the following articulated reasons to rebut a plaintiff's prima facie case. In *Kelly*, the defendant testified that the plaintiff was terminated because he was the least effective salesman. *Kelly*, 640 F.2d at 977(*overruled on other grounds*). Similarly, in *Sakellar*, the defendant alleged that the plaintiff lacked the skills and experience for the position. *Sakellar*, 765 F.2d at 1456. And in *Sutton*, the defendant discharged the plaintiff for "intemperate and impolitic actions." *Sutton*, 646 F.2d at 410.

One common weakness of some novice legal writers is to write topic sentences that merely name the topic. These topic sentences fall under the category of "The next thing I'm going to talk about is . . . ."

Compare the following two topic sentences. Which would a reader find more helpful?

EXAMPLE 1

Another case that discussed actual malice is *Rosenbloom v. Metromedia, Inc.*, 403 U.S. 29 (1971).

EXAMPLE 2

The court extended these protections in *Rosenbloom*, holding that plaintiffs in a defamation action would have to prove actual malice if the published statements were of public or general interest. *Rosenbloom v. Metromedia*, 403 U.S. 29 (1971).

The topic sentence in Example 1 does little more than name a case. The topic sentence in Example 2 is far superior. In addition to naming the case, it sets up the point that the case contributes to the analysis, which is the point the paragraph will develop.

The topic sentence in Example 2 also demonstrates an excellent method for writing topic sentences that introduce a new case: It begins with a transition that relates the point from the new case to the previous discussion and then follows with a paraphrase of the holding. The following example shows how the writer completed the paragraph.

EXAMPLE 3

The court extended these protections in *Rosenbloom*, holding that plaintiffs in a defamation action would have to prove actual malice if the published statements were of public or general interest. *Rosenbloom v. Metromedia*, 403 U.S. 29 (1971). The Court wrote, "If a matter is a subject of public or general interest, it cannot suddenly become less so merely because a private individual is involved, or because in some sense the individual did not 'voluntarily' choose to become involved." *Rosenbloom*, 403 U.S. at 43.

The next two examples also show how to use a court's holding for the topic sentence. In Example 1, the writer develops the topic sentence by setting out the facts in the analogous case and then distinguishing them from the client's case. In Example 2, the writer develops the topic sentence by setting out the facts of the case and then returns to the holding.

EXAMPLE 1

In *Messenger*, the court determined that the trespassory slashing of trees was a permanent form of property damage. *Messenger v. Frye*, 28 P.2d 1023 (Wash. 1934). However, the tree slashing in that case was extensive. It was the extent of the injury, not the type of injury, that made the damage irreparable and therefore permanent. Unlike the slashed trees, the damage to the rosebushes in the Archers' case should not be considered extensive because only four out of twenty rosebushes were destroyed. The rosebushes can probably be replaced, thus restoring the Archers' property to its original condition. Therefore, the damage to the rosebushes and buds is temporary, and the Archers will recover only for the restoration cost of the rosebuds and bushes, as well as the diminished use value of their property.

EXAMPLE 2

In an analogous Arizona case, *State v. Thomas*, the court held that the trial court committed an error of constitutional magnitude when it allowed the prosecution to do exactly as the prosecution did in the present case. *Thomas*, 636 P.2d at 1219. In *Thomas*, the only pertinent evidence was the testimony of the defendant, who was accused of rape, and the testimony of the prosecuting witness. During the trial, the prosecution questioned the witness about her religious beliefs and church-related activities, eliciting from her that she was a religious person. *Id.* at 1217. In closing argument, the prosecution told the jury that the ultimate issue was the credibility of the witnesses, and that before the jury could believe the defendant, it had to believe that the prosecuting witness, an "uprighteous, religious, moralistic type," was a liar. *Id.* The appellate court held that admission of the religious references was an error of constitutional magnitude. *Id.* at 1219.

As we have seen, the first sentence of a paragraph is usually the topic sentence. Topic sentences may, however, appear later in a paragraph, particularly if the opening sentence or sentences are used to provide a transition to or background for the topic.

The following example is taken from the beginning of the second argument in the same memorandum in opposition to the defendants' motion for partial summary judgment. Notice how sentence 1 serves as a transition between the two arguments and sentence 2 provides background for sentence 3, the topic sentence.

EXAMPLE

Sullivan and *Gertz* dealt with individual citizens who had been libeled and who had sought redress in the courts. The case before the court today is different; the plaintiff is a state chartered savings and loan, a business entity. The significance of the different status of a business entity and its reputation, as compared to a private individual, has been recognized in several federal courts. In *Martin Marietta v. Evening Star Newspaper*, 417 F. Supp. 947, 955 (D.D.C. 1976), the court stated that "[t]he law of libel has long reflected the distinction between corporate and human plaintiffs" and that "a corporate libel action is not a basic [sic] of our constitutional system, and need not force the first amendment to yield as far as it would be in a private libel action." The *Marietta* court continued, "Corporations, which do not possess private lives to begin with, must similarly [to public figures] be denied full protection from libel." *Id.*

Margin labels: Transition · Background · Topic sentence

§ 3.5.2 Implied Topic Sentences

Many paragraphs with implied topic sentences occur in statements of fact. Although some statements of fact have paragraphs that are thematically organized and use traditional topic sentences, most have a chronological organization with implied topic sentences. Many use a mix of the two.

Practically all paragraphs in statements of fact depend on their narrative, or storytelling, quality to keep the writing organized. The organizing principle, or topic, of such paragraphs may be what happened in a given time period, what happened to a given person, or what facts make up a given part of the situation.

The following paragraph appeared in the statement of facts from a case about whether service of process was valid when it was left at a spouse's home. The paragraph prior to the one shown here explained that the defendant, Ms. Clay-Poole, has a job and residence in New York and that her husband has a job and residence in California. In the example paragraph, no topic sentence is stated, but one is certainly implied.

> **EXAMPLE**
>
> Ms. Clay-Poole and Mr. Poole usually see each other about once a month for three or four days. They split the traveling about equally, although Ms. Clay-Poole travels to San Diego somewhat more frequently than Mr. Poole travels to Albany. They are happy with this arrangement; consequently, they do not intend to move in together permanently.

The implied topic sentence of this paragraph is that Ms. Clay-Poole and Mr. Poole have a commuter marriage. The writer could have stated the topic sentence, but in this case it was sufficiently obvious to leave it implied.

§ 3.5.3 Concluding Sentences

To be worthwhile, concluding sentences need to do more than just restate the topic sentence. If they don't, then the paragraph will not have advanced the line of reasoning in the memo or brief. Look again at the paragraph about whether a drug informant's testimony is relevant. Notice how the topic and concluding sentences are not simply artful clones of each other.

> **EXAMPLE**
>
> Topic sentence   The fact that the informant is present at the alleged drug transaction is not determinative of whether the testimony of that informant is relevant or necessary. *Lewandowski v. State*, 389 N.E.2d 706 (Ind. 1979). In *Lewandowski*, the Indiana Supreme Court held

that "[m]ere presence of the informer when marijuana was sold   Supporting
to a police officer has been held to be insufficient to overcome the   sentences
privilege of nondisclosure." *Id.* at 710. The court made the same
ruling on nearly identical facts in *Craig v. State*, 404 N.E.2d 580
(Ind. 1980) (informant introduced officer to defendant and was
present during purchase of illegal drugs). The state's informant in
the present case served mainly as a line of introduction and does   Conclusion
not as such automatically become relevant or necessary to the
defendant's case simply because she was present at the scene.

The concluding sentence advances the line of reasoning by taking that topic, or that point, and applying it to the present case. It rather neatly argues that the rationale in *Craig v. State* is applicable in the present case because in both cases the informant "served mainly as a line of introduction." This concluding sentence is not just extra baggage, the obligatory "Now I'm going to tell you again what I told you before." It is a working sentence, perhaps the most significant sentence in the paragraph.

Earlier we saw how a paraphrase of the holding often makes an excellent topic sentence. Paraphrasing the holding can also be an effective way to conclude a paragraph about an analogous case.

EXAMPLE

The Georgia appellate court addressed the issue of consent in relation to the disposal of a stillborn child. *See McCoy v. Georgia Baptist Hosp.*, 306 S.E.2d 746 (Ga. Ct. App. 1983). In that case, the mother delivered a stillborn child in the defendant hospital. Both parents had signed a consent form authorizing the hospital to dispose of the body "in any manner they deem advisable." *Id.* at 747. Thereafter, the mother discovered that the body had been placed in a freezer and left there for approximately one month. The court held that the parents released their quasi-property interests in the child's body to the defendant hospital when they signed the consent form. *Id.*

Another effective technique for writing concluding sentences is to use a particularly apt quotation.

EXAMPLE

The California Supreme Court has decided that an individual's property rights in his cells is not absolute. In *Moore v. Regents of UCLA*, 271 Cal. Rptr. 146 (Cal. 1990), the appellant's diseased spleen was removed by the appellee research hospital. Appellee subsequently discovered that Moore's spleen and other bodily tissue contained cells with unique characteristics that could be used to develop substances with potential commercial value. Moore was never told of appellee's discovery and continued to allow appellee to extract cells from him under the auspices of continuing treatment. The state Supreme Court held that once Moore's cells were removed, he did not retain ownership interest in them. *Id.* at 146-47. The court went on to say, "If the scientific users of human cells are to be held liable for failing to investigate the consensual pedigree of their raw materials, we believe the Legislature should make that decision." *Id.* at 147.

One word of caution, though: Many legal writers overuse quotations. For the technique of concluding with a quotation to be effective, it should be used only occasionally and only when the quotation is unusually well stated.

Remember, too, that every paragraph does not have to have a stated concluding sentence. As with implied topic sentences, implied concluding sentences are permissible as long as the reader can easily surmise the paragraph's conclusion.

§ 3.6 Paragraph Blocks

One reason many paragraphs may not have topic sentences or concluding sentences yet function well is that the paragraphs are part of a larger organizational element: a paragraph block. Like paragraphs, paragraph blocks are mini-compositions, only in this instance the beginning is likely to be a paragraph or two, the middle is usually several paragraphs, and the end is also a paragraph or more.

The beginning paragraph or paragraphs work like a topic sentence. They are general statements that introduce the topic of the paragraph block and assert something about that topic.

The middle paragraphs contain the subpoints—the specifics that support the topic paragraph. Ideally, each of the middle paragraphs will be organized like a mini-composition with its own topic sentence, supporting sentences, and concluding sentences.

The concluding paragraph or paragraphs work in the block the same way a concluding sentence works in a paragraph. They bring the discussion back to the broad general topic, but in a way that advances the line of reasoning.

The following example from an argument section in a brief demonstrates how a typical paragraph block works.

EXAMPLE   Paragraph Block

Topic paragraph

The court in *Colorado Credit Union v. KOAT Television, Inc.*, 656 P.2d 896 (N.M. Ct. App. 1982) held that a financial institution was an all-purpose public figure; however, that case was decided incorrectly. In holding that a credit union was an all-purpose public figure, the New Mexico Court of Appeals extended and broadened the *Gertz* standard in a way the Supreme Court never intended.

By ignoring the Court's mandate to construe the all-purpose public figure standard narrowly, the *Coronado* court extended this standard to include all credit unions. *Id.* at 903. The court considered the following factors to reach this per se rule: (1) Credit unions are chartered by the state to serve the public; (2) Credit unions are regulated by the state through statutes; and (3) Credit unions' financial situation is of public concern. *Id.* at 904.

Supporting paragraph

The fatal flaw in the court's analysis is best illustrated by applying these three factors to the fact pattern in *Gertz*. In *Gertz*, the Supreme Court held that the plaintiff attorney was not an all-purpose public figure. 418 U.S. at 352. But if the *Coronado* analysis had been used, the opposite result would have been reached: (1) Attorneys must be licensed by the state to practice law and must meet certain state requirements to obtain that license; and (2) Attorneys are subject to regulation by the state through professional codes of conduct. In fact, lawyers are officers of the court, and as such, must seek the public good in the administration of justice.

Supporting paragraph

Thus, under the *Coronado* analysis, Mr. Gertz and indeed all attorneys would be classified as all-purpose public figures. Such a result is in direct opposition to the Court's holding in *Gertz*. Consequently, the rule applied in *Coronado* is far too broad and could not withstand constitutional scrutiny.

Concluding paragraph

The following excerpt from a memo shows how two paragraph blocks work together to complete a section under the heading of "negligence." An elements analysis lends itself nicely to paragraph block writing. In the example, notice how the paragraph that concludes one paragraph block also serves as the topic paragraph for the second block.

EXAMPLE

Negligence

If Dennis's negligence created the emergency, then he cannot use the emergency doctrine. Negligence is defined as failing to act as a reasonable person. This general principle is best explained by way of illustration, and the courts provide numerous examples.

Topic paragraph

Speed excessive to conditions can be negligent. For example, when a defendant's logging truck rounded a curve and was unable to stop within 375 feet, his speed was found to be negligent. *Sandberg v. Spoelstra*, 285 P.2d 564 (Wash. 1955). When early morning visibility was restricted to 75 feet by a heavy rainfall, the court held that a speed of 50 miles per hour could be negligent. *Pidduck v. Henson*, 467 P.2d 322

Topic sentence

Supporting paragraph

(Wash. Ct. App. 1970). Finally, when daylight visibility exceeding 100 feet was restricted to about three car lengths at night because of the glare of a street light, the court held that a speed under the 25 miles per hour posted limit could be negligent. *Sonnenberg v. Remsing*, 398 P.2d 728 (Wash. 1965).

Topic sentence

Supporting paragraph

Failure to heed road hazard warnings can also be negligent. Thus, when a driver confronted a multiple car accident on the freeway, where patrol cars were present with flashing lights and other cars were parked along the shoulder and median, the driver was negligent for not slowing down. *Schlect v. Sorenson*, 533 P.2d 1404 (Wash. Ct. App. 1975). Likewise, when a driver was warned of a fog hazard, drove into a deteriorating fog bank, and collided with a stopped vehicle, the driver was negligent. *Hinkel v. Weyerhaeuser Co.*, 494 P.2d 1008 (Wash. Ct. App. 1972).

Topic sentence

Supporting paragraph

Finally, violations of the rules of the road can be negligence per se. When the driver of a semi-trailer observed a car stalled in the road ahead of it, slowed, switched lanes, and passed to the rear of the automobile where it struck one of the occupants on the highway, the driver was negligent. The driver was negligent as a matter of law for failing to obey several rules of the road: (1) reducing speed when confronted with hazards, (2) sounding horn to warn pedestrians of danger, (3) changing lanes only when safe to do so, and (4) signaling a lane change for 100 feet before turning. *Nesmith v. Bowden*, 563 P.2d 1322 (Wash. Ct. App. 1977).

Concluding paragraph/ topic paragraph

Plaintiff is likely to employ all the above arguments. She will probably argue that Dennis was negligent because his speed was excessive, because he failed to heed road hazards, and because he violated the rules of the road.

Topic sentence

Supporting paragraph

Dennis's speed was not excessive for the conditions he faced. Dennis can distinguish the conditions in *Pidduck* and *Sonnenberg* from the conditions that he faced. In both cases, visibility was restricted by unusual circumstances. Dennis faced no unusual circumstances. He was rounding a gradual curve under the speed limit, and there is no indication that the curve was so sharp that it required a reduced speed limit. Nor was there any indication that there was a lower speed limit for night driving as opposed to day driving. In *Sandberg*, the driver had 375 feet in which to stop, and there was no obstruction in his lane when the driver collided with a vehicle in the other lane. Although the exact distance is unknown in Dennis's case, apparently Dennis had much less space in which to stop. Also, he faced an obstruction in his own lane.

Topic sentence

Dennis's situation is analogous to the situation in *Ryan v. Westgard*, 530 P.2d 687 (Wash. Ct. App. 1975), where the driver was found to be not negligent. There, the driver was following approximately 100 feet behind another car. This car swerved into another lane, and the following driver confronted yet another

car going extremely slowly. He attempted to stop, but collided **Supporting**
with the slower vehicle. The court reasoned that the plaintiff **paragraph**
was following the car in front of him at a proper speed until the
moment that vehicle swerved out into the adjoining lane. Like
the driver in *Ryan*, Dennis was travelling at a proper speed until
the moment his vehicle encountered the stalled bus. Therefore, Concluding
Dennis's speed was not excessive.   sentence

Plaintiff will also probably argue that Dennis was negligent Pair of topic
for failing to slow when confronted with a road hazard. Again, sentences
Dennis can distinguish the warning that he had from the warnings
given in *Schlect* and *Hinkel*. Dennis was not warned several miles **Supporting**
in advance of the obstruction as was the driver in *Hinkel*. Nor did **paragraph**
he confront a multiple car accident with flashing patrol car lights
and cars parked along the highway as did the driver in *Schlect*.

Dennis rounded a curve and confronted a bus with flashers Topic
on that was stopped in the left lane of the freeway at 11:30 p.m. sentence
His situation is more analogous to the cases in which drivers faced
sudden and unexpected obstacles after little warning. *See Haynes* **Supporting**
v. Moore, 545 P.2d 28 (Wash. Ct. App. 1975); *Leach v. Weiss*, 467 **paragraph**
P.2d 894 (Wash. Ct. App. 1970). In *Haynes*, the driver confronted
a car, which he first saw when 50 feet away, stopped on a bridge.
He braked, but collided with the car. He was found to be not negligent. Likewise, in *Leach*, the driver confronted a car stopped on a
bridge, braked, crossed the center line, and collided with another Concluding
vehicle. The driver was not negligent. Neither is Dennis negligent. sentence

Finally, plaintiff will probably argue that Dennis was negligent Topic
for violating the rules of the road. Dennis was driving in the left- sentence
hand lane and was not passing or turning. This conduct violates
Wash. Rev. Code § 46.61.100, which requires that a driver stay
in the rightmost lane except when passing or turning. Under
Nesmith v. Bowden, 563 P.2d 1322, 1326 (Wash. Ct. App. 1977), **Supporting**
this violation creates a prima facie case of negligence. However, **paragraph**
Dennis can argue that this conduct was not negligent because it
did not endanger the class of persons that this rule was designed
to protect. The purpose of Wash. Rev. Code § 46.61.100 is to
protect vehicles traveling in the same direction by promoting safe
passing. *Sadler v. Wagner*, 486 P.2d 330 (Wash. Ct. App. 1971).
Evert was not passing Dennis, and Dennis was not passing Evert.
Thus, Evert does not fall within the class of persons this rule was Concluding
designed to protect, and Dennis was not negligent.   sentence

Dennis was not negligent because of excessive speed, he **Concluding**
was not negligent for failing to heed road hazard warnings, and **paragraph**
he was not negligent for failing to obey the rules of the road. His
conduct did not create the emergency. He can submit substantial
evidence in support of this second element, even though he can
expect opposing counsel to make this a difficult issue.

Connections Between Sentences

Transitions are the primary connectors between sentences. Used properly, transitions express the relationship between the ideas in the sentences they serve to connect and signal how the ideas are moving in a line of reasoning.

Three types of transitions connect sentences:

1. Generic transitions
2. Orienting transitions
3. Substantive transitions

Still other transitions, headings and signposts, are used to make connections between paragraphs and over a longer piece of writing. See Chapter 2.

§ 4.1 Generic Transitions

Generic transitions include those words and phrases that are used in every kind of writing. Chart 4.1 lists the most common generic transitions grouped by function.

| **Chart 4.1** | **Generic Transitions** |

A word of warning: This chart of generic transitions categorizes the transitions by function: for contrast, for comparison, for cause and effect, etc. The individual transitions and transitional phrases within any of the categories are not synonyms for each other. Each transition conveys distinct, sometimes subtle, differences in how ideas are connected. Consequently, it is crucial for writers to learn the meaning of any given transition in context in order to use it correctly in their own writing.

For Contrast

alternatively	except	on the contrary
although	however	on the other hand
but	in place of	rather
by (in) contrast	in spite of	still
contrary to	instead (of)	that being said*
conversely	nevertheless*	though
despite	nonetheless*	unlike
even so*	notwithstanding	yet
even though		

For Difference

besides*	otherwise	

For Comparison

analogously	in like manner	likewise
by the same token	in the same way	similarly
for the same reason	like	

For Cause and Effect or Result

accordingly*	because consequently*	now
(and) so	for	therefore*
as a consequence	for that reason	thus*
as a result	hence	

For What Is True in Most Cases

generally	generally speaking	in general

For Addition

additionally	besides*	moreover
also	further	(once) again
and	furthermore	(then) again
as well (as)	in addition	too

For Examples

for example	namely	that is*
for instance	specifically	to illustrate

For Emphasis

above all	clearly	rather
as a matter of fact	in fact	still*
certainly	indeed	

For Evaluation

allegedly	more important	unfortunately
arguably	surprisingly	unquestionably
fortunately		

For Restatement

in other words	simply put	to put it differently
more simply	that is*	

For Concession

after all	granted	of course
all the same*	in any case/event	still*
at any rate	nevertheless*	that said
at the same time*	nonetheless*	to be sure

For Resumption After a Concession

all the same*	nevertheless*	still*
even so*	nonetheless*	that being said*

For Time

afterward	formerly	shortly thereafter
at the same time*	in the meantime	simultaneously
at the time	initially	since
by the time	later	subsequently
earlier	meanwhile	then*
eventually	recently	until now

For Place

adjacent to	here	next to
beyond	nearby	opposite to

For Sequence or Enumeration

final	in the first place	primary, secondary
finally*	later	then*
first, second, third	last	to begin/start with
former, latter	next	

For Conclusion

all in all	in short	to conclude
consequently*	in sum	to (in) review
finally*	in summary	to sum up
in brief	therefore*	to summarize
in conclusion	thus*	ultimately

*Generic transition that falls under more than one category.

§ 4.1.1 Using Generic Transitions

The first question writers have about generic transitions is when to use them. In theory, that seems simple. Because generic transitions signal those shifts or changes inherent in human thought, it would seem that all writers should have to do is insert an appropriate transition to signal each time they make such a shift in their writing.

In practice, transition selection is not so simple. For one thing, there are no hard-and-fast rules for when a writer should use a transition. In fact, experienced writers do not always agree about when a transition is appropriate and when it is cumbersome. For beginning law students and new associates in a firm, such differences in opinion can be confusing: one reader wants more transitions added, and the next reader edits them out.

The truth is that, to some extent, the number and placement of generic transitions is a matter of personal style and preference. That being said, there is still a general consensus about when to use generic transitions. You can find that consensus and develop your own sense about when to use generic transitions in one or more of the following ways.

First, observe how other writers, particularly professional writers, use generic transitions. For example, notice how they rarely omit transitions that signal contrast and ones that show movement up or down the ladder of abstraction. Observe the ways skilled legal writers use generic transitions to keep their readers on track.

Second, read your own writing aloud. Let your ear tell you when a new sentence starts with a jolt rather than a smooth connection.

Third, listen to someone else read your writing aloud. Try stopping that reader at several points along the way (particularly when there is no transition) and asking if he or she can guess what the next sentence will discuss. If the connections between the ideas are so obvious that the reader can anticipate where the writing is headed, then probably no transition is needed. Conversely, if your reader needs more guidance through your points, add the appropriate generic transitions as needed. Law students should take special note that many law school honor codes prohibit unauthorized collaboration. Be sure to check with your professor before asking another person for help on an assignment.

Fourth, and most important, when writing, constantly ask yourself what will help your reader. Keeping the reader's perspective and needs in mind will help you decide when a generic transition is a helpful guide and when it is extra baggage.

§ 4.1.2 Problems with Generic Transitions

Some legal writers have a tendency to write as though others can read their minds. These writers omit transitions because the connections between the ideas are obvious to them. They forget to consider whether these connections are obvious to the reader. For example, in the first pair of sentences that follow, notice how jarring the second sentence seems without the transition for contrast, and then notice how in the revised second sentence the reader easily adjusts once the generic transition for contrast is added.

EXAMPLE

Mr. Wry, the owner of the Fitness Club, may claim that although Singh's restaurant has lost several customers, the majority of the customers will return. Mr. Singh may argue that the loss of several customers is significant to his business.

Revised:

Mr. Wry, the owner of the Fitness Club, may claim that although Singh's restaurant has lost several customers, the majority of the customers will return. Mr. Singh, *on the other hand,* may argue that the loss of several customers is significant to his business.

Other writers omit transitions in hopes of being more concise, forgetting that being concise, although important, is a relative luxury compared to being clear.

Legal writers should also take great care to select the precise transition that best describes the relationship between the two ideas or sentences. In the following example, the writer mistakenly selected a transition for comparison rather than one for addition.

EXAMPLE

Because some overt physical activity and noise are normally generated by fitness and aerobics classes, the Fitness Club's classes are not unreasonably noisy or offensive. *Similarly,* bathing suits are not unusual or unanticipated sights in a waterfront area.

Revised:

Furthermore, bathing suits are not unusual or unanticipated sights in a waterfront area.

The need for precise transitions also means that it is not enough simply to select the right category of generic transition. Generic transitions within the same category often have distinct meanings and connotations. For example, two transitions for conclusion—"to sum up" and "finally"—have entirely different meanings. "To sum up" should signal a brief overview or general statement about the entire piece of writing; "finally" should signal that the last point is about to be made.

In some instances, generic transitions are similar in meaning but quite different in tone. For example, two transitions for cause and effect— "therefore" and "hence"—mean almost the same thing, but "therefore" creates a matter-of-fact tone while "hence" carries with it a feeling of heavy solemnity and old wisdom.

See Quick Tip: Generic Transitions (Meaning) ⊕

Of course, you will find that a few generic transitions in the same category are virtually synonymous. In such instances, you may find that the list offers some variety that may free you from using the same generic transition repeatedly.

Some final advice about transitional expressions: First, because transitions show the connection between two ideas, try to place the transition right at the point of connection. In the following example, the transition showing the cause/effect relationship comes too late to help the reader very much.

EXAMPLE

See Quick
Tip: Generic
Transitions
(Placement) ⊕

Singh was made insecure in the use of his property when patrons threatened not to return. The Fitness Club and its activities constitute a nuisance *as a result*.

Revised:

As a result, the Fitness Club and its activities constitute a nuisance.

Second, the break between paragraphs can also serve as a kind of transition. White space is a strong signal that the writing is moving to a new point. Be careful, though: some legal writers object to generic transitions at the beginning of paragraphs.

§ 4.2 Orienting Transitions

Orienting transitions provide a context for the information that follows. They serve to locate—physically, logically, or chronologically—the ideas or points in the rest of the sentence.

Two of the most common orienting transitions in legal writing are those that include times and dates and those that refer to cases.

EXAMPLE

At 2:00 a.m. on January 1, 2015, Jacob Stein was arrested and charged with reckless driving and driving while intoxicated.

In *Bugger*, the court found that the position of the driver was insignificant.

In the case at hand, there is no indication that the defendant intended to deceive the plaintiff about her rights under the contract.

Other orienting transitions create a context by directing the reader to adopt a certain point of view, by supplying the source of the information that follows, or by locating the information historically or chronologically.

EXAMPLE

From the bank's perspective, granting a second loan would be ill advised and risky.

According to Dallas Police Department Officer James Richardson's report, Officers Richardson and Chon entered the warehouse at 12:30 a.m.

Over the last 20 years, courts have realized that some exceptions to the general principle were necessary.

Orienting transitions frequently occur at the beginning of a section. In such positions, orienting transitions are not so much connections between points within the writing as they are connections between the writing and the mind of a reader first coming to the material.

Orienting transitions also occur at the beginning of paragraphs. From this position, they help readers adjust or "shift gears" as they mentally move along a line of reasoning within a larger idea. Of course, orienting transitions can occur within a paragraph, and when they do, they work like all other transitions to bridge the gap between sentences and between ideas.

§ 4.3 Substantive Transitions

Thus far, we have looked at generic transitions, which are like glue between sentences, and at orienting transitions, which are backdrops for information or sometimes windows through which information can be seen.

The third type of transition, substantive transitions, can best be compared to the interlocking links of a chain. Like the links of a chain, substantive transitions serve two functions: They make a connection and they provide content. In short, they live up to their name—they are both substantive and transitional.

EXAMPLE   Substantive Transition

Bugger and *Zavala* are the only cases in which a conviction was overturned when the motorist's vehicle was totally off the road. While these holdings could be helpful to Mr. Renko, the Montana court will still probably interpret the statute to include the shoulder of the highway.

Here, the substantive transition is "while these holdings could be helpful to Mr. Renko." It serves as a transition connecting the two sentences for two reasons: First, it is placed at or near the beginning of the following sentence, where it can help bridge the gap between the ideas; and second, it uses the phrase "these holdings" to refer back to the information in the previous sentence. In short, the transition looks both forward and back.

But, as we said before, a substantive transition does not serve merely as a transition; it also provides new content. It points out that "these holdings could be helpful to Mr. Renko" before going on to the main point of the sentence, that the court still is likely to interpret the statute as including the shoulder of the highway.

§ 4.3.1 The Structure of Substantive Transitions: Dovetailing

Substantive transitions often employ a technique called "dovetailing" as the basis for their structure.

A carpenter who wants a strong joint between two pieces of wood is likely to use the dovetail, a special joint characterized by the tight fit of interlocking pieces of wood. Similarly, a writer who wants a strong joint between two sentences uses a dovetail of words to connect the ideas. Through the dovetail, he or she interlocks ideas by creating an overlap of language. The overlap of language may be as simple as the repetition of terms from one sentence to the next or the use of pronouns to refer back to an earlier noun.

EXAMPLE

In *Esser*, four people agreed to share costs and build a road. After the road was built, each person used the road under a claim of right.

Sentence 1	*Sentence 2*
. . . four people . . . build a road.	After the road was built, each person used the road . . . .

A slightly more complicated dovetail than the one in the previous example requires the writer to find a word or phrase to use in the second sentence that sums up the idea of the previous sentence.

EXAMPLE Summarizing-Phrase Dovetail

Searches and seizures are governed by the Fourth Amendment to the U.S. Constitution and Article I, Section 7, of the Washington Constitution. Both of these provisions have been interpreted as requiring that search warrants be valid and that searches and seizures be reasonable.

Sentence 1	*Sentence 2*
. . . Fourth Amendment . . . and Article I . . .	Both of these provisions . . . .

Note that in both of these examples the words in the dovetail tend to be toward the end of the first sentence and toward the beginning of the second.

Often the summarizing noun or phrase will be preceded by a demonstrative pronoun, or "hook word," such as "this," "that," "these," "those," or "such."

EXAMPLE   **Hook and Summarizing Phrase**

Realizing that she would not be able to stop in time to avoid hitting the bus, Mrs. Long swerved her vehicle around the bus and into the parallel lane of traffic. This evasive action resulted in her sideswiping another vehicle in the oncoming lane.

Connecting idea	*Connecting idea*	
swerved . . . into . . . traffic	This *(hook word)*	evasive action *(summarizing noun phrase)*

To form an effective dovetail, then, a legal writer can use one or more of the following techniques:

1. Move the connecting idea to the end of the first sentence and to the beginning of the second sentence.
2. Repeat key words from the first sentence in the second sentence.
3. Use pronouns in the second sentence to refer back to nouns in the first sentence.
4. State the connecting idea in a specific form in the first sentence and then restate it in a summarizing noun or phrase in the second sentence.
5. Use hook words such as "this," "that," "these," "those," and "such" before a repeated key word or summarizing noun or phrase. See section 8.5.2 for information about effective use of hook words.

Nouns that tend to make useful summarizing nouns are shown in Chart 4.2.

Chart 4.2   **Nouns That Summarize**

action(s)	concept	facet	rationale
advantage	consequence(s)	form	reason(ing)
angle	course [of action/to follow]	item	result
aspect	criterion(a)	motive	rule
attempt	idea	outcome	stage
branch	disadvantage	period	step
category	drawback	plan	term
circumstance(s)	end	principle	type
class	fact	problem	

Another way to think about dovetailing is to remember that most sentences are made up of two parts: old information and new information. The old information is what has already been named or discussed. It usually appears near the beginning of a sentence. The new information is the point the writer wants to add. It usually appears near the end of a sentence.

Sentence	
old information	new information

A dovetail takes the new information from the end of one sentence and restates it as the now old information at the beginning of the subsequent sentence.

Sentence 1		Sentence 2	
A	B →	B	C
old	new	old	new
information	information	information	information

Obviously, though, all of your sentences cannot realistically follow a strict A + B, B + C, C + D pattern. In reality, and in good legal writing, the pattern is not followed rigidly. Quite often, for example, sentence three will start with old information B.

Sentence 1		Sentence 2		Sentence 3	
A	B	B	C	B	D
old	new	old	new	old	new

EXAMPLE

In 2015, the Montana legislature adopted new and stricter laws to deal with drunk drivers. This legislation increased funding to law enforcement task forces, increased fines, and established stiffer penalties. 2015 Mont. Laws 794, 2015 Mont. Laws 573, 2015 Mont. Laws 1940. This legislation also demonstrated a definite trend in Montana toward greater liability for the individual and a preference toward protecting children who ride with drunk drivers.

Another useful variation of the pattern is to begin a sentence with a combination of two earlier pieces of old information.

Sentence 1		Sentence 2		Sentence 3	
A	B	B	C	B + C	D
old	new	old	new	old + old	new

EXAMPLE

When the defendant entered his hotel room, he was surprised to find two men rummaging through his suitcase. One of the men turned toward him, drew his gun, and aimed it at the defendant. Under these circumstances, the defendant had every reason to believe that he was being robbed and that his life was in danger.

This pattern works well when the writer wants to point out the similarity in two or more cases just cited.

EXAMPLE

Courts in both Illinois and Michigan allowed relocation of children when the court applied the best interests test. *In re Marriage of Coulter*, 2012 IL 113474 (2012), 976 N.E.2d 337; *Pierron v. Pierron*, 782 N.W.2d 480 (Mich. 2010). These cases are significant because in both instances the residential custodial parent wanted to relocate with the child and the courts allowed the relocation.

Some writers unconsciously reverse the old → new pattern. They begin a sentence with new information and tack on the old, connecting information at the end. The result is a halting, disjointed style.

EXAMPLE

Defendants need not ensure the plaintiff's safety; they need exercise only reasonable care. *Potter v. Madison Tavern*, 446 P.2d at 322. Defendants breach their duty to the plaintiff when they do not exercise reasonable care.

Revised:

When defendants do not exercise reasonable care, they breach their duty to the plaintiff.

Occasionally, however, it is awkward, if not impossible, to move the old information to the very beginning of a sentence and the new information to the very end. In such cases, remember that the old → new pattern is a general principle, not an absolute rule.

A final bit of advice about dovetailing: Avoid using hook words without repeating a key term or using a summarizing noun or phrase. See section 8.5.2 on broad pronoun reference.

EXAMPLE

At common law, a duty is established when the defendant stands in a special relationship to the plaintiff. **This can exist** between a specific plaintiff and a specific defendant.

Revised:

This **special relationship** can exist . . . .

§ 4.3.2 The Content of Substantive Transitions

The content in substantive transitions can be compared to half steps in a line of reasoning. Sometimes these half steps are articulated inferences that one can reasonably draw from the previous sentence or idea.

EXAMPLE

The owners of the factory could agree to release the fumes only after certain hours at night or only under certain weather conditions. While these steps may ameliorate the situation, the question remains whether any emission of toxic fumes is reasonable.

In the preceding example, a thoughtful reader would surely be able to infer the content of the substantive transition—"while these steps may ameliorate the situation"—after reading the first sentence. Consequently, some may argue that it would be better to replace the substantive transition with a more concise generic transition such as "even so" or "still." Ultimately, you will need to exercise judgment and weigh the relative merits of completeness versus conciseness.

In the following two examples, notice how the generic transition, although more concise, is less persuasive for the Bells than the substantive transition.

EXAMPLE

Generic Transition:

The Bells' doctor, Peter Williams, advised them that future pregnancies had a 75 percent chance of ending in a stillbirth. Consequently, the Bells decided that Mr. Bell would have a vasectomy.

Substantive Transition:

The Bells' doctor, Peter Williams, advised them that future pregnancies had a 75 percent chance of ending in a stillbirth. Relying on Dr. Williams's advice, the Bells decided that Mr. Bell would have a vasectomy.

Notice how the generic transition "consequently" seems fairly neutral. It suggests that the Bells' decision to have Mr. Bell undergo a vasectomy was the expected consequence of an unfavorable statistical probability. The substantive transition "relying on Dr. Williams's advice," on the other hand, stresses the Bells' dependence on their doctor's professional opinion. Mentioning the doctor again by name not only reminds the reader that the doctor was the source of the information but also emphasizes the role he played in the Bells' decision.

Although it would be impossible to illustrate the many ways substantive transitions are used in legal writing, there are a few common situations in which they are particularly effective.

a. Bridging the Gap Between Law and Application

Perhaps the most common use of substantive transitions in legal writing occurs at junctures between law and application. Compare the following two examples and note how the substantive transition "under the rule announced in *Gibson*" draws the rule and its application together better than a generic transition can.

EXAMPLE

Generic Transition:

A court must be able to infer knowledge by looking at the circumstances around one's possession of the stolen property. *Gibson v. State*, 643 N.E.2d 885, 888 (Ind. 1994). In the case at hand, Bryant was able to assume that he was storing a van for a new friend, and thus, he was not aware of the nature of the property. Therefore, there is sufficient evidence to support the jury's verdict of not guilty.

Substantive Transition:

A court must be able to infer knowledge by looking at the circumstances around one's possession of the stolen property. *Gibson v. State*, 643 N.E.2d 885, 888 (Ind. 1994). In the case at hand, Bryant was able to assume that he was storing a van for a new friend, and thus, he was not aware of the nature of the property. Under the rule announced in *Gibson*, the jury's verdict of not guilty is sustainable.

---

b. Applying Another Court's Rationale

Legal writers often use substantive transitions when the reasoning of one court has been laid out in detail and the writer will now apply the reasoning to the case at hand.

EXAMPLE

Two Washington decisions have developed a more liberal definition of inadvertent. *State v. Henry*, 676 P.2d 521 (Wash. Ct. App. 1984). In *Henry*, officers had learned from an informant that the defendant was heavily armed, and one officer testified that he was looking for guns as well as cocaine, which was specified in the warrant; however, the court held that the guns were found inadvertently. *Id.* at 533. In doing so, the court relied on the definition of "inadvertent" provided in *State v. Callahan*, 644 P.2d 735, 736 (Wash. Ct. App. 1982): "[T]he term 'inadvertent' in the context of the plain view doctrine, simply means that the officer discovered the evidence while in a position that does not infringe upon any reasonable expectation of privacy, and did not take any further unreasonable steps to find the evidence from that position." The *Henry* court concluded that the officers were looking in places that were likely to contain drugs, that a person can harbor no reasonable expectation of privacy concerning a place that is likely to contain drugs, and that the officers took no further, unreasonable steps to find the guns. Therefore, the discovery was inadvertent by the Washington definition. *Henry*, 676 P.2d at 523. The court added that there was no evidence that the drug search was a pretext for a gun search. *Id.*

The state's position in the instant case is stronger. At the time the officers received the search warrant for marijuana, they neither had knowledge nor expected that they might find incriminating photographic evidence of another crime. When he looked in the envelope, Morrison had no reason to believe that the photographs would be evidence of any crime.

Thus, **applying the *Henry* rationale to *Ehrlich***, the court would probably find that Morrison was looking in a place that was likely to conceal drugs (the envelope might have contained drugs as well as photographs), so Ehrlich had no reasonable expectation of privacy. After looking in the envelope, Morrison took no further unreasonable steps to find the photographs. Therefore, the discovery was inadvertent.

c. Gathering Together Several Facts

Another juncture where substantive transitions can be used effectively occurs between a list of numerous individual facts and a statement about their collective significance.

In the following example, the substantive transition "based on these admissions" is essential. It is the one place where the point is made that three facts taken together were the basis for the court's action.

EXAMPLE

In his deposition, Edwards acknowledged that the railroad tie had appeared wet and slippery before he stepped on it. He also stated that he had regularly delivered mail to the Bates residence for two years and that he was familiar with the premises, including the railroad tie. Finally, Edwards acknowledged that he attended weekly postal safety meetings and knew about the hazards posed by wet surfaces. **Based on these admissions**, the trial court granted summary judgment in favor of Bates and dismissed Edwards's negligence action. *Id.* at 942.

---

d. Bridging the Gap Between Sections of a Document

Substantive transitions are more effective than generic transitions at junctures between large sections of a paper. Even when headings are used for larger sections, substantive transitions are still needed to show the similarities or differences between the sections.

In the following example, the writer has just completed a long section on the Ninth Circuit's comments on the inappropriateness of bonuses for services rendered to a bankrupt estate. The following sentence begins the section under the heading Contingency Fees. The substantive transition—"unlike a bonus fee arrangement"—shows the connection between the sections.

EXAMPLE

Contingency Fees:

Unlike a bonus fee arrangement, there is nothing that prevents a contingency fee agreement from being enforced in bankruptcy. *In re Jones*, 356 B.R. 39, 49 (2005).

Transitions: Some Final Thoughts

To sum up, substantive transitions are those special points in writing where the writer pulls two or more thoughts together and, in doing so, creates a powerful bond between ideas. By overlapping the language and merging the ideas, you can do more than just connect the points; you can weave them together.

Although the artificial division of transitions into separate categories makes it easier to understand their separate functions, it also masks the ways in which generic, orienting, and substantive transitions are similar. One can argue, for example, that all transitions, including generic transitions, provide some content or that all transitions orient the reader. Consequently, how you categorize a particular transition is not really important; what is important is that you are able to use all three categories of transitions to create connections in your own writing.

Effective Sentences

Effective sentence writing begins with the subject-verb unit. Those two key sentence positions should contain the crux of the sentence's message. If these two parts of the sentence are written well, then many of the other parts of the sentence will fall into place.

Consequently, our discussion of effective sentence writing begins with four points about the subject-verb unit: the use of active and passive voice, the use of concrete subjects, the use of action verbs, and the distance between subjects and verbs. The remainder of the chapter addresses points that concern the whole sentence: sentence length, emphasis, and sentence structures that highlight similarities or differences.

§ 5.1 Active and Passive Voice

The term "voice" when it is applied to the subject-verb unit refers to the relationship of the subject to the action expressed in the verb. This rather vague concept is easier to understand in terms of the difference between active and passive voice.

§ 5.1.1 Identifying Active and Passive Voice

In active voice, the subject of the sentence is doing the action described by the verb.

The judge overruled the objection.
   (subject) (verb)   *(direct object)*

In the sentence above, the subject "judge" is doing the verb "overruled." Another way to look at it is to remember that in active voice the subject is "active," or acting.

In passive voice, the subject of the sentence is having the action of the verb done to it.

Note: Direct objects are discussed in Chapter 8.

The objection was overruled by the judge.
   (subject)   *(verb)*

In this sentence, the subject "objection" is not doing the overruling; rather, the verb "was overruled" is being done to the subject. Another way to look at it is to remember that in passive voice the subject is "passive." The subject is not acting; it is acted upon.

Notice that in passive voice, the person or thing doing the verb is either mentioned in a prepositional phrase ("by the judge," as in the previous example) or omitted, as in the example below.

The objection was overruled.
   (subject)   *(verb)*

Note that passive voice is different from past tense. Even though both concern the verb, past tense refers to the time of an action and passive voice refers to the relationship of an action to the subject of the sentence.

§ 5.1.2 Effective Use of Active Voice

Legal writers generally prefer active voice over passive voice for several reasons:

1. Active voice is more concise.

EXAMPLES

The marshal left the summons.

(active voice—5 words)

The summons was left by the marshal.

(passive voice—7 words)

2. Active voice uses a more vigorous verb.

The plaintiffs filed a complaint in the Superior Court of Chavez County, New Mexico.

(active voice—the verb "filed" is crisp and vigorous)

A complaint was filed by the plaintiffs in the Superior Court of Chavez County, New Mexico.

(passive voice—the verb "was filed" loses much of its vigor; the auxiliary verb "was" and the preposition "by" dilute the energy of "filed")

---

3. Active voice allows the reader to process information more readily.

The defendant's attorney must offer the deposition into evidence.

This active voice sentence is easy to process mentally. The reader can visualize the subject "defendant's attorney" doing the verb "must offer" to the object "deposition" as quickly as the words are read. The sentence suggests a mini-drama that readers can visualize in their minds.

The deposition must be offered into evidence by the defendant's attorney.

Although the information in this passive voice sentence is not difficult to process, readers must read the entire sentence before they can visualize the sentence in their minds. By the midpoint in the sentence, "The deposition must be offered into evidence," the action has begun, but it is being done by unseen hands. The "actor" in the mini-drama does not appear until the end of the sentence.

4. Active voice emphasizes the actor.

In both objective and persuasive legal writing, active voice is usually preferred when you want to emphasize that someone or something performed a particular action. Active voice emphasizes who or what is responsible for committing an act.

The defendant embezzled over $1 million.

(active voice—emphasizes that the defendant is responsible for the act)

Over $1 million was embezzled by the defendant.

(passive voice—it is still clear that the defendant performed the act, but now the emphasis is on the amount of money)

Over $1 million was embezzled.

(passive voice—doer of the action is either unknown or left unsaid; emphasis is on the amount of money)

§ 5.1.3 Effective Use of Passive Voice

Although active voice is generally preferable to passive voice, passive voice can be more effective in certain situations.

1. **Use passive voice when the person or thing performing the action is unknown or relatively unimportant.**

A portion of the tape was erased.

The safe's hinges must be examined before the manufacturer's liability can be determined.

In both of the examples of passive voice above, the writer was likely unaware of the actors behind the verbs "erased" and "examined" or else decided that the actor was less important than the action. Either way, using passive voice was a conscious, strategic decision on the part of the writer.

2. **Use passive voice when it is undesirable to disclose the identity of the person or thing performing the action.**

The plaintiff's retirement benefits were discontinued.

Toxic fumes were ventilated out of the plant between 2:00 and 3:00 a.m.

3. Use passive voice when the deed, rather than the doer, should be emphasized.

All four defendants were convicted of first degree murder.

In persuasive writing, passive voice allows you to downplay who performed certain actions. For example, counsel for the defendant may want to use passive voice when admitting wrongdoing by the defendant.

A purse was taken from the plaintiff by the defendant.

Counsel for the plaintiff will use active voice to emphasize that it was the defendant who took the purse.

The defendant took the plaintiff's purse.

4. Use passive voice when it allows the writer to keep the focus of the writing where it belongs, as in the following example from a paragraph about a mistake in a contract.

A mistake can also be attributed to Lakeland Elementary School for believing the price of the playground equipment included installation.

5. Use passive voice when it provides a stronger link between preceding and subsequent sentences or clauses. This link is enhanced by moving the connecting ideas to the end of the first sentence (or clause) and then picking up on that point at the beginning of the second sentence (or clause). For more information on dovetailing, see section 4.3.1.

Sentence 1	*Sentence 2*
. . . connecting idea.	Connecting idea . . .

Under Title 62A of the Revised Code of Washington, contracts for the sale of goods are regulated by the Uniform Commercial Code. The UCC outlines the requirements for a valid contract for the sale of goods and the various steps necessary to the contract's performance.

The first sentence uses passive voice so that "Uniform Commercial Code" will be at the end of the sentence. The second sentence begins with "The UCC" to provide a strong link between the sentences.

Sentence 1	Sentence 2
. . . by the Uniform Commercial Code.	The UCC . . .

§ 5.2 Concrete Subjects

Effective subjects of sentences are concrete rather than abstract. They are real people and real things that readers can mentally visualize.

Unfortunately, in legal writing we are often forced to use abstractions as subjects of our sentences. The law and its application often require that we focus on ideas and concepts; consequently, we often end up placing these ideas and concepts in the subject position. Even so, legal readers appreciate having as many concrete subjects as possible to help bring the writing back down to earth.

To find the most effective concrete subject of a sentence, ask yourself, "Who (or what) is doing something in this sentence?" Then place that real person (or thing) in the subject position of the sentence.

Draft: A <u>decision</u> <u>was made</u> by the district manager to eliminate
             (subject)   *(verb)*
             all level four positions.

Revised: The <u>district manager</u> <u>decided</u> to eliminate all level four
                  (subject)   *(verb)*
             positions.

Note that the preceding example illustrates a common problem in legal writing known as nominalization. Nominalization is the process of converting verbs into nouns (for example, "decide" → "decision"). The effect in the sentence is twofold: (1) the real action of the sentence is buried in a noun, making the sentence more ponderous and turgid, and (2) the verb becomes either a passive voice substitute or a "*to be*" verb substitute, making the sentence less energetic.

In many sentences, the real person or thing acting in the sentence has been buried in an abstraction or omitted altogether.

Draft: The <u>awarding</u> of damages <u>will be left</u> to judicial discretion.
          (subject)   *(verb)*

Revised: The <u>judge</u> <u>will decide</u> whether to award damages.
          (subject) *(verb)*

Often the subject position in the sentence is taken up by an almost meaningless abstraction such as "nature of," "kind of," "type of," or "area of." Notice how the sentence improves when these meaningless abstractions are omitted and real people and real things are placed in the subject position.

Draft: The <u>nature</u> of the defendant's argument <u>was</u> that he was
          (subject)   *(verb)*
          "temporarily insane."

Revised: The <u>defendant</u> <u>argued</u> that he was "temporarily insane."
          (subject)   *(verb)*

Both the subject position and verb position are often taken up by the many weak subject-verb combinations that use the "it is _____ that" pattern.

It is important to note that
It is likely (unlikely) that
It is obvious (clear) that
It is essential that

To revise sentences with this weakness, look after the "that" for the real subject and verb.

Draft: <u>It</u> <u>is</u> obvious that the defendant was read his rights.
          (subject/verb)

Revised: The <u>defendant</u> <u>was</u> <u>read</u> his rights.
          (subject)   *(verb)*

Draft: <u>It is</u> unlikely that the defendant will plead guilty.
          (subject/verb)

Revised: The <u>defendant</u> probably <u>will</u> not <u>plead</u> guilty.
                    (subject)   *(verb)*

§ 5.3 Action Verbs

Effective verbs show real action rather than vague action or state of being. To find the most effective verb for a sentence, ask yourself, "What is someone (or something) actually doing in the sentence?" Then place that action in the verb position.

Common Pitfalls to Avoid When Selecting a Verb

1. Avoid overusing a form of the verb "to be" ("am," "are," "is," "was," "were") as a main verb. Use forms of the verb "to be" only as the main verb when the point of the sentence is that something exists. Avoiding these verbs will also help you avoid passive voice.

EXAMPLES

Draft: The <u>owner</u> of the land <u>is</u> East Coast Properties, Inc.
                  (subject)   *(verb)*

Revised: <u>East Coast Properties, Inc.</u>, <u>owns</u> the land.
                       (subject)   *(verb)*

Draft: There <u>are</u> four <u>elements</u> that must be proved to recover
                  (verb)   *(subject)*
                  damages under the family car or purpose doctrine.

Revised: Four <u>elements</u> <u>must be proved</u> to recover damages
                       (subject)   *(verb)*
                  under the family car or purpose doctrine. *OR*

                  Under the family car or purpose doctrine, the <u>plaintiff</u>
                                                               (subject)

                  <u>must prove</u> four elements.
                      (verb)

Notice that the sentence openers "There is" or "There are" or "There was" or "There were" are weak unless the point of the sentence is that something exists. With these four sentence openers, the subject comes after the verb. Notice that the final revision contains the tightest subject-verb unit.

>   2. **Avoid vague verbs such as "concerns," "involves," "deals (with)," and "reveals," which communicate very little about the real action in the sentence.**

EXAMPLE

Draft: *Swanson* <u>dealt</u> with a sales contract that contained an open
        (subject) (verb)
        item and that was signed by a homebuilder and a couple who
        were prospective buyers of a home.

Revised: In *Swanson*, a <u>homebuilder</u> and a <u>couple</u> who were
                    (subject)   (subject)
        prospective buyers of a home <u>signed</u> a contract that
                            (verb)
        contained an open item.

>   3. **Avoid nominalization, that is, burying the real action in a noun, and avoid burying the action in an adjective.**

EXAMPLE

Draft: The <u>corporate officers</u> <u>had</u> an informal meeting at an
                (subject)   (verb)
        undisclosed location.

Revised: The <u>corporate officers</u> <u>met</u> informally at an undisclosed
                (subject)   (verb)
        location.

---

§ 5.4 Distance Between Subjects and Verbs

An effective sentence has its subject and verb close together. When they are close together, the reader can identify the subject-verb unit quickly and comprehend the entire sentence more easily. When they are separated by more than a few intervening words, the reader will find it more difficult to understand the sentence.

EXAMPLE

Draft: Information about Mutual Trust Bank's standard operating
              (subject)
              procedures and about how the contractor drew up his loan
              application will be required by the court.
                          (verb)

Revised: The court will require information about Mutual Trust Bank's
              (subject) (verb)
              standard operating procedures and about how the contractor
              drew up his loan application.

In some cases, the writer will have to rewrite one sentence as two sentences to keep the subjects and verbs close together.

EXAMPLE

Draft: A case in which a section 11-902 charge was dropped because
              (subject)
              the driver was found lying in the highway near his truck shows
                                                                      (verb)
              that a driver's presence in the vehicle is a prerequisite for finding
              him guilty.

Revised: In one case, the court dismissed a section 11-902 charge
                          (subject) (verb)
              because the driver was found lying in the highway near his truck.
              The court reasoned that a driver's presence in a vehicle is a
                  (subject) (verb)
              prerequisite to finding the defendant guilty.

Another reason for keeping subjects and verbs close together is to reduce the chance that they will not agree in number. See section 8.4.1. In the following example, the writer has mistakenly made the verb agree with the singular noun "script" when the plural subject "quality and mutilation" requires the plural verb "are."

EXAMPLE

Incorrect Subject-Verb Agreement:

Inferior quality and mutilation of the musical play *Not Enough Lovin'* as a
                 (subject)
result of Skylark Productions' revisions of the script is hard to establish.
                                                        (verb)

Correct Subject-Verb Agreement:

Inferior <u>quality and mutilation</u> of the musical play *Not Enough Lovin'* as a
              (subject)
result of Skylark Productions' revisions of the script <u>are</u> hard to establish.
                                                        (verb)

A writer must occasionally separate the subject and verb with quite a bit of information. In such cases, if the intervening information can be set off by punctuation, the reader will still be able to identify the subject-verb unit fairly easily. The writer should also take care to avoid creating an awkward sentence that is grammatically correct but nonetheless looks incorrect to the reader.

EXAMPLE

The <u>Lanham Trademark Act</u>, a law primarily designed to prevent
              (subject)
deceptive packaging of goods in interstate commerce, <u>has been</u>
                                                      (verb)
interpreted to include false attribution and distortion of literary and artistic works.

Remember, too, that keeping subjects and verbs close together is desirable, but not absolutely required. There will be times in legal writing when it is all but impossible to keep subjects and verbs close together.

§ 5.5 Sentence Length

Whenever a legal writer asks "how long should my sentences be?" the only possible answer is "it depends." Obviously sentence length is primarily governed by what you are trying to say. In addition, decisions on sentence length should be made based on two other factors: the reader and the context.

§ 5.5.1 The Reader

Effective sentence length is that which the reader can handle comfortably. Educated readers—judges, attorneys, some clients—can comfortably read somewhat longer sentences than the general public. Consequently, legal writers can usually write sentences for their readers that average about 22 words per sentence, with only a rare sentence exceeding a 35-word limit. For readers with less education, shorter sentences are usually more effective.

Notice how the overly long sentence in the following example creates a feeling in the reader of a mental overload. Several overly long sentences written one after another only compound this feeling.

EXAMPLE

The post-trial motion was supported by an affidavit by a juror that stated that a fellow juror discussed the case with a professional truck driver who was familiar with the accident scene and who told the juror that the accident could not have occurred as the plaintiff stated. (48 words in one sentence)

There are several ways to revise overly long sentences so that they become more readable. One way is to break up the sentence into two or more separate sentences. While the following revision uses more total words (53 vs. 48), the revision is easier to read when broken into three short sentences.

EXAMPLE

Revised:

The post-trial motion was supported by an affidavit by a juror. (11 words) In his affidavit, the juror stated that a fellow juror discussed the case with a professional truck driver who was familiar with the accident scene. (25 words) The truck driver told the juror that the accident could not have occurred as the plaintiff stated. (17 words)

Another way to revise an overly long sentence is to create manageable units of meaning within the sentence. You can do this by identifying structural components within the sentence, especially phrases and clauses, and setting them off with appropriate punctuation.

Notice how much more readable the following example becomes when, in Revision 1, the "if" clause is moved to the front of the sentence, where it can be set off from the rest of the sentence by a comma.

EXAMPLE

The Reynoldses will be responsible for both the attacks on the Halversons' chickens and Mr. Halverson's medical bills resulting from the dog bite if the plaintiff can show that the Reynoldses should have known of their dog's viciousness. (38 words)

Revision 1:

If the plaintiff can show that the Reynoldses should have known of their dog's viciousness, (15 words) then they will be responsible for both the attacks on the Halversons' chickens and Mr. Halverson's medical bills resulting from the dog bite. (23 words)

Other punctuation marks, such as the colon, can sometimes be added to create a break within a sentence.

EXAMPLE

Revision 2:

If the plaintiff can show that the Reynoldses should have known of their dog's viciousness, (15 words) then they will be responsible for the following: (8 words) the attacks on the Halversons' chickens and Mr. Halverson's medical bills resulting from the dog bite. (16 words)

This technique of arranging phrases and clauses so that they can be set off by punctuation is particularly helpful when writing issue statements.

EXAMPLE

Under New Hampshire law did the trial court commit prejudicial error by refusing plaintiffs' motion for a new trial because of jury misconduct when the motion was supported by a juror affidavit stating that another juror discussed the case with an alleged expert outside the trial context and then related the information to the entire jury?

In Revision 1, the writer has broken up this same information into more readable units by using a comma to set off the introductory phrase and a conjunction between two main clauses. See Rules 9.1(1) and 9.1(2).

EXAMPLE

Revision 1:

Under New Hampshire law, (4 words) did the trial court commit prejudicial error by refusing plaintiffs' motion for a new trial because of jury misconduct when the motion was supported by a juror affidavit (28 words) and when that affidavit stated that another juror discussed the case with an alleged expert outside the trial context and then related the information to the entire jury? (28 words)

In Revision 2, the writer has used commas between a series of parallel clauses (here, the "when" clauses) to help break up the information into manageable units. See section 8.7. Even though the revised sentence is longer than the original, it is more readable because the reader gets the information in smaller, more manageable units.

EXAMPLE

Revision 2:

Under New Hampshire law, (4 words) did the trial court commit prejudicial error when it refused plaintiffs' motion for a new trial because of jury misconduct

(20 words) when the motion was supported by a juror affidavit (9 words) and when that affidavit stated that another juror discussed the case with an alleged expert outside the trial context and then related information to the entire jury? (27 words)

See Quick Tip:
Problem
Sentences ("All
I'm trying to
say is . . . .")

Another way to solve sentence length problems is to eliminate wordiness. See section 6.2.

§ 5.5.2 The Context

Earlier we said that decisions about sentence length should be based on both the reader and the context. Readers rarely see a sentence in isolation. Most sentences are preceded by other sentences and followed by other sentences. Consequently, how readers respond to the length of any given sentence depends, in part, on the sentences that surround it.

For example, a 40-word sentence that is unwieldy in one context may work in another. A short, snappy sentence that drives a point home in one paragraph may seem trite and unsophisticated in another. Even a steady diet of medium-length sentences is unappetizing. Such writing tends to be monotonous and bland.

When it comes to sentence length, then, consistency is not a virtue. Effective sentences vary in length.

The following example from a statement of facts shows how lack of variety in sentence length makes the writing less interesting to read.

EXAMPLE

On December 15, 2015, Officers Jack Morrison and Wayne Garcia of the Phoenix Police Department searched Victor Ehrlich's apartment. (17 words) They had in their possession a valid search warrant for marijuana. (11 words) Marijuana was found in both the living room and the kitchen. (11 words) While searching the bedroom, Officer Morrison found a large manila envelope in one of the dresser drawers. (17 words) Photographs were protruding from the top of the envelope. (9 words) Morrison looked inside and found photographs of Ehrlich with three young girls sitting on his lap. (16 words) Ehrlich was wearing only boxer shorts, and the girls were nude from the waist up. (15 words) Considering the photographs to be perverse, Morrison showed them to Garcia, who agreed that they looked suspicious. (17 words) They seized the photographs as well as the marijuana. (9 words) The defendant, Victor Ehrlich, has now contested this seizure. (9 words) He has made a motion to suppress the photographic evidence as the result of an unconstitutional seizure. (17 words)

Revised:

On December 15, 2015, Officers Jack Morrison and Wayne Garcia of the Phoenix Police Department searched Victor Ehrlich's apartment. (17 words)

They had in their possession a valid search warrant for marijuana. (11 words) After finding marijuana in both the living room and the kitchen, they searched the bedroom, where Officer Morrison found a large manila envelope in one of the dresser drawers. (29 words) Seeing photographs protruding from the top of the envelope, Morrison looked inside and found photographs of Ehrlich with three young girls sitting on his lap. (25 words) Ehrlich was wearing only boxer shorts. (6 words) The girls were nude from the waist up. (8 words) Considering the photographs to be perverse, Morrison showed them to Garcia, who agreed that they looked suspicious. (17 words) They seized the photographs as well as the marijuana. (9 words) The defendant, Victor Ehrlich, has now contested this seizure and has made a motion to suppress the photographic evidence as the result of an unconstitutional seizure. (26 words)

Part of what makes the revised version effective is its use of short sentences. The revised version is more interesting to read because sentence length now ranges from 6 words in the shortest sentence to 29 words in the longest. The four short sentences were all used to highlight particularly significant facts.

§ 5.5.3 The Power of the Short Sentence

Used sparingly, short sentences can energize writing. Not only can they provide relief to readers who have just labored through several long sentences, they also tend to highlight the information they contain.

Note how in the following example the short sentence serves both as a welcome break after two fairly long sentences and as a way to emphasize the significant point that individuals in both cases were possibly motivated by a reward.

EXAMPLE

In two older decisions, *United States v. Snowadzki*, 723 F.2d 1427 (9th Cir. 1984), and *United States v. Black*, 767 F.2d 1334 (9th Cir. 1985), individuals conducting unlawful searches were considered to have acted as private parties, not as government agents. In both cases, the individuals obtained the documents unlawfully and then turned them over to the government, which later submitted them as evidence at trial. In each instance, a reward was offered.

§ 5.6 Emphasis

Emphasis is a natural part of all writing. In objective writing, the writer uses emphasis to let the reader know where to focus his or her attention. In persuasive writing, emphasis allows the advocate to spotlight those points that favor the client and downplay those that hurt the client. It also allows the advocate to hammer home his or her theory of the case. In the previous section we saw how short sentences can be used to emphasize key points.

EXAMPLE

Original:

The defendant lied when she testified that she was in St. Paul, Minnesota, at the time of the robbery.

Revised:

The defendant testified that she was in St. Paul, Minnesota, at the time of the robbery. She lied.

Besides short sentences, emphasis can be achieved in several other ways:

1. Underlining, italics, or boldface
2. Using positions of emphasis
3. Combining the end position with other strategies for emphasis
4. Using punctuation to highlight a point
5. Using single-word emphasizers
6. Changing the normal order in a sentence
7. Repeating key words
8. Setting up a pattern and
9. Sometimes breaking that pattern.

§ 5.6.1 Underlining

Underlining is undoubtedly the simplest and least sophisticated strategy for emphasis. It requires no restructuring of the sentence and little, if any, planning. If you do decide to use underlining for emphasis, be extremely selective.

EXAMPLE

The contract <u>permits</u> but does not <u>require</u> the tenant to add landscaping and similar outdoor improvements.

It is sometimes tempting to assume that readers will not detect subtle emphasis and must be told which words are crucial. Many writers would consider the underlining in the previous example unnecessary and possibly even condescending. The remaining strategies for emphasis are more subtle and therefore more suitable for sophisticated readers.

Of all the strategies listed, underlining is perhaps the most common and least sophisticated. Some writers consider it too obvious and overused to be effective. Others feel that it can be effective if used selectively.

§ 5.6.2 Using Positions of Emphasis

When it comes to emphasis, all parts of the sentence are not created equal. That is, the beginning, middle, and end of a sentence are not equally emphatic.

In most sentences, writers place new information at the end of a sentence. Also, the end of the sentence is the point of climax. Everything in the sentence builds toward the words at the end. Consequently, in most sentences, the most emphatic position is at the end.

The next most emphatic position is usually at the beginning. Here the writer typically sets the stage for the rest of the sentence. The reader expects the beginning of the sentence to demonstrate how the new information in this sentence is connected with what has already been discussed.

The middle of the sentence is usually the least emphatic. Skillful advocates know that in this part of the sentence they can place information they do not wish to highlight.

SENTENCE

beginning	middle	end
somewhat emphatic	least emphatic	most emphatic

Examine the following two examples, either of which could appear in an objective memo. Example 1 places "are not attractive nuisances" in the end position, so this version should occur in a memo that emphasizes the point that natural streams are usually not attractive nuisances.

EXAMPLE 1

Unless they are concealing some dangerous condition, natural streams that flow through the hatchery are not attractive nuisances.

Example 2 places "unless they are concealing some dangerous condition" in the end position, so this version is likely to occur in a memo that emphasizes that a concealed dangerous condition made a natural stream an attractive nuisance.

EXAMPLE 2

Natural streams that flow through the hatchery are not attractive nuisances, unless they are concealing some dangerous condition.

In the following example from a persuasive brief, note how the end position emphasizes that the error was harmless.

EXAMPLE

Even if the trial court mischaracterized the property, the entire division was fair; thus, the error was harmless.

To emphasize that the entire division of property was fair, the same sentence can be revised.

EXAMPLE

Even if the trial court mischaracterized the property, the error was harmless because the entire division was fair.

As ethical members of the legal profession, legal writers must often include information that is unfavorable to their client. Rather than concede a point in a short sentence, which will highlight the unfavorable point, it is often better to include it with the favorable point and arrange the material so the reader ends with the point favorable to your client.

EXAMPLE

Although Mr. Tucci admits that he raised his voice during the altercation with Ms. Stein, he never threatened Ms. Stein, as Ms. Stein claims, but rather reminded her of his rights as a property owner.

§ 5.6.3 Combining the End Position with Other Strategies for Emphasis

By using the emphatic end position in combination with another strategy for emphasis, legal writers can achieve even more emphasis.

Here the end position, combined with punctuation, is used for dramatic effect.

EXAMPLE

The courtroom fell silent in anticipation of the jury's verdict: guilty.

In the next example, the end position, combined with use of a phrase telling the reader what is important, is used to suggest a climax.

EXAMPLE

Before awarding custody, the court must consider the mental and physical health of all individuals involved, the child's adjustment to home and school, the relationship of the child with his parents and siblings, the wishes of the parents, and, most important, the wishes of the child.

In the next example, the end position, combined with the technique of setting up a pattern and breaking it, is used to startle the reader.

EXAMPLE

Daniel Klein was loyal to his parents, loyal to his wife, loyal to his friends, and disloyal to the company that had employed him for 30 years.

Two final points before leaving the topic of positions of emphasis: First, the positions of emphasis can also be applied at the paragraph and document levels; second, the characterization of most emphatic, somewhat emphatic, and least emphatic for the end, beginning, and middle of sentences is a general, not an absolute, principle. In the following subsections we will see how punctuation, single-word emphasizers, and changing normal word order can make the beginning and even the middle of sentences strong points of emphasis.

§ 5.6.4 Using Punctuation for Emphasis

Commas, colons, and em dashes can all be used to set up a point in an appositive at the end of a sentence. An appositive is a restatement of an earlier word or group of words. It is often a more detailed substitute for the earlier word or group of words. In the following example "brother" is an appositive for "silent partner." Notice how the three different marks of punctuation cast a slightly different light on the words that follow them. The comma, as a rather commonplace punctuation mark, suggests in the first of these examples that there is nothing too surprising about the silent partner being his brother. For more information on appositives, see Rule 9.1(5).

EXAMPLE

The construction contract included a silent partner, his brother.

The colon requires a longer pause; consequently, the phrase "his brother" receives more emphasis in the example that follows. Colons also have an aura of formality that somehow suggests the seriousness of what follows them. For more information on colons, see section 9.3.

EXAMPLE

The construction contract included a silent partner: his brother.

The longer pause created by the em dash gives even more emphasis to "his brother." The em dash also suggests that it is rather surprising that the brother is the silent partner. For more information on em dashes, see section 9.5.6.

EXAMPLE

The construction contract included a silent partner—his brother.

One thing legal writers should consider before using em dashes, however, is that some readers feel dashes also convey a sense of informality. Consequently, many legal writers avoid dashes in legal prose.

§ 5.6.5 Using Single-Word Emphasizers

Certain words in our language ("no," "not," "never," "only," "any," "still," "all," "every," "none") convey natural emphasis because they either dramatically change or intensify the meaning of the word they modify.

EXAMPLE

A change made to the contract must be approved by both parties.

Revision 1:

Any change made to the contract must be approved by both parties.

Revision 2:

A change may be made to the contract only if approved by both parties.

Note that the most effective way to use "not" for emphasis is to place a comma before it and use "not" as a contrasting element. See Rule 9.1(9) for a description of phrases of contrast.

EXAMPLE

It is the taxpayer, not the tax preparer, who is responsible for the accuracy of all information on the form.

Three other single-word emphasizers ("clearly," "obviously," and "very") are so overused that they have lost much of their ability to emphasize. Ironically, sentences that contain "clearly," "obviously," and "very" seem to have more impact when these words are omitted.

Weak:

Clearly, the defendant knew she was committing a crime.

Revised:

The defendant knew she was committing a crime.

§ 5.6.6 Changing the Normal Word Order

Readers expect the traditional subject-verb-object order in sentences. When a writer changes this expected order, the change draws attention to whatever words are out of the traditional order.

The most common change is from active voice to passive voice. See sections 5.1.1 to 5.1.3. Another fairly common change is to insert the words to be emphasized between either the subject and the verb or between the verb and its object.

Martin Fuller, blinded by grief, lost his grip on reality and opened fire on the parking lot.

He shot—apparently at close range—both of the parents of Tim O'Connell.

Another, less frequent change is to delay the subject and verb and open the sentence with a part of the sentence that would normally come at the end.

Ms. Shapiro rewrote her will only one week before she died.

Revised:

Only one week before she died, Ms. Shapiro rewrote her will.

Notice that some of the preceding examples seem to contradict the earlier advice about keeping subjects and verbs close together and using the end position in sentences to achieve emphasis. None of the strategies for emphasis works as an absolute rule. The writer should use his or her judgment in selecting which strategy is effective in each instance.

§ 5.6.7 Repeating Key Words

Many legal writers mistakenly assume that repetition is a weakness. This assumption leads them to search desperately for synonyms of words that recur frequently in a given office memo or brief.

While it is true that needless repetition is ineffective, it is also true that deliberate repetition can be a powerful strategy for emphasis. Key terms and key points should reverberate throughout a piece of legal writing. Like the dominant color in a beautiful tapestry, key words and phrases should be woven throughout to create an overall impression that *this* is what the case is about.

Consider the following excerpt from the respondent's brief in a case where the appellant, a church, wants to operate a grade school without the special use permit required by the city's zoning ordinance for all schools in residential areas. Throughout the excerpt, three different words—"code," "use," and "school"—are deliberately repeated for emphasis. We have bold-faced these three words so you can see how frequently they appear.

EXAMPLE

ARGUMENT

I. THE TRIAL COURT PROPERLY CONSTRUED AND APPLIED BOTH THE ZONING AND BUILDING **CODES** BECAUSE THE CHURCH HAS CHANGED THE **USE** OF ITS BUILDING BY OPERATING A FULL-TIME GRADE **SCHOOL**.

The church must comply with the requirements of the zoning and building **codes** before it may legally operate its **school**. Each of these **codes** makes accommodation for **uses** that legally existed prior to enactment of the **codes**. However, the church never operated a **school** prior to the **codes'** enactment, so full compliance with the **codes** is required for the new **use** involved in operating a **school**.

§ 5.6.8 Setting up a Pattern

The earlier strategy of repeating key words is closely tied to another strategy for emphasis: setting up a pattern. In such cases a pattern is set up and key words are repeated within that pattern.

EXAMPLES

Lieutenant Harris has been described by his superiors as an "exemplary officer"—exemplary in his demeanor and professionalism, exemplary in his management of subordinates, exemplary in his performance of duty, and exemplary in his loyalty to the service.

Both women were abducted in the same locale. Both women were abducted at night. Both women were abducted while alone. Both women were abducted by the same man: Edward Smith.

Note that to achieve a climactic effect, the writer usually used parallel structure (see section 8.7) to create the pattern and then arranged the material in an order of increasing importance.

§ 5.6.9 Variation: Deliberately Breaking a Pattern

A rather dramatic variation of the pattern strategy is to set up the pattern and then deliberately break it. The pattern and repetition of key words create a certain expectation in the reader. The reader's surprise when the pattern is broken creates heightened emphasis.

EXAMPLE

The defendant acted under a common scheme, for a common motive, but with uncommon results.

§ 5.7 Sentence Structures That Highlight Similarities or Differences[1]

Legal writers often need to compare and contrast facts. In arguing that a case is analogous to or distinguishable from the present case, writers must spell out exactly how the two sets of facts are similar or different. All too often, though, novice legal writers are tentative and vague when they set up these comparisons. Instead of making explicit factual comparisons, the novice writer is likely to start a comparison sentence with something such as "Like *Smith*, the defendant in our case . . . ."

This approach has at least two problems. First, the sentence has a basic precision problem. It is comparing a whole case, *Smith*, to a person, the defendant. See section 6.1.5. Second, it is very likely to send the reader scurrying back a page or two to where *Smith* was discussed. "Like *Smith*, the defendant in our case . . ." makes it the reader's responsibility to figure out what the factual similarity is between *Smith* and the present case. What exactly is it in *Smith* that is analogous to the present case?

---

[1] The material and examples in this section first appeared in a column written by Anne Enquist: *Teaching Students to Make Explicit Factual Comparisons,* 12 Perspectives 147 (Spring 2004).

The first problem can be easily solved by simply making sure that the comparison (or contrast) is apples to apples and oranges to oranges: "Like the <u>defendant</u> in *Smith*, the defendant in our case . . ." or "Unlike the <u>driver</u> in *Lee*, the driver in our case . . . ." That lining up of at least one fact (defendant to defendant or driver to driver) gives the reader a start at understanding the argument, but it is still just a start. The second problem can be solved by stating enough of the salient facts about the defendants or the drivers for the reader to see the similarities or differences.

Step one, then, might be to create a table that sets out the parallel similarities or differences before beginning to write sentences.

<u>analogous case</u>	<u>present case</u>
defendants in *Smith*	defendants in our case (the Joneses)
allowed daughter's boyfriend to use the family car to drive to a dance	allowed family friend to use the family car to drive to work
boyfriend used car for a prank	friend used car for work-related errand
and got into an accident	and got into an accident
Holding	*Argument*
family car doctrine does not apply	family car doctrine should not apply
because	because
defendants' permission limited to driving to and from dance, not prank	defendants' permission limited to driving to and from work, not work-related errands
driver acted beyond scope of permission	driver acted beyond the scope of permission
defendants not liable	defendants should not be liable

Step two is to translate the table into sentences. The reader will readily see the comparison if the writer matches the sentence structure in the first and second parts of the sentence so that the information about the analogous case parallels the information about the present case. In the following example, the parallel parts are labeled A and A′, B and B′, and so on.

<u>"Like the defendant in *Smith*, who allowed his daughter's boyfriend to</u>
              A
<u>use the family car to drive to a dance, the defendants in our case</u>
        B   C   A′
<u>allowed their family friend to use the family car to drive to work.</u>
            B′   C′
<u>The *Smith* court held that the defendants were not liable because</u>
                        D
<u>the driver acted beyond the scope of the defendants' permission</u>.
                        E

(cite) <u>Their permission was limited to driving to and from the dance</u>;
                                                  F
<u>it did not extend to using the car for a prank</u>. (cite) Similarly, <u>the Joneses</u>
                          G
<u>should not be held liable</u> <u>because the driver acted beyond the scope of</u>
          D′
<u>their permission</u>. <u>Their permission was limited to driving to and from</u>
          E′   F′
<u>work</u>; <u>it did not extend to work-related errands</u>."
                          G′

Of course, writers do not have to rigidly and mindlessly repeat the exact sentence structure in the second part that they used in the first part, but notice that *some* repetition makes the comparison easier for the reader to follow.

Below are a few more examples of comparing or contrasting tables followed by "like" or "unlike" sentences. An "equals" sign (=) in the chart indicates similarities; an inequality sign (≠) indicates differences.

EXAMPLE

defendant in *Sheldon*	=	Ms. Olsen (the defendant in this case)
used parents' house	≠	used halfway house
for many activities	≠	for only a few activities
indicates	≠	does not indicate
center of domestic activity	=	center of domestic activity

"Unlike the defendant in *Sheldon*, who used her parents' home for many activities indicative of a center of domestic activity, Ms. Olsen used the halfway house for only a few activities indicative of a center of domestic activity."

EXAMPLE

driver in *Cook*, Whitner,	=	Ms. Foster (the driver in this case)
paid room and board	=	paid room and board
family's adult daughter	≠	family friend
lived with parents	≠	lived with Nguyens
since death of husband	≠	while attending university

"Like the driver in *Cook* who paid for room and board, Ms. Foster also paid for room and board; however, unlike Whitner, who was the family's adult daughter who had lived with her parents since the death of her husband, Ms. Foster was only a family friend who was living with the Nguyens while she attended the university."

When the facts in both the analogous and the present case are virtually identical on one or more points, writers often use a sentence structure such as the one below.

EXAMPLE

"As in *Cook*, the driver in our case paid for room and board; however, unlike Whitner, who was the family's adult daughter who had lived with her parents since the death of her husband, Ms. Foster was only a family friend who was living with the Nguyens while she attended the university."

Note, however, that the "As in *case name*," sentence opening should be used with some care. Consider the example below.

EXAMPLE

Chea employee's stress	=	Officer Wu's stress (the employee in this case)
resulted from a series of incidents	=	resulted from three different incidents

Incorrect:

"As in *Chea*, Officer Wu's stress resulted from three different incidents: the Aurora Bridge accident, the City's failure to notify him about his exposure to HIV, and the WTO riots."

The sentence above incorrectly says the employee's stress in *Chea* also came from these same three incidents that caused Officer Wu's stress.

EXAMPLE

Corrected:

"Like *Chea*, in which the employee's stress resulted from a series of incidents, in this case, Officer Wu's stress resulted from three different incidents: the Aurora Bridge accident, the City's failure to notify him about his exposure to HIV, and the WTO riots."

In some situations, writers need to list many facts in order to compare or contrast cases, and doing so in one long sentence would affect readability. For those situations, companion sentences in which all of sentence 1 mirrors all of sentence 2 are often preferable.

EXAMPLE   ## Companion Sentences

Sentence 1:

In *Cook*, because Ms. Whitner ate most meals with the family, had her own room in the family home, was assigned several family-related chores, and was included in the family holiday photo, the court held that she was "treated as a member of the family." *Id.* at 63. Similarly, because Ms. Foster ate three to four times a week with the Nguyens, shared a room with their daughter, and vacationed in Oregon with them, the court should decide that she was treated as a member of the family.

Sentence 2:

In *Cook*, the court noted numerous examples of how Ms. Whitner was treated as a member of the family: She ate most meals with the family, had her own room in the family home, was assigned several family-related chores, and was included in the family holiday photo. Similarly, in our case, Ms. Foster can also point to numerous examples of how she was treated as a member of the family: She ate three to four times a week with the Nguyens, shared a room with their daughter, and vacationed in Oregon with them.

Interestingly, however, distinguishing facts often works best through a series of sentences with juxtaposed parts.

EXAMPLE

Cook is easily distinguishable from our case. Ms. Whitner ate most meals with the family; Ms. Foster ate only three to four times a week with the Nguyens. Whitner had her own room in the family home; Foster shared a room with the Nguyens' daughter, but after October spent most nights at her boyfriend's apartment. Whitner was assigned several family-related chores, including cooking once a week and taking out the trash; Foster was never asked to perform any chores and was instead treated more as a guest. Whitner was included in the family holiday photo and wrote her own paragraph in the family Christmas letter; Foster was included in the Nguyens' Oregon vacation, but she paid for her own room, meals, and souvenirs. Therefore, although Ms. Foster was still living with the Nguyens at the time of the accident, the court is unlikely to find that Ms. Foster was treated as a member of the family.

The examples above are but a few of the many sentence structures for making factual comparisons. The key is to think through how the facts are similar or different and then consciously construct a sentence that highlights those similarities and differences.

CHAPTER 6

Effective Words

A powerful agent is the right word. Whenever we come upon one of those intensely right words in a book or a newspaper the resulting effect is physical as well as spiritual, and electrically prompt.

—Mark Twain,
Essay on William Dean Howells

§ 6.1 Diction and Precision

It is such a seemingly simple thing. Use the right word, Twain tells us, and the effect is physical, spiritual, electric, prompt. But "right" is relative, isn't it? Some words are more right than others. Some words approach the desired meaning; others capture it, embody it, nail it to the wall in a way that leaves both the writer and reader satisfied, almost breathless.

Take the word "right," for example. Twain chose "right" to describe the kind of word he meant, even though the thesaurus suggests that he might have chosen any number of so-called synonyms. How about the "noble" word, the "proper" word, the "suitable" word, the "exact" word, the "accurate" word, the "correct" word, or even the "precise" word?

What is it about "right" that makes it the right choice?

First of all, denotation—that is, the word's definition. "Noble" is the wrong choice because it has the wrong denotation. Webster tells us that "noble" means "possessing outstanding qualities." The definition of "noble" also includes a tie to some kind of superiority. Something is "noble" because it has a "superiority of mind or character or ideals or morals." The kind of words Twain talks about do something different than possess outstanding qualities or superiority.

"Proper" seems to have the right denotation. "Proper" is defined as "marked by suitability, rightness, or appropriateness." Later in the definition we find "strictly accurate" and "correct." These meanings seem closer to Twain's intention. But wait a minute. Further still in the definition we see "respectable," "strictly decorous," and "genteel." But do we have to include all of the possible definitions of a word when we use it? Obviously not, but in the case of "proper," these later definitions are clues about the connotations, or associations, that the word carries.

The word "proper" has close ties with the word "propriety," which means "the quality or state of being proper." "Propriety" also means "the standard of what is socially acceptable." If "the proper thing to do" has overtones of decorum and civility, then "the proper word" might also suggest a bit of politeness in its selection. It's doubtful that Twain meant that a "polite word" is a powerful agent.

"Suitable" has similar denotation and connotation problems. Part of the definition of "suitable" is "adapted to a use or purpose." If "suitable words" are those that are adapted to a certain use or purpose, then it is unlikely anything with such a chameleon-like quality can ever be physical, spiritual, electric, or prompt.

"Exact" has the virtue of meaning in "strict, particular, and complete accordance with fact" and the minor flaw of connoting a kind of mathematical or scientific measurement. Still, it is a far better choice than "noble," "proper," or "suitable."

In fact, "exact," "accurate," "correct," "precise," and "right" all have what dictionaries call "the shared meaning element." They all mean "conforming to fact, truth, or a standard."

What is it then about the word "right" that makes it preferable to the other four words—that makes it just right? It has the right denotation and the right connotation, and it has the right sound.

Go back to the quotation at the beginning of the chapter. Try reading the first sentence aloud as it is. Now, one at a time, substitute the words "exact," "accurate," "correct," and "precise" for "right." Read each of these versions aloud. Notice how much harder it is to get the desired emphasis with the three-syllable "accurate." Even the two-syllable words dilute, albeit just a bit, the punch that we hear in the one syllable "right." Furthermore, "right" has a kind of honesty and simplicity that captures the spirit of Twain's insight.

Now what does all of this mean for a writer of legal documents? The same thing it means for any good writer. Finding the right word to express one's meaning and to reach the reader is critical to clear communication. With anything other than the right word, you have sacrificed precision; you have sacrificed exact meaning.

In cases such as Twain's in which several words can express the intended meaning, the writer can then go beyond precision to eloquence to find the word with just the right sound. See Chapter 7. For now, though, we will focus just on diction and precision and the word choice problems that frequently occur in legal writing. (Three categories of word choice problems, legalese, gender-neutral language, and bias-free language, deserve special attention and are discussed in sections 6.3, 6.4, and 6.5, respectively.)

§ 6.1.1 Colloquial Language

Because legal writing is done for serious reasons and in a professional context, you should strive to select words that reflect seriousness and professionalism. Slang, colloquialisms, or informal expressions that are acceptable in everyday spoken language are usually out of place in legal writing.

EXAMPLE

Poor:

The prosecutor noted that Mr. Webb is **hung up on** how clean his car is, what gas is used in it, and how it is driven.

Revised:

The prosecutor noted that Mr. Webb is **obsessed** about how clean his car is, what gas is used in it, and how it is driven.

The only exception to the general ban on using slang, colloquialisms, and informal language in legal writing exists when the writer is quoting. While a writer of a trial brief would be ill-advised to call the defendant "a bad dude," he or she may effectively use that expression, in quotation marks, if it appeared in the record.

§ 6.1.2 Reader Expectations and Idioms

Your choice among synonyms should also be governed by your reader's expectations. Legal readers, for example, expect to hear about "analogous" cases or "similar" cases, not "comparable" cases or "matching" cases.

Read the following example and see if any word is jarring for legal readers.

EXAMPLE

Beaver Custom Carpets will probably argue that there are significant **parallelisms** between its case and *Flowers*.

Revised:

Beaver Custom Carpets will probably argue that there are significant **similarities** between its case and *Flowers*.

Likewise, some synonyms have the correct denotation and connotation, but their use is jarring because the reader expects certain idiomatic combinations.

Consider the following example. Which word doesn't seem quite right?

EXAMPLE

Corporations can elude liability by dissolution.

Although the thesaurus may list "elude" as a synonym for "avoid" and "escape," legal readers expect either the idiom "avoid liability" or the idiom "escape liability."

Numerous verbs have certain prepositions with which they commonly combine. In common usage, for example, one always "infers *from*" something. A client may "agree *to*" sign a contract, but she may "agree *with*" the way you are handling her case.

When in doubt about which idiom or preposition is appropriate, consult a reliable dictionary or a usage guidebook. Another strategy is to read the sentence aloud. Native speakers of English can usually "hear" which preposition is correct. If your senses aren't "tuned" to correct usage, try to pay attention to how other legal writers use these prepositions as you read.

See Quick Tip:
Its vs. It's ⊕

EXAMPLE   **Wrong Preposition**

Publishers must be able to publish matters of public concern without fear **for** a lawsuit.

Revised:

Publishers must be able to publish matters of public concern without fear **of** a lawsuit.

---

§ 6.1.3 Not-Really-Synonymous Synonyms

Of the many types of imprecision, the most common is the simple substitution of a not-really-synonymous "synonym." In the following example, the writer knew that there were several things he had to prove under the doctrine of adverse possession, but he forgot what to call those "things."

EXAMPLE

The adverse possessor must prove the **condition** of hostility.

"Condition" is not completely wrong; the reader can probably figure out what the writer intended. But "condition" is not precise. By using the precise term "element," the writer conveys the exact intended meaning, and he makes it clear that he is doing an elements analysis of the problem.

EXAMPLE

Revised:

The adverse possessor must also prove the **element** of hostility.

Notice that in the above example the term "element" is used when there are indeed "elements" that must be proved. Some legal writers mistakenly use the terms "element" and "factor" as if they were synonyms. The term "element" refers to a requirement—something that must be proved or met. "Factors," on the other hand, refers to what a court must consider. For example, courts must examine several factors to determine which parent gets custody of a child.

Another group of problematic terms that some legal writers use imprecisely includes the words "part," "prong," and "step." If there is a two-part test, then both parts must be satisfied. If there are two prongs to a test, then the test can be satisfied in either of the two ways. If there is a two-step test, both steps must be satisfied in sequence.

Unfortunately, however, you may find that courts themselves sometimes use the terms "factor," "element," "part," "prong," and "step" imprecisely when describing a test. In such instances, you will probably want to adopt the court's word choice if you are writing to that same court. In writing for others, however, you will probably want to adopt the precise term.

Yet another precision problem occurs when writers try to dress up a simple idea in a fancy vocabulary word and end up instead with a word choice that misses the mark.

EXAMPLE

The McKibbins may argue that rugs **are totally diverse** from closed circuit television camera security systems because few consumers have a need for such elaborate security systems.

Revised:

The McKibbins may argue that rugs **differ** from closed circuit television camera security systems because few consumers have a need for such elaborate security systems.

The most serious type of "not-really-synonymous synonym" problem occurs when writers attempt to use words they are not quite sure of. Needless to say, it can be embarrassing to find that you have used a word that only sounds like the word you intended. Undoubtedly, the writer of the following example intended the point to be "salient," not salty.

See Quick Tip:
Commonly
Confused
Words ⊕

EXAMPLE

Mrs. Harris's most **saline** point is that Mr. Harris intends to move the children over 250 miles away.

---

§ 6.1.4 The Same Term for the Same Idea

Another common precision problem in legal writing is the misuse of elegant variation. In other words, legal writers sometimes try to use synonyms for key terms in their writing in the mistaken belief that using the same term over and over again bores their readers.

What they have forgotten, though, is that their legal readers have been carefully trained to read statutes and, according to the rules of statutory construction, a different term signals a different idea. Many legal readers carry this rule over into their memo and brief reading. A change in a key term starts them wondering: "Does the writer mean the same thing as before, or is this really something new?" A character in Tom Robbins's novel *Jitterbug Perfume* echoes a theme largely true to legal writing: "There are no such things as synonyms! . . . Deluge is not the same as flood." To the trained legal mind, words mean what they mean, and any other word could potentially mean something else, something unexpected.

Notice how in the following example the writer uses the term "stability" and its variations consistently but floats back and forth among the terms "factor," "principle," and "element."

EXAMPLE

Under the applicable case law, the relevant **factors** used by the courts in deciding custody disputes are the stability of the parent and the role of the primary caregiver. *In re Marriage of Maddox*, 641 P.2d 665 (Or. Ct. App. 1982). Oregon courts seem to use stability as the overriding **principle** to decide custody disputes. If the court can determine that one parent is more stable than the other, custody is usually granted to the more stable parent. Another **element** appears, as in *Maddox*, in which the father argued that he devoted a significant amount of time to the children, even though the mother was the primary caregiver during the marriage. *Id.* at 667. Both of these **factors** relate back to the first part of the statute, which deals with the emotional ties and interest and attitudes.

In cases such as the example above, the reader does not know whether to accuse the writer of sloppy writing or to try to make some fine distinction between "factor," "principle," and "element." In many cases, there is a legal distinction between "factor" and "element" or between "factor" and "principle." In those cases, substituting the terms for each other would be more than confusing; it would be legally inaccurate.

In short, then, legal readers appreciate appropriate variety, but they do not appreciate variety at the expense of clarity.

§ 6.1.5 Precise Comparisons

In the preceding sections, we saw how disconcerting it can be for readers when writers aren't careful about precise word choice. Equally disconcerting for readers are situations in which writers are sloppy about the comparisons they make.

Because a case includes more than just the facts, it is incongruous to compare just the facts of one case to another entire case.

EXAMPLE

The facts of *Turner* are **similar to our case**.

Revised:

The facts of *Turner* are **similar to the facts in our case**.

In the following examples, the writer has forgotten that the italic type signals the case, not the defendant.

EXAMPLE

Unlike *Callahan*, Richardson was not just a temporary visitor.

Revised:

Unlike *Callahan*, Richardson was not just a temporary visitor.

EXAMPLE

Like *Collins*, Richardson had personal possessions on the premises.

Revised:

Like the defendant in *Collins*, Richardson had personal possessions on the premises.

As in *Collins*, in our case, Richardson had personal possessions on the premises.

See section 5.7 for more on precise comparisons and examples on how to correct problems.

§ 6.1.6 Subject-Verb-Object Mismatch

Not all problems of precision are a matter of just one poorly chosen word. All too frequently, the problem is a poorly chosen combination of words. In the following example from a case about a custody dispute, note that the subject, verb, and object are mismatched.

EXAMPLE

> Dr. Davis's <u>occupation</u> as an obstetrician <u>has shown</u> a <u>diminished ability</u>
>   *(subject)*   *(verb)*   *(object)*
> to provide consistent care and guidance for her children.

Can an occupation show a diminished ability to do anything? Obviously not. What the writer wants to say is that Dr. Davis is an obstetrician and that people who are obstetricians often have demanding, irregular schedules and therefore less time and energy to give consistent care and guidance to their own children.

EXAMPLE

Revised:

Dr. Davis's occupation, obstetrician, may impair her ability to provide consistent care and guidance for her children.

To determine whether this or any other subject-verb-object combination is mismatched, lift those three parts out of the sentence and see if they make sense as a unit.

> occupation   may impair   ability
> *(subject)*   *(verb)*   *(object)*

Does "occupation may impair ability" make sense? Most readers would say that it does; some, however, would argue against the personification of "occupation" and suggest that occupations cannot "impair" anything. Precision, as we said earlier, is a relative thing.

One common personification used in law that many readers consider imprecise is the use of a case in the subject position when the writer actually means the court that presided over that case.

EXAMPLE

The case *In re Miller*, 670 P.2d 819 (Colo. Ct. App. 1983), reversed the trial court's decision because of the trial court's undue emphasis toward "motherly instincts."

Using the "lift-out" strategy, we get the following combination:

> case   reversed   decision
> *(subject)*   *(verb)*   *(object)*

To be more precise, place the real actor, the appellate court, in the subject position.

Occasionally, legal writers mistakenly end up with a combination that essentially means "X equals X"; that is, the subject or beginning of the sentence and object or end of the sentence are the same.

EXAMPLE

The purpose of the legislation is compensatory intent.

---

purpose   is   intent

(subject)   *(verb)*   *(predicate nominative)*[1]

There is virtually no difference between "the purpose of the legislation" and "the intent of the legislation." More than likely, the writer intended to say that the purpose of the legislation was to compensate someone.

EXAMPLE

Revised:

The purpose of the legislation is to compensate victims of such crimes.

Part of matching the right subject with the right verb is understanding how the legal system works. Knowing exactly what courts, juries, parties to litigation, legislatures, and agencies do and don't do makes it easier to select appropriate verbs. Chart 6.1 lists some typical subject-verb-object combinations.

For example, "the court found" is the right combination for describing the action a court takes in making a finding of fact. "The court held" is the right combination for describing the court's decision on a question of law. "The court ruled" is the right combination for describing the actions a court takes on a particular issue, such as a motion or an objection, in a particular case. Courts can also "deny motions" or "grant injunctions"; they can "take something under advisement."

Courts can "apply the law," they can "apply a standard," and they can "apply a test"; they never "apply the facts."

Chart 6.1   **Typical Subject-Verb-Object Combinations**

the court found (findings of fact)
the court ruled (ruling on an objection or a motion)
the court held (law applied to facts of a specific case)
the court determined (or must determine)
the court granted an injunction

---

[1] The term "predicate nominative" is used instead of "object" with linking verbs. See section 8.1.

the court granted the motion
the court denied the motion
the court applied the law (the test, the rule, the standard)
the court adopted the test
the court ordered (psychological testing, discovery)

the court relied on
the court followed
the court concluded
the court examined
the court reasoned

the appellate court affirmed the trial court's decision
the appellate court modified the trial court's decision
the appellate court reversed the trial court's decision
the appellate court upheld the trial court's decision
the appellate court remanded the case

In *Smith*, the court criticized the court's holding in *Jones*.
In *Smith*, the court explained the court's holding in *Jones*.
In *Smith*, the court followed the court's holding in *Jones*.
In *Smith*, the court limited the court's holding in *Jones*.
In *Smith*, the court questioned the court's holding in *Jones*.
In *Smith*, the court expanded upon the court's holding in *Jones*.
In *Smith*, the court overruled *Jones*.

the jury found the defendant (guilty or not guilty)
the jury acquitted the defendant
the jury determined that the defendant was (was not) liable
the jury awarded damages

the defendant (or plaintiff, State, prosecutor, defense counsel) argued,
    stated, maintained, asked, claimed, alleged, asserted, contended,
    responded, rebutted, countered, moved

the defendant was arrested, charged, arraigned, tried, convicted/found not
    guilty

the legislature passed, enacted, amended
the legislature intended to (promote, encourage, prevent, protect)
the legislature wanted to (promote, encourage, prevent, protect)

the agency determined, decided
the agency ruled
the agency promulgated, investigated, proposed, mediated

In cases in which the court is both the decider of law and the trier of fact, courts perform an additional set of duties. When no jury is present, the court will "find" the criminal defendant guilty or not guilty, and the court will "award" civil damages.

As both the decider of law and the trier of fact, the court may "make determinations" or simply "determine" something about the law or the facts. Even so, "determine" is more commonly used for findings of fact.

For cases up on appeal, appellate courts have a variety of actions they can perform. They can "affirm," "modify," "reverse," or "remand" a case; they can also "criticize," "distinguish," "explain," "follow," "limit," "overrule," or "question" the decisions in another case.

The court never takes on the role of one of the parties to litigation. Consequently, as a general rule, the court does not "claim," "allege," "assert," "contend," or "argue." The court is in a position to "say," not to "claim."

Even though it is technically incorrect to say "the court claimed," "the court asserted," or "the court argued," there are a few times when these combinations may be strategic word choices. In instances in which you are disagreeing with another court, for example, you may deliberately use "the court claimed" as a pejorative attack on another court's reasoning. The effect, of course, is the subtle undermining of the court's authority.

Another instance in which you can use a combination such as "the court argued" occurs when members of the same court differ. Consequently, a law professor or the author of a law review article may say "Justice X argued" to describe a position that a justice took when trying to persuade the other members of the same court.

Juries, on the other hand, are charged with different tasks from judges. They "find" that a defendant is guilty or not guilty, they "determine liability," and they "award damages," but they do not "rule" on the law. Consequently, "a jury found," "a jury determined," and "a jury awarded" are appropriate combinations. In a jury trial, the jury, not the judge, "renders a verdict," and the judge, not the jury, "enters a judgment" based on that verdict. In a bench trial, the judge "renders a verdict."

Defendants and plaintiffs perform certain acts as well. They "argue," "state," "ask," "claim," "contend," "allege," "assert," "respond," "rebut," and "counter," but they do not "apply" the law. That is for the court to do.

EXAMPLE

Incorrect:

Applying the majority rule, the defendant will argue that the benefit of having a healthy baby outweighs the burden.

Correct:

The defendant **will argue** that the court should apply the majority rule and hold that having a healthy baby outweighs the burden.

Either party to litigation can make a preliminary motion. Although you often hear, for example, that "the plaintiff made a motion for summary judgment," it is more concise to say "the plaintiff moved for summary judgment."

Legislatures, of course, perform entirely different functions from judges, juries, and litigants. The legislature may "enact a statute," it may "amend a statute," and it may "pass a law." It does not "hold" or "find." When it comes to policy, it is appropriate to say that the legislature "intended," "wanted to promote," "wanted to encourage," "wanted to prevent," or "wanted to protect."

Like judges, agencies "make determinations" (or just "determine"), and they "decide" things. Rarely does an agency "hold"; save "hold" for the few times when an agency issues an opinion. Even then, it is more likely to "rule." And of course, agencies perform many other functions such as "promulgate," "investigate," "propose," and "decide."

Perhaps the most glaring errors in word choice made by novice legal writers are those that stem from confusion over criminal and civil cases. Chart 6.2 lists some examples of appropriate word choice depending on whether a case is criminal or civil. Use "accused," "prosecuted," and "charged" for criminal cases. The defendant in a civil suit may be "sued" or "an action may be filed" against him or her; a civil suit defendant is not "accused," "prosecuted," or "charged."

Similarly, defendants in civil suits are not found "guilty" or "not guilty"; they are found "liable" or "not liable."

The outcome of a trial is a "judgment," not a "settlement." Use "settlement" for those agreements reached by parties through negotiation, not litigation. Parties may "settle out of court."

Chart 6.2

Criminal Cases	Civil Cases
accused (verb)	sued
charged	action filed against
guilty	liable
not guilty	not liable
defendant	defendant
state (or commonwealth)	plaintiff
prosecutor	plaintiff's counsel

§ 6.1.7 Grammatical Ambiguities

Before leaving the topic of precision, we must consider those times when writing becomes ambiguous and imprecise because the writer has not paid close attention to the grammar of the sentence. Modifiers, in particular, can create unintended meanings because modifiers seem to be free-floating spirits that can find a home in many different spots in a sentence. If you write, "The sketch of the contested surgical clamp was written by the man on a cocktail napkin," your reader may be forced to speculate as to how the man got on the cocktail napkin in the first place. See section 8.6 for more on modifiers.

§ 6.2 Conciseness

Imagine for a moment that a colleague is at a great steak house. Because it's a special occasion, he orders the best steak on the menu. However, when the meal arrives, he sees that the steak is surrounded by an inch of fat. Appealing? Hardly. The meat itself may be tender and juicy, but your colleague finds it hard to appreciate its flavor with all that fat staring up off the plate at him. Why, he wonders, didn't the chef trim off the fat before serving the meal? Wordy writing is like a steak surrounded by fat. It may have great analysis and brilliant arguments, but if you haven't trimmed the fat, the reader is likely to find the writing unappealing.

The question for most legal writers is how to transform fatty writing into writing that is lean and appealing. What follows are numerous strategies for trimming excess verbiage.

§ 6.2.1 Don't State the Obvious

Judges, lawyers, and most clients are busy people. They don't want to spend time reading the legal equivalent of "the sky is blue" or "people breathe air," unless, of course, you have something new to say about what is obvious.

Wasting time with sentences such as "Now I am going to discuss the cases that are relevant to this issue" or "The appellate court will not reconsider factual issues" annoys legal readers. Legal readers know that an office memo will discuss cases that are relevant to the issue; they know that appellate courts do not retry a case on its facts.

Novice legal writers often state the obvious because it reminds them of the steps they must go through in legal analysis. For example, a writer who begins the discussion section of a memo with "To determine the answer to this question, we must first look at the rule that . . . ." has not recognized that a legal reader would be shocked to find something other than the rule at this point in the memo.

Consider the following excerpt from a draft of a memo.

EXAMPLE

Our client bears the burden of establishing that the action meets the federal removal requirements. Some of these requirements are more important than others, but all are required before removal may occur. To understand these requirements, it is easiest to break down 28 U.S.C. § 1441(a) (2011) into its component parts and discuss each part separately.

Besides the wordiness that comes from the redundancy in the first two sentences—requirements are required—the last sentence is no more than an announcement that one should do the obvious: analyze the requirements.

Novice and experienced legal writers often fall into the "stating the obvious" trap when they are trying to compose topic and transitional sentences within a discussion or argument section.

Suppose, for example, that a writer has just completed a paragraph about the holding, rationale, and facts of an analogous case. The writer now wants to compare the facts of the analogous case with those of the present case. At first the writer may be tempted to begin with something such as "*Moore* and our client's case are factually similar." This announcement should be quickly obvious, however, and unworthy of mention. What the writer needs to discuss in this topic sentence is the nature of these similarities or why those similarities suggest a certain outcome.

§ 6.2.2 Don't Start Too Far Back

Some novice legal writers fall prey to a cousin of the "stating the obvious" problem—starting too far back. They forget that there is common knowledge among legal readers. Consequently, the writing problem is determining where to begin and what not to say.

Consider the following example of starting too far back from a draft of a memo about a case in which criminal charges had been filed against the client who had photocopied a dollar bill and, after a friendly bet, had tried it in a change machine.

EXAMPLE

Counterfeiting has been classified as an offense affecting the administration of governmental functions because the power to coin money was expressly granted to Congress and denied to the states by the terms of the Constitution. Hence, counterfeiting is a federal crime and the penalty for passing counterfeit money is found in the *United States Code*. Congress has enacted statutes making counterfeiting a federal offense; the various counterfeiting crimes are defined by these statutes, and these statutes determine the essential elements of the respective crimes.

The background information in the preceding example is unnecessary. The writer of this excerpt seems to have forgotten who the reader is and what that reader is likely to know.

Writers who have a tendency to start too far back often fill their writing with background information that *they* needed in order to focus their ideas or to clarify a point. Even if they needed the information to analyze the problem, that does not automatically mean that their reader will need it too.

For example, because of a lack of experience, the writer may have had to do a fair amount of spade work to fill in a skimpy background in a given area of law. Unless the writer believes the reader needs the same kind of review or preliminary discussion, it should be omitted from the reader's version.

Furthermore, writers are obliged to save their readers from at least some of the blind alleys they explored. New legal writers who were successful writers as undergraduates often have a difficult time adapting to the new expectations of the legal profession. In law, you don't receive extra credit for arguments that don't work.

Thus far, we have primarily discussed legal writing that starts too far back analytically. Occasionally legal writers start too far back historically. They give long, careful explanations of how a particular area of law has evolved when all the reader wants is a discussion of how the end result of that evolutionary process applies to the facts of a case at hand.

This is not to say that tracing the history of a statute or a judicial trend is never appropriate. The point is to consider your specific reader and the reader's purposes, and then ask yourself if it is appropriate in the document you are writing. Put another way, don't write a law review article when the senior partner has assigned you an office memo.

§ 6.2.3 Don't Overuse Quotations

When to quote and how much to quote—these are two tough questions for all legal writers. Like many other issues in legal writing, there is a range of opinion about when quoting is appropriate, even required, and when the writer should merely paraphrase and cite to authority.

Most legal readers agree that relevant portions of statutes should be quoted. The trick, of course, is to pare the quotation down to that which is relevant.

In the following example, the writer has mistakenly quoted more of the statute than her reader needs. The case she is working on does not have anything to do with obstruction of a highway or the closing of a channel, but rather with whether a noisy aerobics club with patrons in skimpy attire is a private nuisance.

EXAMPLE   Overquoting a Statute

In determining whether there is a cause of action for private nuisance, the court is guided by Washington Revised Code § 7.48.010 (2016), which provides the following:

> The obstruction of any highway or closing the channel of any stream used for boating or rafting logs, lumber or timber, or whatever is injurious to health or indecent or offensive to the senses, or an obstruction to the free use of property, so as to essentially interfere with the comfortable enjoyment of the life and property, is a nuisance and the subject of an action for damages and other and further relief.

First, edit out all of the statute that is extraneous to the case:

The obstruction of any highway or closing the channel of any stream used for boating or rafting logs, lumber or timber, or whatever is injurious to health or indecent or offensive to the senses, or an obstruction to the free use of property, so as to essentially interfere with the comfortable enjoyment of the life and property, is a nuisance and the subject of an action for damages and other and further relief.

Appropriately pared down then, the quotation looks like this:

[W]hatever is . . . indecent or offensive to the senses, or an obstruction to the free use of property, so as to essentially interfere with the comfortable enjoyment of the life and property, is a nuisance . . . .

Note the use of ellipses to indicate words omitted in the middle and at the end of the quotation. The brackets, which are used to show that the "w" was not capitalized in the original, also show that the original did not begin at the word "whatever." See sections 9.5.2 and 9.5.3 for more on the use of ellipses and brackets in quotations.

Although most legal writers agree about quoting relevant portions of statutes, some disagree about whether common law should be set out verbatim. As a general rule, if a specific phrase reappears in the cases, then that phrase has become the standard or familiar "rule" and should therefore be quoted.

Generally, you can paraphrase the holding and rationale and cite to authority. Occasionally, however, the particular language of the holding or court's reasoning is so apt or well stated that a quotation is effective. This tactic works best when used sparingly.

Never quote facts of a case, although you may want to quote the exact words of a person in a fact statement when those words suggest the person's attitude, motive, or intention. Think of it this way: quote the quotations in the facts section when it helps your writing, but don't quote the narrative.

When deciding how much to quote, also consider your purpose. In persuasive writing, you will probably use fairly extensive quoting from the record to make points about errors and conflicting testimony. You might also use a few more quotations from analogous cases because they allow you to create emphasis and effective repetition. A well-written lead-in to a quotation, which makes your point, followed by a carefully selected quotation, which also makes your point, allows you to make that point twice without being tedious. The same tactic used in objective writing, however, would be tedious.

The cardinal rule of quotations can be summed up as follows: *Quote only when the language itself is worth attention.* The language of statutes is always worth our attention; the specific language of common law is sometimes worth our attention; and, occasionally, the language of a court stating its holding or expressing its rationale is so memorable that it should not escape our attention. In all three instances, quote; otherwise, don't.

§ 6.2.4 Create a Strong Subject-Verb Unit

The quickest way to achieve an energetic yet lean writing style is to make sure that the subject-verb unit carries the core of meaning in the sentence. In other words, put the real action in the verb; put the doer of that action in the subject.

All too frequently in ineffective legal writing, the real action of the sentence is buried in a noun. This practice of changing verbs to nouns, known as "nominalization," tends to make sentences wordy (see section 5.3). Because the real action in the sentence is somewhere other than the verb, the writer must find a substitute to fill the verb slot in the sentence, usually either a form of the verb "to be" or some other filler verb that expresses no real action.

EXAMPLE

This case <u>is</u> an <u>illustration</u> of this point.
    (verb)(nominalization)

Revised:

This case <u>illustrates</u> this point.
    (verb)

The following examples are but a few of the many ways legal writers can make their writing more concise by finding the real action in the sentence.

> See Quick Tip:
> Finding and
> Correcting
> Nominalizations

made the assumption	→	assumed
made a recommendation	→	recommended
made a statement	→	stated
perform a review	→	review
reached an agreement	→	agreed
supports an inference	→	infers

If the real doer of the action is somewhere other than in the subject, then the subject of the sentence is also inevitably wordy because the writer has had to manufacture some language to fill that slot in the sentence.

Sometimes writers fill the subject slot with wordy expletives such as "there is," "there are," "there was," "there were," "it is," or "it was." Avoid these expletive constructions unless the point of the sentence is that something exists.

EXAMPLE

It was his intention to return to Maryland.

Revised:

He intended to return to Maryland.

See Quick Tip:
Conciseness
(Strong Verbs) ⊕

When writers inadvertently slip into the passive voice (see section 5.1), they inevitably create a wordy sentence with a weak subject.

EXAMPLE

Authorization for the contract was given by the district manager.

Revised:

The district manager authorized the contract.

---

§ 6.2.5 Avoid Throat-Clearing Expressions

Frequently, legal writers create wordy sentences because they fill both the subject and verb slots with throat-clearing expressions that add little, if any, meaning to the sentence.

EXAMPLE

It must be remembered that the statute requires that service be made at the dwelling house or usual place of abode.

Revised:

The statute requires that service be made at the dwelling house or usual place of abode.

Most, but not all, of these throat-clearing expressions fall into the pattern "It is _____ that":

It is expected that
It is clear that
It is apparent that
It is generally recognized that
It has been determined that
It is significant that
It is a known fact that
It is obvious that
It is essential that
It is crucial that
It is conceivable that

Notice how the following throat-clearing expressions may be reduced to one word or completely edited out.

It seems more likely than not that   → probably
It can be presumed that   → presumably
It may be argued that   → arguably *or* say who may argue

A fair number of the throat-clearing expressions spend time saying that someone should take note of something.

> It should also be noted that
> It is interesting to note that
> It should be noted that
> It is worth noting that
> It is crucial to note that
> It is important to note that

If the writer can presume that the reader is already taking special note of all that is written, then such expressions are superfluous.

For an extended discussion on writing strong subject-verb units, see sections 5.2 and 5.3.

Three additional thoughts:

See Quick Tip:
Conciseness
(in Sentence
Openers) ⊕

1. Do not edit out every conceivable bit of wordiness from your writing. If you do, your writing will become sparse and lifeless.
2. Do not focus on wordiness in the early stages of drafting. Being concerned about wordiness at that point is premature. First efforts and early drafts are, by nature, wordy and overwritten. In fact, at the beginning of the writing process, it may even be healthy for you to have an excess of words to work with. Thus, you should try to apply all the suggested strategies for conciseness in this section late in the writing process.
3. Do not use throat-clearing sentence openers just so you can avoid writing in the first or second person. "It may be argued that . . ." and "I will argue . . ." are both problematic.

§ 6.2.6 Don't Use Pompous Language

A traveling geological formation acquires little vegetative growth. Translation: A rolling stone gathers no moss.

If only that were true. All too often, legal writers who are really "rolling" through an analysis begin gathering all kinds of moss in the form of stuffy, overly formal words. Instead of valuing their ideas for their clarity and simplicity, legal writers sometimes feel that they have to "dress them up" so that they look lawyerly and sound smart. They may have forgotten that their readers want to understand what they are saying, not be impressed by their vocabulary. If you read some of the best legal writers in the country, you will notice their prose avoids the trappings of pompous language. In the words of one former student, "The real big-shots don't write like big-shots."

The following are but a few of the many words and expressions that legal writers sometimes use to dress up an otherwise simple point. Resist the temptation. Keep it simple. Your readers will love you for it.

allocate	→	give, divide
ascertain	→	make sure
cease	→	stop

commence	→	begin
constitute	→	make up
emulate	→	copy
endeavor	→	try
finalize	→	complete, finish, end
implement	→	carry out, put into effect
initiate	→	begin
objective	→	goal, aim
originate	→	start
preclude	→	shut out, prevent
prior to	→	before
promulgate	→	issue, publish
pursuant to	→	under
render	→	make, give
secure	→	get, take, obtain
subsequent	→	after
terminate	→	end, finish
utilize	→	use
verification	→	proof

§ 6.2.7 Don't Repeat Yourself Needlessly

Language seems to be inherently redundant. Start trying to string a few words together and fairly soon some of those words will start making the same point. No matter how hard we try, words just keep coming out at a faster rate than the ideas, so naturally some words double up and say the same thing.

Some of this doubling up seems to come from a lack of faith in the words themselves. For example, why does anyone ever say or write "close proximity"? Isn't proximity always close? How about "mutual cooperation"? When is cooperation not mutual?

What logic is there in the expression "sworn affidavit"? If an affidavit is a "sworn statement in writing," then is a "sworn affidavit" a "sworn sworn statement in writing"?

The following is a sampling of many common redundancies, adapted from a list called "Dog Puppies" compiled by writer and editor Yvonne Lewis Day.[2] A few extra redundant phrases have been added by the authors. The word or words in parentheses should be omitted.

3:00 a.m. (in the morning)	(advance) warning
11:00 p.m. (at night)	alongside (of)
red (in color)	(and) moreover
(a distance of) 20 feet	appreciate (in value)

---

[2] Adapted from "The Economics of Writing" by Yvonne Lewis Day, reprinted with permission from the August 1982 issue of *The Toastmaster*.

(a period of) six months
(absolute) guarantee
(absolutely) clear
(actual) experience
(advance) planning
at (the) present (time)
(basic) fundamentals
belief (system)
(but) however
(but) nevertheless
(close) scrutiny
combine (together)
(complete) monopoly
(completely) destroyed
consensus (of opinion)
crisis (situation)
(current) trend
daily (basis)
depreciate (in value)
descend (down)
(different) kinds
(direct) confrontation
during (the course of)
during (the year of) 2006
each (and every)
each (separate) incident
free (of charge)
(future) plans
(general) public
healing (process)
(important) essentials
indicted (on a charge)
(integral) part
is (now) pending
join (together)
(local) residents
(major) breakthrough
(many) (different) ways
(mass) media
merged (together)
my (own) opinion
my (personal) opinion
never (at any time)
never (before)
off (of)
(over) exaggerate
(past) experience

(as) for example
ascend (up)
ask (a question)
(as to) whether
(at a) later (date)
emergency (situation)
(empty) space
(end) result
eradicate (completely)
(essential) element
(established) pattern
estimated (roughly) at
(false) pretenses
few (in number)
(foreign) imports
(past) history
(past) records
permeate (throughout)
(personal) friendship
(plan) ahead
postponed (until later)
(pre-) planned
probed (into)
protest (against)
(provision of) law
(rate of) speed
recur (again)
refer (back)
reflect (back)
reiterate (again)
repeat (again)
reported (to the effect) that
revert (back)
risk (factor)
scrutinize (carefully)
(separate) entities
shooting (incident)
(specific) example
(State's) prosecutor
(subtle) nuance
(sudden) outburst
(suddenly) exploded
(temporary) reprieve
(thorough) investigation
(underlying) (basic) assumption
(unexpected) surprise
(usual) custom

Many redundancies and wordy expressions have an "of" in them. Some legal writers find that they can spot many wordy constructions simply by searching for "of" and editing out about half of them.

The preceding list of redundancies includes those expressions that are common to writers in all disciplines. The language of law is much worse; it has made redundancy an art. In fact, to the average reader, the lawyer's motto seems to be: "When in doubt, say it twice."

One source of these redundancies, according to David Mellinkoff,[3] has been the law's tendency to draw on more than one language at a time to describe a single idea. Consequently, we get tautologies such as "null and void" when either "null" or "void" alone would be sufficient.

attorney (French) or lawyer (Old English)
buy (Old English) or purchase (French)
constable (French) or sheriff (Old English)
larceny (French) or theft or stealing (Old English)
minor (Latin) or child (Old English) or infant (French)
own (Old English) or possess (French)
property or chattels (French) or goods (Old English)
pardon (French) or forgive (Old English)
will (Old English) or testament (Latin)

Mellinkoff adds that other redundancies such as "aid and abet," "part and parcel," and "safe and sound" come from law's early oral tradition when the rhythm and sound of the words made them not only more memorable but also more powerful in the minds of the people.[4]

The question for modern legal writers, then, is whether doubling phrases serve any purpose for their readers. Is there some important distinction between "perform" and "discharge"? Is "cease and desist" more memorable or more emphatic than just "cease" or "desist" or "stop"?

If the answer to these questions is no, then what the writer has done by using doubling phrases is to double the words the reader must read. No new content, just more words—not exactly the way to win over a busy reader.

See Quick Tip: Conciseness (Needless Repetition) ⊕

(Admittedly, some repetition in legal writing is done for effect. Used properly, repetition can be persuasive and even eloquent. Obviously, the discussion in this section refers to mindless, not deliberate, repetition.)

§ 6.2.8 Clean Out the Clutter

Clutter in writing takes several forms, including prepositional phrases, "of" phrases, and adverbs.

---

[3] David Mellinkoff, The Language of the Law 58 (1963).

[4] *Id.* at 42-44.

Prepositional Phrases

One of the most common is the extraneous prepositional phrase. Notice how easily prepositional phrases can begin to grow and multiply.

EXAMPLE

We are filing a motion for summary judgment.

Clutter:

We are in the process of filing a motion for summary judgment.

More Clutter:

At this point in time, we are in the process of filing a motion for summary judgment.

Still More Clutter:

At this point in time, we are in the process of filing a motion for summary judgment with the court.

Eight words have quickly grown to 20, with no real gain in content.

"Of" Phrases

As we saw in the earlier list of redundancies, the "of" preposition tends to be a frequent offender. Although we cannot write without *any* "of" phrases, in most people's writing about half of them can be eliminated.

EXAMPLE

In the absence of any evidence of drugs on the premises, the police officers' actions can be given the interpretation of an invasion of privacy.

Revised:

Without evidence of drugs on the premises, the police officers' actions were an invasion of privacy.

Notice that the "of the" can be eliminated from some phrases and made into possessives in others.

all of the defendants	→	all defendants
none of the witnesses	→	no witness
the family of the victim	→	the victim's family
the reasoning of the court	→	the court's reasoning

Adverbs

Adverbs are sly little creatures. They like to creep in legal writing sentences, often in the disguise of precision. You can usually (there's one!) spot adverbs by their *-ly* ending, but look out for "quite," "rather," "somewhat," and "very," too.

EXAMPLE   **Adverb Clutter**

Basically, the witness seemed quite relaxed as she carefully outlined the rather long list of extremely technical calculations she had made.

Revised:

The witness seemed relaxed as she outlined the long list of technical calculations she had made.

See Quick Tip: Finding Adverbs ⊕

One adverb that deserves special mention is "clearly." It is so overused in legal writing that one has to wonder if it has any meaning left. **Clearly**, it is time to think of a more sophisticated way to begin sentences.

§ 6.2.9 Focus and Combine

A clear focus will help you decide which sentences can be combined and, when combining, which parts to keep as the main subject and verb and which parts to subordinate. For example, two sentences can often be combined into one by changing one of the sentences into a relative clause beginning with "which," "who," "whom," "whose," or "that."[5]

EXAMPLE

The State's main witness was Arthur Hedges. Arthur Hedges agreed to testify after reaching a favorable plea bargain.

Combined:

The State's main witness was Arthur Hedges, who agreed to testify after reaching a favorable plea bargain.

In some cases, these same relative clauses can be reduced to phrases by deleting unnecessary *who*'s, *which*'s, and *that*'s.

---

[5] Use "who" for persons and the nominative case; use "whom" for the objective case; use "whose" when you need the possessive. Use "that" and "which" for things, but use "that" for restrictive clauses and "which" for nonrestrictive clauses. (See Glossary of Usage on "who/whom" and Rule 9.1(4) on "that" and "which.")

EXAMPLE

The defendant lived in a room that was over the garage.

Revised:

The defendant lived in a room over the garage.

Frequently, two sentences can be combined when one of them defines or identifies part of the other.

EXAMPLE

Upon entering the house, the police smelled phenyl-2-propanone. Phenyl-2-propanone is an organic chemical that is a necessary precursor ingredient of amphetamine.

Combined:

Upon entering the house, the police smelled phenyl-2-propanone, an organic chemical that is a necessary precursor ingredient of amphetamine.

You can use a colon to combine two sentences when the first sentence introduces a list or an explanation that will be given in full in the second sentence.

EXAMPLE

To assert the emergency doctrine, the defendant must be able to satisfy four elements. The four elements are (1) that he was suddenly confronted by an emergency; (2) that he did not cause the emergency by any negligence on his part; (3) that he was compelled to decide a course of action instantly; and (4) that he made such a choice as a reasonably careful person placed in such a position might have made.

Combined:

To assert the emergency doctrine, the defendant must satisfy the following four elements: (1) he was suddenly confronted by an emergency; (2) he did not cause the emergency by any negligence on his part; (3) he was compelled to decide a course of action instantly; and (4) he made such a choice as a reasonably careful person placed in such a position might have made.

Occasionally, you can combine two or more sentences that have the same subject using compound verbs or by changing one set of verbs into participles. See section 5.7 for more information on how to keep compound verbs parallel.

EXAMPLE

The police officers discovered the laboratory used to make the amphetamine. The officers found a propane burner.

Combined (compound verbs):

The police officers discovered the laboratory used to make the amphetamine and found a propane burner.

To reduce phrases to words, be on the lookout for wordy constructions such as "the fact that," most phrases built around "regard," "of" prepositional phrases, and phrases that end in "that."

a number of	→ many
because of the fact that	→ because
by means of	→ by
by virtue of	→ by, under
despite the fact that	→ although, even though
due to the fact that	→ because
during the course of	→ during
except for the fact that	→ except for
for the purpose of	→ to
for the reason that	→ because
has the option of	→ may
in the absence of	→ without
in compliance with your request of	→ as requested, as you requested
in the course of	→ during
in the event that	→ if
in favor of	→ for
in light of the fact that	→ because, given that
in the neighborhood of	→ about, approximately
in point of fact	→ in fact
in regard(s) to	→ about, concerning
in spite of the fact that	→ although, even though
in view of the fact that	→ because, considering that
on the basis of	→ from
over the signature of	→ signed by
owing to the fact that	→ because
the fact that he asked	→ his question
with regard to	→ about, concerning

Legal writers are divided over whether (or not) to omit the "or not" in the expression "whether or not." Notice, for example, that the "or not" can be deleted from the preceding sentence with no loss in meaning. In such cases, it is better to delete it. Sometimes, however, the sentence becomes nonsensical if the "or not" is omitted. Usually, the "or not" can be omitted when the word "if" can substitute for "whether." Retain "or not" if the substitution of "if" for "whether" changes the meaning.

Some phrases are deadwood and can be omitted or replaced with one word.

at this point in time   → omit or use "now"
at that point in time   → omit or use "then"
in this day and age   → omit or use "now," "nowadays"
in the case of   → omit or use "in"
in reality   → omit
in terms of   → omit
in a very real sense   → omit

§ 6.2.10 Avoid Excessive Conciseness

The question, of course, with the reducing and combining advocated in this section, is how much is too much? When does editing for conciseness improve the writing, and at what point does it hinder the readability of sentences?

Properly done, reducing and combining can make your writing more focused and concise. Overdone, it can ruin writing by packing it too tightly and by creating overly long and overly complicated sentences.

One result of overdone combining is compound noun phrases, also known as noun strings. Like those Russian dolls that have a seemingly endless progression of smaller and smaller dolls inside each doll, compound noun phrases have a modifier modifying a modifier modifying a modifier to the point that the reader forgets where the whole thing began. Such overpacking in a sentence strains even the most cooperative reader.

EXAMPLE

Alabama's silent prayer statute's failure to satisfy "the purpose" prong of the *Lemon* test renders it unconstitutional.

Revised:

Alabama's silent prayer statute fails to satisfy "the purpose" prong of the *Lemon* test; therefore, it is unconstitutional. *OR*

Alabama's statute on silent prayer fails . . . .

Notice that in the preceding example a nominalization, "failure," became the verb and the revision eliminated one of the possessives, "statute's." Because multiple possessives are always awkward, avoid them whenever possible.

Also remember that some nominalizations can be unpacked and improved by changing the noun into the participle, or adjective form, as is done with "exclusion" in the following example.

EXAMPLE

a broad prior conviction evidence exclusion rule

Revised:

a broad rule excluding evidence of prior convictions

Like all tricks of the trade, then, editing for conciseness must be used with discretion and an eye toward what the reader will find easier to read and understand.

§ 6.3 Plain English vs. Legalese

Early in law school there seems to be an almost irresistible urge to clothe everything in the diction and style of the most incomprehensible insurance policy.

—Norman Brand and John O. White[6]

To communicate upon matters of technicality and complexity . . . is impossible with (and for) the nontechnical and simple person; and to use the language of simplicity in addressing a learned profession is to insult that profession.

—Ray J. Aiken[7]

Above are but two samplings of the heated, ongoing debate over legalese. Proponents of the traditional style of legal writing argue that legalese is part of the specialized discourse of lawyers and that it serves worthwhile purposes for lawyers and their readers. Proponents of "Plain English," on the other hand, argue that legalese is responsible for many of the ills that plague legal writing, not the least of which is that lay readers cannot readily comprehend what their attorneys are writing.

If you read the law journals, you may get the impression that the advocates for simplified, Plain English are winning the debate. Article after article decries the use of such mainstays of legal writing as Latin phrases and legal argot. Perhaps a more significant indication that legalese is on the way out is that several state legislatures have passed legislation requiring "simple," "clear," "understandable" language that uses "words with common and everyday meanings" in consumer contracts and insurance policies.[8]

If you read the writing of most practicing attorneys, however, you might get the impression that the advocates for the traditional style of legal writ-

---

[6] Legal Writing: The Strategy of Persuasion 107 (1988).

[7] *Let's Not Oversimplify Legal Language*, 32 Rocky Mtn. L. Rev. 364 (1960).

[8] See, for example, Minn. Stat. § 325G31, N.Y. Gen. Oblig. Law § 5-702, N.J. Rev. Stat. § 56:12-2, and Conn. Gen. Stat. § 38a-295, the Insurance Plain Language Act.

ing have won the day. Corporate lawyers rely heavily on boilerplate, and most practitioners seem to have absorbed the language of their law school casebooks. They may have heard that legalese is dead, but they don't write like they believe it.

And so the debate rages on, and although the Plain English vs. legalese issue has been before the collective "court" of legal professionals and their clients for some time now, we have yet to reach a verdict. The trend seems to be toward Plain English, but the resistance is strong. In short, in the matter of Plain English vs. legalese, the jury is still out.

So what is a legal writer to do? While the profession continues to wrestle with this issue, we would like to offer a simple test for determining whether any given bit of legalese should be used or relegated to the dustbin.

The Test

Given the document's reader, writer, purpose, and surrounding circumstances, does the legalese increase or decrease communication between writer and reader?

With the test as a backdrop, let's examine legalese and its characteristics.

First of all, there is no agreed-upon definition of "legalese." One law review author has defined a legalism as "a word or phrase that a lawyer might use in drafting a contract or a pleading but would not use in conversation with his wife."[9]

With a bit of editing, we can modify the definition to omit the sexism and to describe legalese: Historically, "legalese" is language a lawyer might use in drafting a contract or a pleading but would not use in ordinary conversation. In short, legalese is distinct from human talk; it is law talk.

What then are the characteristics that distinguish law talk from ordinary human talk?

Group 1

- long sentences, especially those with excessive modification and qualification
- abstractions as subjects—the real "doers" or actors are often omitted or relegated to a prepositional phrase
- weak verbs—both passive voice and nominalizations sap the sentences of their natural energy

Group 2

- archaic word choice
- foreign phrases

---

[9] George R. Smith, *A Primer of Opinion Writing, for Four New Judges*, 21 Ark. L. Rev. 197 (1967).

- terms of art and argot
- use of "said" and "such" as articles
- omission of articles, especially "the"
- use of "same" as a noun
- avoidance of the first and second person (I, we, you)
- doubling phrases

The first group of characteristics primarily involves sentence structure. These characteristics are discussed in the following sections: long sentences, section 5.5; abstractions as subjects, section 5.4; and weak verbs, sections 5.1 and 5.3.

The second group of characteristics occurs at the word level. Is it better to use a formal word, an unfamiliar word, a foreign word, or a simple word? When is a word or phrase an unnecessary legalism, and when is it a term of art? When is one word enough, and when should it be bolstered by one or more synonyms to cover every possible contingency?

These characteristics of legalese are the focus of this section.

§ 6.3.1 Archaic Word Choice

Consider a story told by an attorney who is an advocate of Plain English. Her client wanted her to draft a will. She drafted two versions: a Plain English version and a traditional version. Although the attorney recommended the Plain English version, the client selected the traditional version because it "sounded like a will." For this document and its purpose, the formality of "I hereby give, devise, and bequeath" was appropriate. It created the tone, the solemnity, and the timeless quality that the client wanted.

But what about client letters, office memoranda, and briefs to the court? Although these documents are formal in nature, do they require archaic language? Most authorities on legal language agree that they don't.[10] In fact, research shows that appellate judges, who are the readers of the most formal of these documents, appellate briefs, strongly prefer Plain English.[11]

The standard argument that "if I don't sound like a lawyer, I won't be believable" was strongly refuted in this research. In fact, the research showed that the judges were more likely to categorize writing in legalese as "poorly worded, unconvincing, vague, not concise, unpersuasive, uncreative, unscholarly, from a non-prestigious firm or an ineffective appellate advocate, unpowerful, incomprehensible and ambiguous."[12]

The legalese-ridden documents that the judges read included Old and Middle English words such as "thereby" and "herein." Below is a fairly comprehensive list of other Old and Middle English words and phrases that

---

[10] Joseph Kimble, Writing for Dollars, Writing to Please: The Case for Plain Language in Business, Government, and Law 134 (1st ed. 2012).

[11] Robert W. Benson & Joan B. Kessler, *Legalese v. Plain English: An Empirical Study of Persuasion and Credibility in Appellate Brief Writing*, 20 Loy. L.A. L. Rev. 301-19 (1987).

[12] *Id.* at 315.

should be avoided in client letters, office memoranda, and briefs. In some cases, a more appropriate substitute word or phrase follows in italics.

Compound words that begin with *here-*, *there-*, and *where-*

hereafter
herebefore
hereby
herein
hereinabove → *above*
hereinafter
hereinunder → *below*
hereof
heretofore → *before, up to this time*
hereunder
herewith (enclosed herewith → *enclosed*)
thereabout
thereafter
thereby
therefrom
therein
thereof
thereon
thereto
thereunto
therewith
whereas[13]
whereat
whereby
wherefore
wheresoever
wherein → *there*
whereof
whereon
whereupon

aforementioned (omit or substitute *previously mentioned*)
aforesaid (omit or substitute *above*)
behoove → *to be necessary, to be proper*
comes now the plaintiff
foregoing (for the foregoing reasons) → *for these reasons*
forthwith → *immediately*

---

[13] "Whereas" can often be eliminated or replaced with "because," "considering that," "while on the contrary," or "inasmuch as." At other times, it can be used but with care. Frequently, writers use it without seeming to know what it means. At times, "whereas" is the best choice; for example, using "whereas" is certainly better than the wordy "in view of the fact that."

henceforth[14]
hitherto → *until this time, up to now*
pursuant to → *under* or *according to*[15]
thence → *from there, from that place, time or source, for that reason*
thenceforth → *from that time on, after that*
thereafter → *from that time on*
to wit → *namely, that is to say*
whence → *from where*
whensoever → *whenever*

§ 6.3.2 Foreign Phrases

Many of the Latin phrases that appear in legal writing create a barrier between writer and reader. Only a student on the way home from Latin class (or possibly a lawyer specializing in property) will be comfortable with a phrase such as *cujus est solum ejus est usque ad coelum et usque ad inferos*. The rest of us would do one of two things: use the context to try to figure out what the writer meant or reach for the *Unabridged Black's Law Dictionary*. In either case, the Latin has not aided communication. Even the conscientious consulter of the dictionary will understand the writer's meaning only by looking up the explanation the writer should have given the reader in the first place.

More often, the Latin is not so much confusing as it is unnecessary. Why say "*supra*" when "above" works just as well? Unnecessary Latin phrases make the writing appear stuffy and pretentious. When a simple English equivalent can be used without loss of meaning, use it.

Latin Words or Phrases to Avoid

arguendo → for the sake of argument
et al. → and others
infra → below
inter alia → among other things
per curiam → by the court
seriatim → in turn, serially, one after another
sui generis → unique
supra[16] → above
viz. (abbreviation for "*videlicet*") → namely, that is to say

Not all Latin should be replaced, however. Some Latin phrases ("gratis," "per diem") are sufficiently familiar to educated readers that their use does

---

[14] Many would not object strenuously to "henceforth" but find it a bit dated. "From now on" is a satisfactory Plain English substitute.

[15] Sometimes "pursuant to" is a useful legalism that lawyers and judges find acceptable. Avoid using it, however, with non-lawyers.

[16] The word *supra* continues to be used in footnotes and citations. These uses are permissible.

not impair communication. In fact, these phrases are often accepted as English.

Other Latin phrases ("*amicus curiae*," "*per se*") are equally familiar to lawyers and judges and can be used for these readers without a second thought. They are the "shop talk" of law. The same phrases, though, may need substitutes or explanation for client readers.

A final group of Latin phrases are so useful that few are willing to discard them. "*Respondeat superior*," for example, sums up a whole doctrine in tort law; "*res judicata*" is a fundamental rule of Civil Procedure. While these phrases will probably need clarification for readers who are not lawyers, the average legal reader would find them not only familiar but indispensable.

Latin Words or Phrases to Keep for Readers Who Are Lawyers

ad hoc	*mens rea*
ad litem	*modus operandi*
amicus curiae	*nexus*
bona fide	*nolo contendere*
caveat emptor	*non sequitur*
certiorari	*penumbra*
consortium	*per diem*
corpus delicti	*per se*
de facto, de jure	*post mortem*
de novo	*prima facie*
dicta, dictum	*pro bono*
ex parte	*quorum*
ex post facto	*quid pro quo*
gratis	*res ipsa loquitur*
habeas corpus	*res judicata*
id. (abbreviation for *idem*)	*respondeat superior*
in limine	*scintilla*
in personam	*stare decisis*
ipso facto	*sua sponte*
mandamus	*supersedeas*

Of course, Latin is not the only foreign language that appears frequently in legal writing. Thanks to the Norman Conquest of England in 1066 and its subsequent effect on the English language, French plays an important role in the language of law.

The vast majority of the words derived from French are common terms that are already fully incorporated into English and as such pose few if any problems for readers ("assault," "defendant," "heir," "larceny," "mortgage," "plaintiff," "pleadings," "tort," "reprieve," and "verdict," to name just a few).

More likely troublemakers are those words and phrases that are Old French. For the following French terms, use the suggested Plain English substitutes.

alien or *aliene* (used as a verb)→ to convey or to transfer
cestui que trust→ beneficiary
cy-pres→ as near as possible

en ventre sa mere→ in its mother's womb
en vie→ alive
feme covert→ married woman
feme sole→ single woman
save→ except
seisin→ possession or ownership

As we saw with Latin, though, there are French words and phrases that are terms of art for which we have no satisfactory Plain English substitute. Although they will almost certainly require explanation for readers who are not lawyers, they are indispensable vocabulary for a lawyer.

French Words and Phrases to Keep

estoppel   laches   voir dire

§ 6.3.3 Use of Terms of Art and Argot

Terms of art, by definition, do not have satisfactory substitutes. Even though one might be able to give a short explanation of a term of art's meaning, complete understanding would take an extensive explanation.

A term of art, according to David Mellinkoff, is "a technical word with a specific meaning."[17] In *The Dictionary of Modern Legal Usage,* "terms of art" are defined as "words having specific, precise significations in a given specialty."[18]

Given these requirements, it should not be surprising that there are relatively few terms of art in law. "Certiorari," for example, is a true term of art. Perhaps a satisfactory short explanation is that it refers to the order written by a higher court to a lower court requiring the lower court to produce a certified record of a certain case.

For a full understanding of "certiorari," however, one would have to lay out a much larger context: how discretionary review and the appellate process work in general and, specifically, how the Supreme Court of the United States chooses cases it wishes to hear.

Argot, by contrast, is legal jargon, or lawyers' shop talk. It is the shorthand of law, the quick-and-easy term or phrase that lawyers use among themselves. For this reason, argot is inappropriate when communicating with non-lawyers. Used with discretion, argot can help you effectively communicate with the legal community.

"Case on all fours" is a classic example of argot. Other common examples include "adhesion contract," "attractive nuisance," "Blackacre," "case at bar," "case-in-chief," "clean hands," "cloud on title," "court below," "four corners of the document," "horse case," "instant case," "off the record," "pierce

---

[17] David Mellinkoff, The Language of the Law 16 (1963) (quoting *Webster's New International Dictionary* (2d ed. 1934)).

[18] Bryan A. Garner, The Dictionary of Modern Legal Usage 872 (2d ed. 1995).

the corporate veil," "reasonable person," "*res ipsa loquitur*," "sidebar," and "Whiteacre."

In writing, avoid argot that has degenerated into slang. "Cert. denied" or "resipsey case" sounds cute rather than professional.

§ 6.3.4 Use of "Said" and "Such" as Adjectives

If you were a stand-up comic trying to make fun of the way lawyers write, all you would have to do is put "said" or "such" before almost every noun.

EXAMPLE

It was snowing and icy on January 9, 2011, when Mr. Smith, the plaintiff, was driving home from work along a deserted highway in his 1995 Honda Accord with chains on said vehicle's tires. Suddenly said plaintiff felt said vehicle jerk violently, and then said plaintiff heard a loud clanging of metal. Such clanging continued until such time as said plaintiff was able to pull said vehicle over to the shoulder of said highway. Upon inspection of said vehicle, said plaintiff realized that such clanging was caused when said chains had broken and then wrapped around the axle of said plaintiff's said vehicle. "Oh, *!?/*!" said plaintiff.

In client letters, office memos, and briefs, rigorously avoid all use of "said" as an adjective. Replace with "the," "that," "this," or an appropriate, unambiguous pronoun.

"Such" can be used as an adjective with categories of persons, things, or concepts. For example, "such instances of neglect," "such witnesses as these," and "such an example of compassion" are not legalese. These phrases are good writing.

Do not, however, use "such" with singular nouns that are not categories of persons, things, or concepts but rather specific references to the same, previously mentioned singular noun. For example, "such payment" should be revised to "this payment"; "such stock certificate" should be changed to "the stock certificate." See section 8.5.2 for more information on broad pronoun reference.

§ 6.3.5 Omission of the Article "The"

Occasionally, one sees legal writing that has the sound of a police report.

EXAMPLE

Defendant denies that she struck victim.

This rather terse style is achieved by omitting the article "the." The reason for omitting "unnecessary" articles in police reports may be that information needs to be recorded on forms. Happily, lawyers do not have these requirements, so they do not have to sacrifice a fluid writing style. Some novice legal writers will inadvisably drop articles in order to stay under a specified word limit for a document.

EXAMPLE

Revised:

The defendant denies that she struck the victim.

---

§ 6.3.6 Absence of First- and Second-Person Pronouns

By convention, legal writers rarely use the pronouns "I," "me," "we," "us," "you" and "your." Occasionally, in a client letter, a lawyer might write "I recommend" or, more commonly, "in my opinion." Much less frequent would be the phrase "I think" or (horrors!) "I feel" (the common explanation for the horrified reaction being that lawyers are paid to think, not to feel) in an office memorandum. Pity the naive attorney, though, who writes in a brief "you should rule" or "you must determine."

To get around the using "I," "we," or "you" in legal writing—because after all it is I, the writer, who is recommending and thinking, and it is you, the judge and reader, who is ruling and determining—legal writers resort to all sorts of linguistic gymnastics. Before discussing which of these gymnastic moves work and which lead to new problems, let's examine why the first- and second-person pronouns are *persona non grata* in legal writing.

First, remember the long-standing tradition of avoiding first and second person pronouns in any formal writing. While the recommendations about this issue have relaxed considerably for undergraduate research papers and the like, the original rationale applies to most legal writing. The facts and the application of law to those facts are the focus of attention for both writer and reader. As such, the law and facts should occupy center stage.

Second, the use of "I" and "you" often creates an inappropriately informal tone. While a bit of informality and familiarity may be appropriate in some client letters and an occasional office memo, these documents should generally be formal and professional in tone. (Remember, though, formal does not mean stilted.)

Third, indiscreet use of "you" in client letters and especially in briefs may make the writer appear arrogant, pushy, and disrespectful. Readers rarely like to be ordered around. Not surprisingly, "you must" or "you should" language often backfires. Rather than encouraging the reader to act as the writer wants, such language sets the stage for resistance to the writer's recommendations and arguments.

In the following example, the inclusion of "my," "I," and "you" is both distracting and inappropriate. The first-person references incorrectly place the emphasis on the writer, and the second-person references may even anger the judge.

EXAMPLE

In my research, I found that you must apply Washington Rule of Evidence 609(a) to determine the admissibility of evidence of a criminal defendant's prior convictions.

Revised:

In Washington, the admissibility of evidence of a criminal defendant's prior convictions is governed by ER 609(a). *OR*

Washington ER 609(a) governs the admissibility of evidence of a criminal defendant's prior convictions.

The first revision of the example illustrates one of the common gymnastic moves that legal writers use to avoid the first- and second-person pronouns: using the passive voice. While the passive voice is a good choice in some instances (see section 5.1.3), it can easily lead to dull, lifeless writing. Use it with care.

Some legal writers use the pronoun "one" to get around using "you." This tactic works reasonably well as long as the writer does not use "one" several times and then shift—incorrectly—from "one" to the third-person pronoun "he," "she," "him," "her," "it," "they," or "them."

EXAMPLE

Incorrect:

One should avoid first-person pronouns in his or her legal writing.

Revised:

One should avoid first-person pronouns in one's legal writing.

Better:

Avoid first-person pronouns in legal writing.

In office memos, some writers slip into a *we-they* style as they describe the various arguments the two sides can make: "They will argue . . . and we will rebut this argument by showing . . . ." This practice is accepted in some firms. Other firms simply name the parties: "Smith will argue . . . and Jones will rebut this argument." Generally, placing a concrete noun (e.g., plaintiff, defendant, opposing counsel) at the beginning of the sentence will solve the problem.

Frequently, a writer of an office memo is tempted to use "we" in the following situation. The writer has just explained the law or just described an analogous case to the reader. Now the writer wants the reader to follow along as he or she applies that law or case.

The writer might begin by saying "If we apply the plain meaning of statute X to our facts, we can see that the photocopy is a similitude" or "If we compare the actions of the defendant in *Smith v. Jones* to the actions of Brown, we can see that Brown, unlike Jones, knew he was lying to the F.B.I." This is not a serious writing sin, of course, but it can be easily avoided.

Unfortunately, some writers try to write around the "we" in such instances and end up with a dangling modifier. See section 8.6.2.

There is a better way. The writer does want the reader to follow along as he or she makes the next logical connection, but the writer also wants to suggest that the court must see the same logical connection. Therefore, it makes good sense, both in terms of writing style and strategy, to say "If the court applies the plain meaning of statute X to our facts, it will find . . ." or "Applying the plain meaning of statute X to our facts, the court will find . . . ."

One final note about first- and second-person pronouns: Because these pronouns have gained acceptance in some other types of formal writing, they are likely to gain increasing acceptance in all but the most formal documents in legal writing. Watch the trend, and you will be able to adjust accordingly.

§ 6.4 Gender-Neutral Language

The language of law, while a bit slower to change than the language in other disciplines, is moving in the direction of gender-neutral word choices. Numerous states now require gender-neutral language in their legislation. Increasingly, legislators, practitioners, and jurists are realizing that some language they previously considered to be inclusive has just the opposite effect: It excludes.

For legal writers, there are at least four good reasons for making the effort to use gender-neutral language: fairness, clarity, precision, and reader reaction. These reasons more than justify the effort it takes to master the five problem areas legal writers face when trying to use gender-neutral language.

§ 6.4.1 Generic Use of "Man"

Avoid using the term "man" to mean all people or all of humanity. Similarly, avoid using expressions and other derivatives built on this broad use of the term *man*.

Sexist Terms	*Gender-Neutral Substitutes*
man (as a noun) or mankind	people, persons
man (as a verb) as in "man the office"	staff, operate, run

a man who . . .	an individual who . . . , a person who . . . , one who . . . , someone who . . .
the common man, the average man, the man in the street	the common person, the average citizen, ordinary people
man-made	hand-crafted, handmade, manufactured, machine-made, fabricated, synthetic, created

§ 6.4.2 Generic Use of "He"

Grammar and writing texts used to advise writers to use masculine pronouns when the gender of the antecedent noun or pronoun could be either male or female. Now most grammar and writing texts advise writers to avoid the generic use of "he." Unfortunately, though, we have been unable to agree on a gender-neutral singular pronoun as a substitute. Until we do, we will need to use one or more of several approaches for avoiding the generic use of the masculine pronouns.

a. Revise the Sentence So That the Antecedent and Its Pronoun Are Plural

EXAMPLE

The holding suggests that a defendant waives his constitutional rights only through an affirmative or overt act.

Revised:

The holding suggests that defendants waive their constitutional rights only through affirmative or overt acts.

b. Revise the Sentence So That a Pronoun Is Not Needed

EXAMPLE

As a general rule, an employer is not liable for the work performed by his independent contractors.

Revised:

As a general rule, an employer is not liable for the work performed by independent contractors.

c. Replace the Masculine Noun and Pronoun with "One," "Your," or "He" or "She," as Appropriate

EXAMPLE

Every man has a right to defend his home.

Revised:

One has a right to defend one's home.

You have a right to defend your home.

Everyone has a right to defend his or her home.

d. Alternate Male and Female Examples and Expressions

EXAMPLE

If a student enrolls at a university with the promise that he will receive an athletic scholarship and he later finds out that his scholarship has been revoked, he can sue the university for breach of contract. If, on the other hand, a student enrolls at a university with the promise that he will receive an athletic scholarship and he later refuses to play the sport, the university can sue him for breach of contract.

Revised:

If a student enrolls at a university with the promise that she will receive an athletic scholarship and she later finds out that her school scholarship has been revoked, she can sue the university for breach of contract. If, on the other hand, a student enrolls at a university with the promise that he will receive an athletic scholarship and he later refuses to play the sport, the university can sue him for breach of contract.

e. Repeat the Noun Rather Than Use an Inappropriate Masculine Pronoun

EXAMPLE

Joinder of counts should not be used to embarrass or prejudice a defendant or to deny him a substantial right.

Revised:

Joinder of counts should not be used to embarrass or prejudice a defendant or to deny that defendant a substantial right.

One approach that is occasionally recommended for avoiding the generic "he" is to use the plural pronouns "they" and "their" for singular nouns and indefinite pronouns, such as "everyone" or "anybody." While using this approach may arguably solve the sexism problem, it still leaves the legal writer with an error in pronoun agreement (see section 8.5.4) as well as with more than a few logical inconsistencies, for example, "Everyone is entitled to their opinion." Rather than trade one problem for another, use one of the other five strategies outlined above for avoiding the generic "he."

§ 6.4.3 Gender-Neutral Job Titles

Avoid job titles that suggest it is nonstandard for women to hold the position.

Sexist Terms	Gender-Neutral Substitutes
businessman, chairman	business executive, manager coordinator, presiding officer, head, chair
Congressman	Representative, member of Congress, congressional representative, Senator
councilman	council member
fireman	firefighter
foreman (as the head of a group of workers)	supervisor, head worker, section chief
foreman (as the head of a jury)	foreperson
insuranceman	insurance agent
juryman	juror
landlord	owner, manager, lessor
mailman, postman	postal carrier, postal worker, mail carrier
middleman	negotiator, liaison, intermediary
newspaperman	reporter, editor
policeman	police officer
salesman	sales associate, sales representative
spokesman	representative, spokesperson
steward, stewardess	flight attendant
watchman	guard, security officer

§ 6.4.4 Sexist Modifiers

Unconsciously, writers sometimes assign needless sexist modifiers to words. Avoid modifiers that suggest that it is unusual for either a woman or a man to occupy a certain position.

Sexist Modifier	Revised
female judge	judge
lady lawyer	lawyer
male nurse	nurse
woman attorney	attorney

§ 6.4.5 Other Sexist Language

Avoid feminizing a word with a suffix, for example, "actress," "executrix," "testatrix." Such endings suggest that it is nonstandard for women to fill certain roles.

Avoid terms with connotations of youth (girl), decorum (lady), or informality (gal) unless the comparable terms for males (boy, gentleman, guy) are also appropriate.

When using titles (Miss, Mrs., Ms.) before women's names, follow the particular woman's preference, if known, or, if unknown, use no title. In professional contexts, professional titles take precedence over social titles for both women and men, for example, Justice Ruth Bader Ginsburg, not Mrs. Ginsburg. In salutations in letters, avoid using the outdated "Dear Sir" or "Gentlemen" when the gender of the receiver is unknown. Acceptable substitutes include "Dear Sir or Madam," "Ladies and Gentlemen," or the title of the receiver(s), as in "Dear Members of the Board." Some writers omit the salutation and use a reference line such as "To the Director of Operations" or "Re: Credit Department."

Sexist Term	Gender-Neutral Substitutes
coed	student
divorcee	divorced person
forefathers	ancestors, forerunners, forebears
girl or girls (when applied to adult females)	woman or women
househusband, housewife	homemaker
lady or ladies	woman or women (unless the equivalent "gentleman" or "gentlemen" is also used for men)
man and wife	man and woman, husband and wife
old wives' tale	superstitious belief or idea

§ 6.5 Bias-Free Language

In addition to the concern that legal writers use gender-neutral language in their documents, there are related concerns that the language of law be free of bias against other groups, such as racial, religious, and ethnic minorities, homosexual persons, elderly people, poor people, and persons with disabilities.

Making bias-free language choices is not always easy, though, particularly when one realizes that the preferred terms are constantly changing and not all members of any given group have the same preferences. These challenges tempt some to ignore or just give up on the issue of bias-free language in law. The argument seems to go something like this: "Why should I bother when they can't decide what they want to be called?"

The temptation to avoid the issue is easier to resist, however, when one considers the power of language and its ability to shape perception. How we label something or someone affects our perception. Thus, language can serve to perpetuate stereotypes, or it can bring new insight and perspective. Choices in language can suggest that members of a group are inherently inferior or that they are valued members of society. In short, what we call ourselves or someone else matters. Naming, or labeling, is both an enormous power and an enormous responsibility, and like all legal writing, it should be done with a lot of thought and care.

§ 6.5.1 Avoid Irrelevant Minority References

Perhaps the most subtle and possibly the most insidious forms of prejudice in some legal writing are unnecessary references to race, ethnic origin, or other minority categories. In a case in which the description of an individual is necessary to the analysis (such as a case in which the police apprehended an individual based on the individual matching a victim's description), including the race of the individual is obviously appropriate. Unless a crime was racially motivated, however, it is probably inappropriate to include the race of a victim.

The same principle also applies to persons who are adopted. Include references to a person being adopted only when it is relevant.

§ 6.5.2 Stay Abreast of the Preferred Terminology

All language changes over time. Some parts of language tend to change more rapidly, however, because of rapid changes in sensibilities and society's collective thinking about certain issues.

Notice, for example, the changes in terminology for the following groups of people:

Colored People → Negro → Black → Black American[19] → African American or Afro-American
Indian → American Indian → Native American[20]
Oriental → Asian American
Mexican American → Chicano/Chicana or Hispanic or Latino/ Latina

---

[19] While early forms of many terms that combined races or nationalities often had hyphens ("African-American," "Mexican-American," "Asian-American"), the current trend is toward omitting the hyphen. The argument for omitting the hyphen is that it conveys something less than full membership in both groups.

[20] Note, however, that when the 1995 census asked members of this group for their preferences, 49.76% indicated that they preferred "American Indian," 37.35% preferred "Native American," 3.66% preferred "some other term," 3.51% preferred "Native Alaskan," and 5.72% had "no preference." Bureau of Labor Statistics, U.S. Census Bureau Survey, May 1995. The more recent censuses did not ask the same questions regarding preference regarding their identification.

Handicapped → Disabled → Physically Challenged or Persons of
    Differing Abilities or Persons with Exceptionalities or Excep-
    tional Persons
Bums, Hobos → Homeless Persons
Elderly → Senior Citizens

Notice, too, that several of these progressions end with two or more choices, indicating a lack of consensus among the members of the group about the current preferred term.

How then does a legal writer decide what term to use? Legal writers can use the following general guidelines when deciding which words or labels will work best in any given situation:

a. Prefer self-chosen labels (and avoid terms that may offend members of that group)
b. Choose precise, accurate terms
c. Whenever possible, prefer the specific term over the general term
d. Prefer terms that describe what people are rather than what they are not
e. Notice that a term's connotations may change as the part of speech changes (e.g., the same word that is offensive as a noun may be acceptable as an adjective)
f. In selecting terms, emphasize the person over the difference
g. Avoid terms that are patronizing or overly euphemistic or that paint people as victims
h. Avoid idioms that are steeped in prejudice

Below is a guide to navigate these decisions. However, you will still want to do research to stay abreast of the preferred terminology.[21]

a. Prefer Self-Chosen Labels

While it may be difficult to determine what a whole group of individuals prefers to be called, it is often simple to determine what a given person wants to be called. One can just ask. If a client prefers to be labeled as "black" rather than "African American," for example, that preference should be honored. See Chart 6.3. If an individual describes herself as a "gay woman" rather than as a "homosexual" or "lesbian," the self-chosen term is the obvious choice.

If the applicable law uses a specific label for a group that differs from the individual's preferred term, the sensible solution is for the lawyer-writer to explain to the client why it might be preferable to use the term used in the law but then leave the final decision about word choice up to the client. For example, the law may refer to an "illegal alien" but an individual may

---

[21] For example, for updated information on terminology for the lesbian, gay, bisexual, and transgender community, consult the NLGJA Stylebook Supplement, which can be found on the National Lesbian & Gay Journalists Association website at http://www.nlgja.org.

prefer to be called an "undocumented worker." Each label carries with it strong connotations, which should also be considered before deciding which term to use.

Equally important to preferring self-chosen labels is to avoid offensive labels. Perhaps the best example of a term that members of a group find offensive is the label "Oriental" when used to refer to persons of Asian origin. The objections to the term are twofold. First, the word "Oriental," which means "eastern," identifies people from Asian countries in relationship to being east of Europe; hence the term smacks of a Eurocentric perspective. Second, and probably more important, the word "Oriental" has connotations of Asian countries as being "exotic" and the people being "inscrutable." As a result, many Asian Americans consider it nothing short of an ethnic slur to be called "Orientals." Using the word "Oriental" as an adjective in phrases such as "Oriental rug," "Oriental cuisine," or "Oriental medicine," however, is generally considered acceptable.[22]

Some whites, most notably the Irish, find it offensive to be labeled "Anglos." The alternate term "Caucasian" is still used in many police departments, but "Caucasian" is not generally a recommended term because it is based on an outmoded notion of a Caucasian race that is no longer accepted in the scientific community. The preferred term, "white," is also not without problems, not the least of which is that its parameters are ambiguous. The term obviously refers to skin color, and its generally accepted meaning is any white or light-skinned person of non-Latin extraction. In some cases, however, "white" includes Latinos and Latinas.

Chart 6.3	**Honoring Personal Preferences[23]**

The words used to describe African Americans have a history. The short way I explain it to my non-African American friends and my students is as follows:

My grandparents are **Colored**
My parents are **Negroes**
My siblings are **Black**
I was **Black** when I was born and now I am **African American**
My nieces and nephews are **People of Color** (and alternately **African American**)

---

[22] The term "retarded" is also considered offensive by many. Preferred terms are persons with an "intellectual disability" or who are "developmentally disabled." Recently the term "special needs" has come under close scrutiny with some individuals noting that it may evoke unwanted sympathy and concerns about scarce resources, as well as contribute to exclusion and marginalization of the children so described. One possible replacement for "children with special needs" is "children with cognitive difficulties."

[23] Included with permission from and thanks to Professor Teri Mcmurtry-Chubb, Mercer University School of Law.

Not surprisingly, my siblings still refer to themselves as Black. I refer to myself alternately as Black or African American. The point is that depending on the historical period you are discussing, any of the words in the above list is valid. You want to make sure that your audience is aware that you know the history of the words you are using. Your audience should also know that your present understanding is that the terms "African American" and "person of color" are current and acceptable.

I use exercises involving cases from the Civil Rights era all of the time, and I give the little talk that I outline above. It never fails to break the tension in the room so that we can get back to the lesson.

As for my personal preference, I do not like the term colored, and don't use "person of color" to refer to myself because it reminds me too much of colored. I do like Mark Wojik's "person with color,"[24] but I prefer Teri.[25]

b. Choose Precise, Accurate Terms

Precision and accuracy are highly valued in all word choices in legal writing, and even more so when selecting words that describe race, ethnicity, national origin, and religion. For this reason it is important not to assume that terms are interchangeable. "Mexican American," for example, should be used only to refer to a person who is a United States citizen or permanent resident with Mexican ancestry. "Spanish" refers to persons whose ancestors were from Spain. "Latino" and "Latina" are accurate terms only for persons who have Latin American ancestry.[26]

Similarly, the terms "Arab," "Middle Easterner," and "Muslim" are not synonyms; they refer to language, geography, and religion respectively. The term "Arab," for example, refers to persons who speak the Arabic language. The term "Middle Easterners," which focuses on geography, is obviously accurate only for those individuals from the Middle East and not for people from Algeria, Tunisia, Morocco, and Libya. Remember, too, that there are non-Arab countries—Iran, Turkey, and Israel—in the Middle East.

---

[24] Mark Wojik is a Professor at the John Marshall Law School in Chicago, IL.

[25] Professor Mcmurtry-Chubb's response was to the question "What word is proper?" asked on the Legal Writing Institute listserv, September 26, 2011.

[26] In addition to accuracy, some terms are self-chosen and others are rejected because of their varying emphasis on geographic, historical, cultural roots or political identity. For example, although "Hispanic" is an accurate term for people in the United States who trace their ancestry back to one or more Spanish-speaking countries, some Spanish-speaking persons resent the term, not only because it homogenizes so many diverse peoples but also because it came into common use by way of the government (particularly through the census), the media, and the public at large. Other people resent the term "Hispanic" because they associate it with Spanish colonialism and feel it overemphasizes Spanish ancestry and ignores the African and indigenous roots of Latino culture. "Latino," on the other hand, is preferred by many because it has both a Spanish sound and connotations of ethnic pride. Whether a given individual prefers to be called "Hispanic," "Latino," or "Chicano" may also depend on where the person resides in the United States or on the person's politics. "Hispanic" is the more popular choice in Florida and Texas; "Latino" is more commonly used in California; "Chicano" has connotations of political activism.

The term "Muslim" refers to a person who believes in the Islamic religion. Thus, not all Muslims are Arabs, nor are all Arabs Muslims. Likewise, not all Israelis are Jewish, nor are all Jewish people Israelis.

c. Whenever Possible, Prefer the Specific Term Over the General Term

Unnecessarily lumping groups of people with varying histories, cultures, and languages under a generic term can be interpreted as not making the effort to understand or respect the differences captured by the specific terms. Thus, while there are differences within the group over whether to use "American Indian" or "Native American" or even the newest term, "First American," what is consistently preferred is to use a more specific term, such as "Mohawk" or "Navajo," whenever possible rather than a generic term. This principle also applies to the term "Asian American." Although "Asian American" is appropriate when a generic term is needed, it is better to use a more specific term, such as "Japanese American," whenever possible. Note as well that many people who come from the republics that used to be part of the former Soviet Union are offended when they are lumped together and labeled "Russians." Here again, use specific terms such as "Armenians."

d. Prefer Terms That Describe What People Are Rather Than What They Are Not

Three terms that designate a person as a member of a group other than the majority white population—"nonwhite," "minority," and "person of color"—demonstrate the interplay of several principles related to bias in language. "Nonwhite" is often considered offensive because it classifies people by what they are not rather than by what they are. The term "minority" does not seem to create the same level of resentment as "nonwhite," although some members of minority communities that are not African American complain that the term "minority" is often treated as synonymous with the black community. All three terms have the disadvantage of grouping widely disparate peoples together and, at least in some instances, should be replaced by a specific reference. In some situations, long lists of specific references are impractical. In such cases, the generic term "person of color" is currently the preferred option.[27]

e. Notice That a Term's Connotations May Change as the Part of Speech Changes

Earlier we saw that while the term "Oriental" is considered offensive when used as a noun to label a person, it is acceptable as an adjective in such

---

[27] In custody disputes over the children of a lesbian couple, the choice in labels for each of the parents often foreshadows the legal arguments, for example, one side may use a term such as "co-mother" and the other use "nonbiological mother."

phrases as "Oriental rug" or "Oriental food." This same principle comes into play in the preferred terminology for sexual orientation, disability, and aging. "Homosexual," for example, is not considered offensive as an adjective in a phrase such as "homosexual relationship," but its use as a noun describing an individual is offensive to many members of this group. Those who object to the noun form cite its emphasis on the sexual life of an individual rather than on the broader cultural or social life of that person. The self-chosen terms are "gay man," "gay woman," or "lesbian." "Gay" by itself is not preferred as a noun.

Members of the disability community tend to prefer the adjective form of "disabled," as in "disabled persons," over the noun form, "the disabled." The adjective form of "elderly" as in "an elderly man" is less offensive than the noun form "the elderly." Members of this community tend to prefer the term "senior citizen."

f. In Selecting Terms, Emphasize the Person Over the Difference

The disability community has endorsed what is known as the "person first" principle, which is selecting terms that put the person before the disability whenever possible. The idea is that the individual should be emphasized over the difference and that the difference should not be treated as the person's total identity. Consequently, although as we saw in the last section, members of the disability community prefer the adjective form of "disabled," as in "disabled persons," over the noun form, "the disabled," others further recommend "persons with disabilities" over "disabled persons" because it puts the person before the disability. Similarly, "person with epilepsy" is preferred over the term "epileptic," "person with an amputated leg" over "amputee," and "person with diabetes" over "diabetic."

g. Avoid Terms That Are Patronizing or Overly Euphemistic or That Paint People as Victims

While there is a temptation to move toward more euphemistic terms for persons who have physical and mental disabilities, that temptation should be tempered not only by the importance of communicating clearly but also by the realization that sugarcoated euphemisms can be patronizing. Some options also seem to be too long to be practical. Consider the following progression:

Handicapped → Disabled →   Physically challenged OR
                            Persons of differing abilities OR
                            Differently abled persons OR
                            Persons with exceptionalities OR
                            Exceptional persons

Well-meaning persons have tried to introduce terms such as "persons of differing abilities," "differently abled persons," "persons with exceptionalities," and "exceptional persons" to try to put a positive gloss on having a disability. Such euphemisms tend to fail because they are both imprecise and patronizing. The term "physically challenged" is more acceptable because it finds a balance between being sensitive to those described and being clear about the relevant condition.

Within the disability community, there is also a controversy over verbs that paint persons with disabilities as being weak and helpless victims. Some argue that writers should omit or replace the clichéd verbs in phrases such as "person *confined* to a wheelchair"—replace with "person in a wheelchair" or "person who uses a wheelchair"; "person *stricken* with multiple sclerosis"—replace with "person with multiple sclerosis"; "person *suffering* from arthritis"—replace with "person who has arthritis"; and "person *afflicted* with AIDS"—replace with "person with AIDS". In some instances, of course, a lawyer may feel that the "language of victimization" works to the client's advantage. The question, of course, is whether to use this kind of short-term "advantage" when it contributes to a particular cultural bias and stereotyping. As with so many decisions such as this, it may be appropriate to consult the described individual to determine his or her preference.

For an in-depth discussion of bias in legal language and argument, see Lorraine K. Bannai & Anne Enquist, *(Un)Examined Assumptions and (Un)Intended Messages: Teaching Students to Recognize Bias in Legal Analysis and Language*, 27 Seattle U. L. Rev. 1 (2003).

h. Avoid Idioms That Are Steeped in Prejudice

Idioms, or figurative phrases that have different meanings than those directly suggested by the words, are present in every culture and language. American English is especially rich in idioms, including clever, well-worn phrases such as "piece of cake," meaning "easy," and "hit the nail on its head," meaning "aptness" or "precision." Many of these colloquial idioms are innocent and fun, although not always appropriate in the formal context of legal writing. Others come from darker corners of history and can accidentally be hurtful or insensitive.

Writers may innocently use idioms like "off the reservation" or "beyond the pale" to refer to an individual's erratic or unauthorized behavior, forgetting or being unaware of the history of these idioms as racist or prejudicial ways to refer to the perceived "savage" behavior of Native American and Irish people, respectively.

While the idiom "sold down the river" might be a colorful way to signify betrayal by a party in a business deal, its history refers to the practice of selling slaves from northern states to southern states, where the work was harder and more physically demanding.

Even the seemingly innocent idiom "grandfather clause," often used in building codes or zoning laws, refers back to nineteenth century legislation aimed at disenfranchising African Americans from voting because their grandparents were ineligible to vote.

A list of all idioms that ought to be avoided would be inevitably incomplete. You should, however, investigate and replace potentially offensive idioms when you are able.

CHAPTER 7

Eloquence

Is it unrealistic for legal writing to be eloquent? After all, lawyers write under enormous time pressure. Who has the time to massage language to the point at which someone would call it "eloquent"?

Further, is it appropriate for legal writing to be eloquent? Should an office memo sound like it was written by Shakespeare? What client is willing to pay for a client letter that waxes poetic? Are judges more impressed by arguments or by the language they are wrapped in?

All these good questions really boil down to one question: Should a lawyer strive to write eloquently?

Yes, at least sometimes.

While it wouldn't hurt if every office memo and client letter were written eloquently, the one area in which eloquence undoubtedly pays off is briefs. An eloquent brief is a more persuasive brief. Of course your arguments must be sound and persuasive in and of themselves, but you cannot divorce the content of the argument from the form in which it is written. What you say and the way you say it are inextricably linked.

One striking bit of evidence that eloquent briefs are persuasive is the frequency with which well-articulated arguments from briefs reappear in judicial opinions. If imitation is the highest form of flattery, there can be nothing more flattering to a brief writer than to have a judge "lift" a phrase or more from the brief and incorporate it into the opinion.

But as we suggested before, eloquence is not something legal writers can add as a kind of finishing touch. Eloquence is not a tuxedo or an evening gown. A writer cannot "put on" eloquence any more than an artist can put on originality.

Eloquence in legal writing and originality in art are there throughout the creative process, often at the point of conception, again through the drafting and revising, and yet again in the final polishing.

§ 7.1 Purple Prose

Like artists who try to force themselves to be original, legal writers who try to force themselves to be eloquent will probably end up creating something that is either absurd or monstrous.

The following excerpt is from the Statement of Facts in a case about whether racial slurs create a cause of action for the tort of outrage.

EXAMPLE

Our client, Mr. Silvino Gomez, is a 20-year-old of Mexican American descent. Mr. Gomez's prowess as a basketball player brought him to the delighted attention of enthusiastic recruiters from several private colleges. He ultimately accepted an athletic scholarship from the University of Newton, where he matriculated and began playing his chosen sport in September 2011. His maiden voyage into the waters of college life was off to a promising start: Barely out of the starting gate, he showed himself to be as talented in the classroom as on the court, and his grades reflected his academic acumen. His interests that fall also included the very beautiful Elizabeth Jaynes, former steady of the team's star guard, Michael Wilson.

Silvino's freshman year was not to be without troubles, however. Storm clouds gathered on the horizon as the season got under way. Gomez, playing well, sensed that Wilson considered him a threat, and tension between the two stirred the air as Wilson harassed Gomez on the court. Although there was no "name-calling" during October, the dust flew in November when Wilson thundered at Gomez, "You fucking spic!" At first, the insults were made only when the coaches were absent, but in late November Wilson hurled them like lightning bolts during several practices in the presence of the coaches. In December, even the fans at several games were listening as Wilson's insults fell like hailstones on Gomez.

Some call writing like the example above "purple prose." Instead of focusing the reader's attention on the point being made, it calls attention to itself. What's worse, the effort shows.

How does one prevent the purple prose syndrome? The best safeguard is the axiom "when in doubt, don't." If you think the writing may be "too much," it probably is. Err on the side of subtlety.

Or if you are fortunate enough to have a candid colleague, get a second opinion. If you fear that something you have written may be overdone, ask that colleague to read the writing and let you know if you have stepped over the invisible line and into the realm of purple prose.

You might also try watching out for some of the common features of purple prose, many of which appear in the example above.

- Excessive use of adjectives and adverbs: *delighted* attention, *enthusiastic* recruiters, *the very beautiful* Elizabeth Jaynes
- Cliché-ridden phrases and images: *the dust flew, hurled them like lightning bolts*
- Mixed metaphors: *maiden voyage* mixed with *out of the starting gate*
- Overdeveloped metaphors: the weather metaphor in the second paragraph
- Pretentious vocabulary: academic *acumen*

Other common features of purple prose not demonstrated in the previous example include the following:

- Too much of any one of the poetic devices (for example, excessive alliteration, or the "Peter Piper" effect)
- Heavy-handed use of stylistic devices
- Excessive use of underlining and italics for emphasis

§ 7.2 Common Features of Eloquent Writing

Before writing can be considered eloquent, it must be clear, competent, and readable. Eloquent writing, however, goes a step beyond competence. The language is more than clear and energetic: It is memorable, striking, even poetic because the writer has paid attention to the sound, rhythm, and imagery of language.

Features of language that one may not have thought about since that last class in poetry—alliteration, assonance, cadence, stressed and unstressed syllables, onomatopoeia, simile, and metaphor—may be used, but they should not overwhelm eloquent legal writing. Rhetorical features you might have noticed in aphorisms—parallelism, balance, antithesis—may also be used, particularly at key points.

Other features, such as effective verbs (see section 5.3), occasional short sentences (see section 5.5), variety in sentence length and sentence openers, and subtle devices for creating emphasis (see section 5.6), are fairly common.

Best of all, all of this occurs naturally, apparently effortlessly, even though we know better. Like a pair of dancers who move as one body or a well-executed double play in baseball, eloquent writing is the perfect, harmonious matching of form and content. The reader feels satisfied, perhaps even uplifted, by the writing.

§ 7.2.1 Repetition of Sound

Eloquent writing begs to be read aloud. One wants to savor the language. Every word and phrase seems to be just the right choice. Quite simply, the writing sings.

Of the numerous features that affect the sound of a piece of writing, alliteration and assonance are probably the easiest to identify. Alliteration, or the repetition of consonant sounds, must be subtle or the writing will begin to sound like "Peter Piper picked a peck of pickled peppers." One way accomplished writers work in alliteration without overpowering the prose is to use it in the middle of words as well as at the beginning.

The following example demonstrates a subtle use of alliteration. The example is taken from the amicus brief for the United States in the landmark Supreme Court case *Wallace v. Jaffree*, which concerned the constitutionality of a state statute authorizing public school teachers to allow a moment of silence at the beginning of the school day for "prayer or meditation."

EXAMPLE   Subtle Alliteration

Moment of silence statutes are libertarian in the precise spirit of the Bill of Rights: they accommodate those who believe that prayer should be an integral part of life's activities (including school), and do so in the most neutral and non-coercive spirit possible. The student may pray, but is equally free to meditate or daydream or doze. No one can even know what the other chooses to do: silence is precious because it creates the possibility of privacy within public occasions. To hold that the moment of silence is unconstitutional is to insist that any opportunity for religious practice, even in the unspoken thoughts of schoolchildren, be extirpated from the public sphere. It is to be censorial where the Religion Clauses are libertarian; it would make the very concept of religious accommodation constitutionally suspect.

The alliteration in this example is unobtrusive. In fact, most of us can read this passage and never consciously notice that it includes alliteration. Look again at these phrases:

the most <u>n</u>eutral and <u>non</u>coercive spirit possible
<u>d</u>ay<u>d</u>ream or <u>d</u>oze

The brief writer could have said "the most impartial and noncoercive spirit possible" or "the most objective and noncoercive spirit possible" or even "the most equitable and noncoercive spirit possible," but didn't. "Neutral," when coupled with "noncoercive," has both the right meaning and the right sound.

The same is true of "daydream and doze." Rather than select "doze," the writer could have easily said "nap," "rest," "sleep," or "snooze." All have similar meanings, but try substituting any one of the four in the original sentence to see what is gained by the alliterative "doze."

The brief writer saves the most subtle and arguably the most powerful alliteration for the clause "silence is precious because it creates the possibility of privacy within public occasions." This clause has two layers of alliteration. The more obvious is the repetition of the "p" sounds: "silence is precious because it creates the possibility of privacy within public occasions." The second layer is the repetition of "s" sounds, which is done by both the letters *s* and *c*: "silence is precious because it creates the possibility of privacy within public occasions."

The soft "s" and "sh" sounds work perfectly in this context. They underscore the writer's meaning by gently, almost imperceptibly reminding the reader of the kind of quiet the writer wants the schoolchildren to have.

Assonance, or the repetition of vowel sounds, is similar to alliteration. In the following example, the brief writer repeated the "a" sound.

EXAMPLE   **Assonance**

The absurdity of this implicit assumption is apparent when applied to the motivations of those responsible for the First Amendment itself.

Is the assonance overdone in the example above? Read it aloud to determine if it works.

§ 7.2.2 Cadence

Cadence is the rhythmic flow of the writing, what musicians might call "the beat." Unlike music, though, writing has no apparent time signature and few overt signals for where to place the emphasis. Even so, good writers control the pace and emphasis in their sentences by artful use of sentence structure, sentence length, punctuation, and stressed and unstressed syllables. Like good musicians, they "hear" what they are creating.

Read aloud the following example from the writing of Supreme Court Justice Louis Brandeis.

EXAMPLE

In a government of laws, existence of the government will be imperiled if it fails to observe the law scrupulously. Our Government is the potent, the omnipresent teacher. For good or for ill, it teaches the whole people by its example. Crime is contagious. If the Government becomes a lawbreaker, it breeds contempt for law; it invites every man to become a law unto himself; it invites anarchy. To declare that in the administration of the criminal law the end justifies the means—to declare that the Government may commit crimes in order to secure the conviction of a private criminal—would bring terrible retribution. Against that pernicious doctrine this Court should resolutely set its face.

This excerpt is rich with the features of eloquent prose, but for now let's look just at the rhythm in the language. Consider, for example, the phrase "the potent, the omnipresent teacher." The more common way to write two adjectives before a noun is "the potent, omnipresent teacher," without the extra "the." Why the extra "the" in the Brandeis version? Try scanning the phrase as you would a piece of poetry.

⌣ / ⌣ / ⌣ / ⌣ / ⌣

the po-tent, om-ni-pres-ent teach-er

The unvarying unstressed, stressed, unstressed, stressed syllable pattern is flat and lifeless, particularly when it comes in two-syllable, sing-song units. It does not give "omnipresent" enough emphasis. Add the extra "the," however, and the rhythm is more interesting and, more important, more compatible with the desired emphasis.

Now look at the last sentence of this selection.

. . . this Court should resolutely set its face.

This clause is easy to read aloud. It is a grand, solemn conclusion. Why? Scan the last four words.

/ ⌣ / ⌣ / ⌣ /

res-o-lute-ly set its face

The three one-syllable words "set its face" break up any sing-song effect. Further, notice where the stress falls—on "set" and "face." Thus, by ending the selection on a stressed syllable, a strong note, Justice Brandeis creates the sound of finality and conviction. Had Brandeis arranged the last clause so that it ended on "resolutely" (as he had the earlier one, "to observe the law scrupulously"), the unstressed syllable at the end of "resolutely" would have fought against the decisive closure he wanted.

/ ⌣ / / ⌣ / ⌣

set its face res-o-lute-ly

Does this mean Justice Brandeis scanned his prose for stressed and unstressed syllables as he was writing it? That's highly unlikely. What is likely is that he *heard* the sound he was creating and, perhaps through trial and error, manipulated the words until he achieved the aural effect he wanted.

The preceding examples show that an extra syllable here or there or changing a stressed to an unstressed syllable or vice versa can make a difference in how writing sounds. Adding or deleting an extra word or syllable also makes a difference in the pace of the writing. Such a change in pace is particularly obvious when the word added or omitted is a conjunction in a series.

A typical series reads like "red, white, and blue." Asyndeton, or the deliberate omissions of conjunctions in a series, quickens the pace. The same series without the conjunction—"red, white, blue"—sounds slightly rushed. See Rule 9.1(10) for more information on creating lists.

Polysyndeton, or the deliberate use of many conjunctions in a series, slows the pace and drags out the prose. Now the series takes more time: "red and white and blue."

Compare the following examples from a child custody case, in which the court looks at which of the parties was the child's primary caregiver. In an objective, neutral discussion of the father's care of the child, the following series may appear.

EXAMPLE

Mr. Lundquist had certain responsibilities regarding his daughter Anna's care: He drove her to school, checked her homework, and took her to medical appointments.

The attorney for Lundquist's former wife may use asyndeton to create the impression that Mr. Lundquist's care of his daughter was minimal.

EXAMPLE

Mr. Lundquist had few responsibilities regarding his daughter Anna's care: He drove her to school, checked her homework, took her to medical appointments.

Mr. Lundquist, on the other hand, will probably want to create the impression that he was an involved parent who spent a great deal of time with his daughter. Notice how the use of polysyndeton, in combination with other persuasive devices such as characterizing the facts and adding detail, creates the desired effect.

EXAMPLE

Mr. Lundquist had several significant responsibilities regarding his daughter Anna's care: He drove her to school each day and checked her homework every evening and took her to all regularly scheduled and emergency medical appointments.

§ 7.2.3 Variety in Sentence Length

In section 5.5, we said that legal readers can comfortably read sentences that average around 22 words in length. We also suggested that long sentences, 35 words or more, are difficult to read unless they are broken into manageable units of meaning. Finally, we briefly touched on the power of the short sentence. All of these points apply to eloquent writing.

Let's look again at the earlier example from Justice Brandeis.

In a government of laws, existence of the government will be imperiled if it fails to observe the law scrupulously. Our Government is the potent, the omnipresent teacher. For good or for ill, it teaches the whole people by its example. Crime is contagious. If the Government becomes a lawbreaker, it breeds contempt for law; it invites every man to become a law unto himself; it invites anarchy. To declare that in the administration of the criminal law the end justifies the means—to declare that the Government may commit crimes in order to secure the conviction of a private criminal—would bring terrible retribution. Against that pernicious doctrine this Court should resolutely set its face.

A reader's sense of how long a sentence is depends partly on the number of words in the sentence but also on the number of syllables in the sentence. Here's how the sentences in the Brandeis excerpt break down, both in the number of words they contain and in the number of syllables.

sentence 1	20 words	32 syllables
sentence 2	8 words	15 syllables
sentence 3	13 words	17 syllables
sentence 4	3 words	5 syllables
sentence 5	24 words	38 syllables
sentence 6	37 words	62 syllables
sentence 7	11 words	18 syllables

The variety in sentence length in this selection is remarkable—from 3 words to 37 words. Having variety, though, is not an end in itself. Notice how Brandeis uses sentence length. The one extremely short sentence, "Crime is contagious," is startling in its brevity. It hits the reader like a slap in the face. Its terseness creates the emphasis this point deserves.

The longest sentence in the selection has to be longer just to get across its points, but it also needs more words to create the effect of building to a climax. This sentence needs time to gather momentum. And even though it is fairly long—thirty-seven words or sixty-two syllables—this sentence is easy to read because it comes in manageable units of meaning: 15 words, 18 words, and 4 words.

Such variety in sentence length helps create an interesting and varied pace. Deliberately breaking the "rules" can be another effective way to create reader interest. In the following example from *Edwards v. Aguillard*, Justice Scalia used a marathon sentence to help make a point.

But the difficulty of knowing what vitiating purpose one is looking for is as nothing compared with the difficulty of knowing how or where to find it. For while it is possible to discern the objective "purpose" of a statute (*i.e.,* the public good at which its provisions appear to be directed), or even the formal motivation for a statute where that is explicitly set forth (as it was, to no avail, here), discerning the subjective motivation of those enacting the statute is, to be honest, almost always an impossible task. The number of possible motivations, to begin with, is not binary, or indeed even finite. In the present case, for example, a particular legislator need not have voted for the Act either because he wanted to foster religion or because he wanted to improve education. He may have thought the bill would provide jobs for his district, or may have wanted to make amends with a faction of his party he had alienated on another vote, or he may have been a close friend of the bill's sponsor, or he may have been repaying a favor he owed the Majority Leader, or he may have hoped the Governor would appreciate his vote and make a fundraising appearance for him, or he may have been pressured to vote for a bill he disliked by a wealthy contributor or by a flood of constituent mail, or he may have been seeking favorable publicity, or he may have been reluctant to hurt the feelings of a loyal staff member who worked on the bill, or he may have been settling an old score with a legislator who opposed the bill, or he may have been mad at his wife who opposed the bill, or he may have been intoxicated and utterly *un*motivated when the vote was called, or he may have accidentally voted "yes" instead of "no," or, of course, he may have had (and very likely did have) a combination of some of the above and many other motivations. To look for *the sole purpose* of even a single legislator is probably to look for something that does not exist.

The fifth sentence is a linguistic *tour de force*. At 202 words, it must set some kind of record for sentence length, yet the sentence is quite readable because it is broken up into manageable units that vary between 8 and 24 words.

But no one thinks Justice Scalia wrote this sentence to demonstrate that he could write a long sentence that is readable. Rather, in this rare instance, an extremely long sentence dramatically made his point that there is an extremely long list of reasons why any single legislator may vote for a bill.

§ 7.2.4 Variety in Sentence Openers

It is risky to suggest that legal writers should occasionally vary the openings of their sentences. In the hands of the wrong writer, this advice can lead to some clumsy prose.

For the most part, writers should follow the more traditional advice and begin the majority of their sentences with the subject. Writers who use all sorts of sentence openers other than the subject tend to write prose that sounds jumpy and disjointed. But writers who oversubscribe to the idea of starting sentences with the subject write incredibly boring prose.

The question then is when should a writer use something other than the subject to begin a sentence? Even in garden-variety prose, subjects are frequently preceded by phrases or clauses that establish a context or pick up

See Quick Tip:
Over-Reliance
on Common
Sentence
Patterns ⊕

on a previously established theme. (See sections 4.2 and 4.3.1 on orienting transitions and dovetailing.)

What is far more unusual and, when done well, more striking, is the inverted word order of some sentences. Such an inversion, known in classical rhetoric as "anastrophe," focuses particular attention on whatever words are out of their normal or expected order. The Brandeis excerpt ended with an example of inverted word order.

EXAMPLE

Against that pernicious doctrine this Court should resolutely set its face.

As always, to understand the drama and power this arrangement creates, all one has to do is read the sentence in the normal, expected word order.

This Court should resolutely set its face against that pernicious doctrine.

Here is another example from an amicus brief in *Wallace v. Jaffree*:

EXAMPLE

The public schools serve as vehicles for "inculcating fundamental values," including "social, moral, or political" ones. *Bd. of Educ. v. Pico*, 102 S. Ct. 2799, 2806 (1982). Pointedly absent from this list are religious values. Education in those values is not, under the Constitution, the responsibility of the public schools; it is that of family and church.

The expected word order of the second sentence in the second example is "Religious values are pointedly absent from this list." Notice that by inverting the order, the brief writer not only places emphasis on what is out of order, "pointedly absent," but also strengthens the emphasis on "religious values" by moving it to the end of the sentence. Keep in mind, though, that this technique works best when used sparingly.

§ 7.2.5 Balance and Symmetry

Parallelism, or the use of similar grammatical structures in a pair or series of related words, phrases, or clauses, is required in some contexts. (See section 8.7.) Accomplished writers, however, treat parallel language not just as a grammatical requirement, but as a stylistic opportunity. They use balance and symmetry to create special effects, emphasis, and euphony.

Here's an example from the appellants' brief in *Wallace v. Jaffree*:

This development is a tribute not only to the good sense of the American people, but also to the genius of the Framers of the body of the Constitution.

| *not only* | *to the good sense of the American people,* |
| *but also* | *to the genius of the Framers of the body of the Constitution* |

Look again at the Scalia excerpt. Justice Scalia used a specialized rhetorical technique called "isocolon" when he matches both the structure and the length of the parallel elements in the following sentence.

In the present case, for example, a particular legislator need not have voted for the Act either because he wanted to foster religion or because he wanted to improve education.

| *either* | *because he wanted to foster religion* |
| *or* | *because he wanted to improve education* |

The same excerpt from Justice Scalia demonstrates an effective use of rhetorical balance. In the sentence below, notice how the first half of the sentence is balanced against the second half.

To look for the sole purpose of even a single legislator is probably to look for something that does not exist.

To look for	*is*	*to look for*
the sole purpose	*probably*	*something that*
of even a		*does not exist.*
single legislator		

Balance can also be created in a number of other ways. Here's an excerpt from Cardozo's opinion in *Hynes v. New York*:

The approximate and relative become the definite and absolute.

approximate	*become*	*definite*
and		*and*
relative		*absolute*

From the brief of the appellees in *Wallace*:

EXAMPLE

The First Amendment is as simple in its language as it is majestic in its purpose.

| *as simple* | *as (it is) majestic* |
| *in its language* | *in its purpose* |

Also fairly common in eloquent legal writing is a rhetorical technique known as "antithesis." Like balance, antithesis repeats similar parallel structures on both sides of the equation, but unlike balance, the ideas are in contrast.

The structure of antithesis is usually quite simple and falls into one of two patterns:

> not _____ but _____
> _____, not _____

Examples from the amicus brief of the United States in *Wallace*:

EXAMPLE

The touchstone is not secularism, but pluralism.

. . .

We believe that provision for a moment of silence in the public schools is not an establishment of religion, but rather a legitimate way for the government to provide an opportunity for both religious and nonreligious introspection in a setting where, experience has shown, many desire it. It is an instrument of toleration and pluralism, not of coercion or indoctrination.

Yet another way to balance your prose is to use parallel openers. Parallel openers can start sentences, clauses, or phrases, and they often have the effect of building to a climax or suggesting that a point is well established.

From the Brandeis excerpt:

EXAMPLE

If the Government becomes a lawbreaker, it breeds contempt for law; **it invites** every man to become a law unto himself; **it invites** anarchy. **To declare that** in the administration of the criminal law the end justifies the means—**to declare that** the Government may commit crimes in order to secure the conviction of a private criminal—would bring terrible retribution.

---

§ 7.2.6 Onomatopoeia

"Snap," "crackle," and "pop"—these words are examples of onomatopoeia; that is, they sound like what they mean. So do "sizzle," "plop," "hiss," "click," "twang," "crinkle," and a host of others. These words sound like the natural sounds they represent.

Other words have an onomatopoetic quality even though the words don't represent a sound. Consider the word "weird." Not only does it sound weird, it is even spelled weirdly. The word "bizarre" works the same way; it looks and sounds bizarre. The list goes on. There is something grotesque in the look and sound of "grotesque," and it is hard to imagine a word that looks and sounds more unattractive than "ugly."

Consider the sound of words such as "sensual," "lascivious," "salacious," and "licentious." Notice how the rolling "s" and "l" sounds combine in various ways to give the words a lazy, even erotic sound. "Sultry" works the same way.

The "slippery slope" one hears so much about in law puts the "s" and "l" together as a consonant blend and achieves a different effect. The words seem to *slide* off the tongue with slow ease. Like a judicial system that has started down that slippery slope, there are no natural brakes to stop these words once they are formed on the lips. Notice too that "slick," "slime," "slink," "slither," "slush," and "sludge" all somehow share this same slippery, even oily quality.

Should legal writers use onomatopoeia in their writing? Consider the following versions of essentially the same point.

EXAMPLE

Harris suddenly took the keys and ran out the door.

Harris snatched the keys and ran out the door.

"Snatched" says in one word—even one syllable—what the first of the examples takes two words and four syllables to say. Its quickness mirrors the quickness in the action. It *sounds* like a quick grab at those keys.

§ 7.2.7 Simile and Metaphor

Similes are indirect comparisons that often use the words "like," "as," "so," or "than."

EXAMPLE

Lowell's mental irresponsibility defense is like the toy gun he used in the robbery—spurious.

Metaphors are direct comparisons.

Our Government is the potent, the omnipresent teacher.

To be effective, similes and metaphors need to be fresh and insightful. Unfortunately, all too many metaphors used in legal writing are cliché-ridden. How often must we hear that something or other is "woven into the fabric of our society"? When was the last time you actually thought about wolves and sheep when something or someone was described as a "wolf in sheep's clothing"?

Timeworn similes and metaphors suggest that the writer's thought processes are on autopilot, and no more than that will be expected of the reader. We can all mentally coast.

A fresh simile or metaphor makes demands of the reader. It asks the reader to bring to the new subject matter all the associations it has with the other half of the metaphor.

So powerful is metaphor that metaphors have become issues themselves. Consider, for example, the same landmark Supreme Court case from which we drew earlier examples, *Wallace v. Jaffree*, which involved the Alabama "silent meditation or prayer" in public schools statute. Throughout that case's history, both sides argued whether there was "an absolute wall of separation" between federal government and religion.

§ 7.2.8 Personification

Like so many of the suggestions in this chapter, personification, or giving human traits or abilities to abstractions or inanimate objects, must be used with a light hand if it is to be used at all in legal writing.

In the brief of the appellees in *Wallace v. Jaffree*, the writer used personification to make a point about the intent of the Alabama legislature.

In 1982, in order to breathe religious life into its silent meditation statute, the Alabama legislature amended § 16-1-20 to expressly include "prayer" as the preferred activity in which the students and teachers may engage during the reverent moment of silence.

In his dissenting opinion in *Hoffa v. United States*, Chief Justice Warren used personification to make a point about the government's actions and its witness.

EXAMPLE

Here the Government reaches into the jailhouse to employ a man who was himself facing indictments far more serious (and later including one for perjury) than the one confronting the man against whom he offered to inform.

Eloquent language does one of two things. It creates a satisfying sound or, as in the Warren excerpt above, it creates a memorable image. The best of the best does both. Such writing is memorable, even unforgettable. It grabs the reader's attention long enough to make the reader see something new or see something old in a new way.

See Quick Tip: Affect vs. Effect ⊕

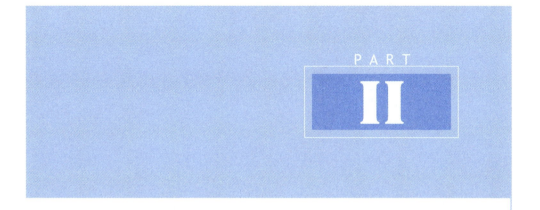

A Guide to Correct Writing

This section is a review of grammar and punctuation. While many legal writers have a good command of these aspects of writing, some complain that they never really understood how to use a semicolon or that they have heard about dangling modifiers but what in the world are they, anyway?

This section is designed to be a quick refresher and explanation for those who have forgotten some of the basic rules or who, for some reason, never learned some of them. Even those who have strong backgrounds in grammar and punctuation may find it helpful to review some of the chapters in this section simply because legal writing puts more demands on the writer than do most other types of writing. Consequently, it may make your writing more efficient and more effective if you have all the rules, and hence all the options, at your fingertips.

Finally, although this Part is entitled "A Guide to Correct Writing," the term "correct" is slightly misleading because it may suggest that the choices outlined in these chapters are absolutely the "right" ones in all circumstances. This is not true. In informal language, for example, certain other usage choices are not only acceptable but preferred. In legal writing, however, standard legal English is the norm and therefore the "correct" choice.

Grammar

§ 8.1 Basic Sentence Grammar

Grammar, like law, is a system. Once you understand the basic workings of the system, you can begin to use the system effectively and efficiently.

Much of Part I, "A Guide to Effective Writing," and Part II, "A Guide to Correct Writing," depends on understanding the grammar of an English sentence. This section is a quick review of basic sentence structure and the various components of most English sentences.[1]

§ 8.1.1 Sentence Patterns

In law, as in most other writing, most sentences are statements. These statements name someone or something (the subject) and then describe an action that that someone or something is performing (the predicate).

---

[1] Although modern grammarians have persuasively argued that structural and transformational grammars more accurately describe the English sentence, the authors have elected to use traditional grammar, partly because it is more familiar to most readers and partly because it is sufficient for our purposes.

Smith   hit Jones.
(subject)   *(predicate)*

Smith's car   smashed into the railing.
(subject)   *(predicate)*

Occasionally, the predicate describes the state in which the subject exists, or the subject's state of being.

Smith's car   is a total loss.
(subject)   *(predicate)*

At the heart of every subject is a noun or a pronoun. Nouns name persons (Supreme Court Justice Anthony Kennedy), places (Austin, Texas), things (savings bond), and concepts (negligence). Because pronouns are substitutes for nouns, they too can serve as subjects.

At the heart of every predicate is a verb. Some verbs express an action (argue, allege); others show a state of being (such as forms of the verb *to be*). Frequently, the main verb is preceded by other verbs known as auxiliary, or helping, verbs (*might have been* assaulted), which express time relationships and shades of meaning. See section 10.1.2.

Pattern 1: Subject + Verb

To write a sentence, you need at least one noun or pronoun for a subject[2] and at least one verb for a predicate. This is the simplest sentence pattern.

subject   **predicate**
Lawyers   argue.
(noun)   *(verb)*

Pattern 2: Subject + Verb + Direct Object

Many verbs, however, cannot stand alone. They require a noun that will receive the action of the verb. We cannot, for example, simply say "lawyers make" and call that a sentence. "Make" what? To make sense, the verb needs a direct object. Notice that the direct object is part of the predicate.

subject   **predicate**
Lawyers   make arguments.
(noun)   *(verb)   (noun)*
                (direct object)

Another way of thinking about this point is to say that the subject performs the action of the verb, and the verb "is done to" the direct object.

---

[2] Some English sentences seem to lack a subject while still being grammatical. The imperative mood contains an implied subject. See section 8.3.2.

You can often find the direct object in a sentence by simply asking the question "what?" after the verb. Make what? Make *arguments*.

Pattern 3: Subject + Linking Verb + Subject Complement

Similarly, state-of-being verbs, or linking verbs, need nouns (or sometimes adjectives) to complete the idea. Because these words do not directly receive the action of the verb in the same way as a direct object, they are not called direct objects. Instead, they are called "subject complements" because they complement the subject by renaming or describing it.

subject	**predicate**	
Lawyers	are	advocates.
(noun)	*(linking verb)*	*(noun)*
		(subject complement)

subject	**predicate**	
Lawyers	are	aggressive.
(noun)	*(linking verb)*	*(adjective)*
		(subject complement)

Note that some of the same words (am, is, are, was, were) function as linking verbs in some sentences and as auxiliary, or helping, verbs in other sentences. You can always tell whether one of these words is a linking verb or a helping verb by checking to see whether it is the only main verb in the sentence (then it is a linking verb) or whether it is followed by another main verb (then it is an auxiliary, or helping, verb).

EXAMPLE

The judge is the trier of fact.

In the preceding example, "is" is the only verb; therefore, it is a linking verb.

EXAMPLE

The judge is speaking to the jury.

In the preceding example, "is" is followed by another main verb, "speaking"; therefore, "is" is an auxiliary, or helping, verb in this example. Notice that the combination "is speaking" is an action verb.

Pattern 4: Subject + Verb + Indirect Object + Direct Object

In another common pattern, the verb is followed by two nouns. The second noun after the verb, the direct object, receives the action of the verb. The first noun after the verb, the indirect object, identifies to whom or for whom (or what) the action is performed.

subject	predicate		
Lawyers	tell	clients	their options.
	(verb)	*(noun)*	*(noun)*
		(indirect object)	***(direct object)***

Pattern 5: Subject + Verb + Direct Object + Object Complement

In this last pattern, we also have two nouns following the verb, but in this pattern, the first noun is the direct object and the second noun is an objective complement. An objective complement renames or describes the direct object.

subject	predicate		
Smith	called	Jones	a liar.
	(verb)	*(noun)*	*(noun)*
		(direct object)	***(objective complement)***

Using these basic sentence patterns, we can now begin adding all those extras that make sentences interesting and complex.

§ 8.1.2 Single-Word Modifiers

Modifiers change, limit, describe, or add detail. Words that modify nouns or pronouns are, by definition, adjectives (*illogical* argument, *bearded* suspect).

Words that modify verbs, adjectives, or adverbs are adverbs (*quickly* responded, finished *soon, extremely* angry, *very* recently). Notice that adverbs often end in "-ly."

Any of our basic sentences can be expanded by using adjectives and adverbs as modifiers.

EXAMPLES

Thoughtful lawyers make very persuasive arguments.
(adjective)   *(adverb)(adjective)*

Too many lawyers are overly aggressive.
(adv.)(adj.)   *(adverb)(adjective)*

§ 8.1.3 Phrases

When expanding the basic sentence patterns, we are not limited to single-word modifiers. Groups of related words, or phrases, can also serve as modifiers. A phrase is easily distinguished from other groups of related words because a phrase always lacks a subject or a verb or both.

Probably the most common type of modifying phrase is the prepositional phrase, which is made up of a preposition (a word that shows a relationship between other words, such as "about," "at," "by," "for," "in," "of," "on," "to"), its object, and any modifiers.

Preposition	Modifiers	Object
at......................	the same.......	time
for.....................	a new...........	trial
under.................	this..............	section

Prepositional phrases can modify nouns, verbs, adjectives, or adverbs.

EXAMPLE

At 10:00 p.m. on April 5, 2016, a two-truck collision occurred in Delaware between a truck driven by Ms. Constance Ruiz and a truck driven by Mr. Fred Miller.

Basic sentence patterns can also be expanded with verbals. Verbals are made from verbs, but they cannot serve as the main verb of a sentence. Instead, verbals are ways of using verb forms in other roles in a sentence. The three types of verbals—gerunds, infinitives, and participles—are described below. Notice that each can be expanded into a phrase.

a. Gerunds

Gerunds always act as nouns, so they are found in slots in the sentence that require nouns (subject, objects). They are formed by adding "-ing" to the base form of a verb. However, not all words ending in "-ing" are gerunds.

EXAMPLES

Impeaching his testimony will be difficult.
  (gerund)

Forgery includes writing a bad check.
            (gerund)

---

b. Participles

Participles act as adjectives. Present participles are formed by adding "-ing" to the base form of the verb; past participles usually add "-d" or "-ed." Irregular verbs have a special past participle form (for example, *brought, given, stolen*).

EXAMPLES

A laptop <u>wrapped</u> in a blanket was in the defendant's trunk.
   (participle)

<u>Applying</u> this rule, the New York Supreme Court held that the
(participle)
appellant's constitutional rights were not violated.

<u>Given</u> that assault is not a crime of dishonesty, the court found that
(participle)
evidence of the prior conviction was inadmissible.

Notice that the only way to distinguish between a gerund and a present participle is to determine the role they perform in a sentence.

c. Infinitives

Infinitives can act as nouns, adjectives, or adverbs. The infinitive form is always "to" plus the base form of the verb.

EXAMPLE

<u>To extend</u> the all-purpose public figure standard <u>to include</u> all financial institutions ignores the Supreme Court's mandate <u>to construe</u> the standard narrowly.

---

d. Absolutes

One additional type of phrase, the absolute phrase, can also be used to expand the basic sentence patterns. Absolute phrases do not modify any one word or phrase in a sentence; instead, they are whole-sentence modifiers. Absolute phrases are made up of a noun (or pronoun), a participle, and their modifiers.

attention   diverted
   (noun)   +   *(participle)*

EXAMPLE

<u>His attention diverted by the fire</u>, the witness is unlikely to have viewed the fleeing arsonist for more than a second.

---

§ 8.1.4 Clauses

A clause is a group of related words that has both a subject and a verb. There are two types of clauses: main (or independent) clauses and subordinate (or dependent) clauses. A main clause can stand alone as a sentence. A subordinate clause cannot stand alone as a sentence because a subordinate clause is introduced by a subordinating conjunction or relative pronoun. For a list of subordinating conjunctions, see section 8.2.2.

Relative Pronouns

that	which	whom
what	who	whomever
whatever	whoever	whose

Notice that in subordinate clauses introduced by a relative pronoun, the subject of the clause is often the relative pronoun. ("Defendants *who do not take the stand* risk having jurors infer that they are guilty.")

EXAMPLES

Main Clauses:

Martin retained full possession of the stock.

The trial court abused its discretion.

It failed to consider the statutory factors.

Subordinate Clauses:

although Martin retained full possession of the stock

that the trial court abused its discretion

when it failed to consider the statutory factors

Subordinate Clauses Attached to Main Clauses:

Although Martin retained full possession of the stock, the trial court awarded the stock to Judith.

The appellate court found that the trial court abused its discretion when it failed to consider the statutory factors.

§ 8.1.5 Appositives

Appositives are words or groups of words that follow a noun and rename, further describe, or identify the noun.

EXAMPLES

Conrad Murray, <u>Michael Jackson's personal physician</u>, was found guilty of involuntary manslaughter.

In *Texas v. Johnson*, a <u>case about a state criminal statute forbidding</u> "the desecration of a venerated object," the Supreme Court ruled that burning the

American flag as an expression of political discontent is protected by the First Amendment.

Appositives are frequently introduced by phrases—*that is, such as, for example*.

EXAMPLE

Evidence of some crimes, <u>such as fraud, embezzlement, and false pretense,</u> may be probative of a defendant's credibility as a witness.

§ 8.1.6 Connecting Words

The five basic sentence patterns can also be expanded by using connecting words that allow us to combine words or word groups of equal rank. For example, we can add one or more nouns to a subject to create a compound subject ("Smith and Wilson hit Jones"), or we can add one or more verbs to the predicate to create a compound predicate ("Smith hit and kicked Jones").

a. Coordinating Conjunctions

The most common connecting words are the seven coordinating conjunctions,

and	nor	yet
but	for	so
or		

"And," "but," "or," "yet," and "nor" can connect any two (or more) of the same kind of word or word group. "For" and "so" connect main clauses.

EXAMPLES

Connecting Two Nouns:

Crimes of dishonesty involve **fraud** <u>**or**</u> **deceit**.

Connecting Two Verbs:

The complaint stated that the defendants **had published** <u>but</u> not **retracted** a defamatory article about Vashon Savings and Loan.

Connecting Three Phrases:

Copies of the article were distributed to **subscribers, newsstands,** <u>and</u> **three civic groups**.

Connecting Two Subordinate Clauses:

Because there are only two witnesses <u>and</u> because each witness has a different version of the facts, the jury will have to choose which one to believe.

Connecting Two Main Clauses:

Vashon Savings and Loan has not assumed a role of special prominence in the affairs of society, <u>nor</u> does it occupy a position of pervasive power or influence.

b. Correlative Conjunctions

Correlative conjunctions come in pairs.

both…and	either…or	whether…or
not…but	neither…nor	as…as
not only…but also		

EXAMPLES

The plaintiff's contact with the community is <u>both</u> **conservative** <u>and</u> **low-key**.

The jury <u>either</u> **will not hear the defendant's testimony** <u>or</u> **will completely disregard it** if his prior convictions are admitted.

c. Conjunctive Adverbs

Even though conjunctive adverbs do not connect parts of the sentence grammatically, they are useful because they show the relationship between two or more ideas.

The Most Common Conjunctive Adverbs

accordingly	further	likewise	similarly
also	furthermore	meanwhile	still
anyway	hence	moreover	then
besides	however	nevertheless	thereafter
certainly	incidentally	next	therefore
consequently	indeed	nonetheless	thus
finally	instead	otherwise	undoubtedly

EXAMPLES

Ms. Davis admits that her physician told her that she has a drinking problem. She refuses, <u>nevertheless</u>, to attend Alcoholics Anonymous. <u>Instead</u>, she claims that she drinks only an occasional glass of wine.

Ms. Davis will have $63,872 a year to spend as she sees fit; <u>therefore</u>, she has no need for the dividend income from the stock.

See Quick Tip:
Finding and
Correcting
Comma Splices
and Fused
Sentences ⊕

§ 8.2 Fragments

Simply defined, a sentence fragment is an incomplete sentence. Theoretically, it may be missing its subject,[3] but more than likely it is missing a main verb or a subordinate clause trying to pose as a sentence.

§ 8.2.1 Missing Main Verb

All verbals—gerunds, participles, and infinitives—are formed from verbs, but they cannot fill verb slots in a sentence. Consequently, verbals cannot serve as the main verb of a sentence. Some legal writers who are prone to writing fragments mistake verbals for main verbs. (See section 8.1.3 for definitions and explanations of verbals.)

EXAMPLE   **Fragment**

The attorney objecting to the line of questioning.

In the example above, "objecting" is not a verb; it is a participle modifying "attorney." Because the example has no main verb, it is a fragment, not a sentence. To make it a sentence, either add a main verb or change "objecting" from a participle to a main verb.

EXAMPLES   **Possible Revisions**

The attorney objecting to the line of questioning <u>rose</u> to her feet.

The attorney <u>objected</u> to the line of questioning.

The attorney <u>was objecting</u> to the line of questioning.

Notice that the same word, "objecting," can be a participle or, with an auxiliary verb added, can be a main verb.

§ 8.2.2 Subordinate Clauses Trying to Pose as Sentences

Take any main, or independent, clause and add a word such as "although," "until," or "when" in front of the word and it becomes a subordinate, or dependent, clause.

$$until + \text{main clause} = \text{subordinate clause}$$

---

[3] Imperative, or command, sentences such as "Sit down" or "Hang your coat in the cloakroom" may appear to have a missing subject, but the subject is always understood to be "you." Therefore, imperative sentences are not fragments even if they are only one word long, such as "Run!" Generally, it is best to avoid imperatives in legal writing unless quoting.

Main Clause:

The attorney objects to the line of questioning.

Subordinate Clause:

Until the attorney objects to the line of questioning

Subordinate clauses must be attached to a main, or independent, clause.

Until the attorney objects to the line of questioning, the judge will
                   (subordinate clause)   *(main clause)*
not rule.

"Although," "if," "until," "because," and "when" are not the only words, or subordinating conjunctions, that can change a main clause into a subordinate clause. Below is a fairly complete list of the most common subordinating conjunctions used in legal writing. Remember: If one of these words or phrases introduces a clause, that clause will be subordinate. If a subordinate clause stands alone, it is a fragment.

Subordinating Conjunctions

after	before	now that	till
although	even if	once	unless
as	even though	provided	until
as if	if	rather than	when
as long as	if only	since	whenever
as soon as	in order that	so that	where
as though	in that	than	whereas
because	no matter how	that	wherever
		though	while

Notice, too, that subordinate clauses may follow a main clause. In fact, many fragments are written because the writer should have attached a subordinate clause to the preceding main clause.

Fragment:

Kaiser's statement acknowledging Sloan's ownership of the land may have no effect on the hostility of his claim. Because he never acted in subordination to the true owner.

Corrected:

Kaiser's statement acknowledging Sloan's ownership of the land may have no effect on the hostility of his claim because Kaiser never acted in subordination to the true owner.

The relative pronouns—"who," "whoever," "whom," "whomever," "whose," "what," "whatever," "which," and "that"—also lure some writers into writing fragments.

EXAMPLE

Fragment:

The admission of a defendant's prior convictions may affect that defendant's decision to take the stand. Which would interfere with his right to testify freely on his own behalf.

Corrected:

The admission of a defendant's prior convictions may affect that defendant's decision to take the stand. Therefore, admission of his prior convictions would interfere with his right to testify freely on his own behalf.

In short, to determine if you have written a sentence and not a fragment, (1) make sure you have a verb, (2) make sure you have a subject, and (3) make sure your subject and verb are not preceded by a subordinating conjunction or a relative pronoun.

§ 8.2.3 Permissible Uses of Incomplete Sentences

There are a handful of permissible uses for incomplete sentences in legal writing.

    a. In issue statements beginning with "whether"
    b. As answers to questions
    c. In exclamations
    d. In quoted material
    e. For stylistic effect
    f. As transitions

a. In Issue Statements Beginning with "Whether"

Many issue statements, or questions presented, begin with the word "whether."

EXAMPLE

Whether, under Washington tort law on wrongful death or conversion, the Hoffelmeirs may collect punitive damages for the destruction of their pet cat when the cat was impounded and when, after Mr. Janske of the Humane Society tried unsuccessfully to contact the Hoffelmeirs, the animal was destroyed before the time required by the Sequim city ordinance.

Although a grammarian would not consider the example above to be a complete sentence, most attorneys and judges find this format acceptable in legal writing. It is as though legal readers read in an implied "the issue is" before "whether."

b. As Answers to Questions

Many office memos contain a brief answer section. Typically, a brief answer will begin with an incomplete sentence that is a short response to the legal question, such as "Probably not." This is an acceptable use of a fragment. The following example is the brief answer to the question presented in the preceding example.

EXAMPLE

Probably not. In Washington, there is a strong policy against the award of punitive damages and, unless there is a statutory provision allowing for punitive damages, the courts will not award them. In this instance, there is no statutory provision allowing for punitive damages.

---

c. In Exclamations

Exclamations rarely occur in legal writing because they make the tone of the writing appear inflammatory, effusive, or sarcastic. The one place exclamations do appear in legal writing is in quoted dialogue. On such occasions, quote exactly what the speaker said and how he or she said it, including fragments.

d. In Quoted Material

From time to time, you will certainly find instances when another writer used a sentence fragment for stylistic effect or to capture a particular sentiment. You should remain faithful to the original source material in both writing and quoted dialogue; human speech often deviates from established grammatical conventions for writing.

e. For Stylistic Effect

Sophisticated writers who are well schooled in the rules of grammar can occasionally use an intentional fragment for stylistic effect. Most writers, however, should avoid writing any fragments.

EXAMPLE

It may have been unavoidable, but it still took courage. <u>More courage than most of us would have had</u>.

---

f. As Transitions

As with fragments for stylistic effect, intentional fragments as transitions are a risk. Use them only if you are secure about and in complete control of your writing.

If you have already read sections 3.4 and 3.5 of this book, you may have noticed that we, the authors, used two incomplete sentences as transitions to begin those sections.

EXAMPLES

First, the truth.

Again, the truth.

---

§ 8.3 Verb Tense and Mood

§ 8.3.1 Tense

Verb tense does not pose problems for most legal writers who are native speakers of English. Native speakers tend to "hear" when the verb is right or wrong. Some academic disciplines, including English and philosophy, write in a perpetual present tense. Other disciplines use present tense to add a sense of excitement to prose. Consequently, verb tense is one of those areas of writing that is best left alone, unless a writer is having problems.

For those native and non-native speakers of English who are having problems with verb tense in legal writing, the following is a quick review of the basic verb tense structure. (See Chapter 10 for more on verbs and verb tense, particularly how auxiliary verbs create shades of meaning.)

Throughout this review of verb tense, we will use a capital "X" to indicate the present on all time lines.

The term "tense" refers to the time in which the verb's action occurs in relation to the time when the writer is writing. For example, present tense is used for actions that occur in the present, that is, at the time the writer is writing.

EXAMPLE   **Present Tense**

The defendant <u>pleads</u> not guilty.

Time line:_____ X _____
the present
(the action is occurring
at the same time
the writer is writing)

Notice, however, that the "X" on the time line that represents "the present" may be as short as a fraction of a second or as long as several centuries, depending on what time frame the writer sets up.

Past tense refers to actions that occurred before the writer is writing.

EXAMPLE   **Past Tense**

Two years ago, this same prosecutor <u>charged</u> the defendant with aggravated assault.

> Time line: _____ X _____
> **←the past→**

Legal writers usually use the past tense when describing analogous cases.

EXAMPLE

In *Colorado Carpet*, the court <u>rejected</u> the argument for the specially manufactured goods exception because the carpet <u>was</u> not <u>cut</u> to a room size.

Future tense refers to actions that will occur after the writer is writing.

EXAMPLE   **Future Tense**

The plaintiff <u>will call</u> an expert witness.

> Time line: _____ X _____
> **←the future→**

The simple tenses—present, past, and future—are just that: simple and easy to use. Only the present tense offers a few noteworthy wrinkles.

In addition to its common use for actions that occur in the present, present tense is also used to express general truths and to show habitual actions.

EXAMPLES

Appellate courts <u>do</u> not <u>retry</u> a case on its facts.

The defendant <u>drinks</u> a six-pack of beer every Friday night.

Present tense can also be used to indicate the future when the sentence contains other words and phrases to signal a future time.

EXAMPLE   **Present Tense**

The court <u>hears</u> oral arguments later this afternoon.

The perfect tenses are a bit more complicated. Perfect tenses are designed to show that an action is completed before a certain time.

For example, the present perfect tense usually shows that an action is completed at the time of the statement. It is formed by using "have" or "has" before the past participle. In the sentence below, the present perfect "have tried" occurred before the present.

EXAMPLE 1   **Present Perfect Tense**

The plaintiffs <u>have tried</u> this strategy before, but it is not working this time.

Time line: _____ X _____
                              ————→
                         (action begun in the
                         past and completed
                         before the present)

The present perfect tense is also used when the action was begun in the past and it continues on into the present.

EXAMPLE 2   **Present Perfect Tense**

The prosecutor <u>has offered</u> Mr. Pemberque a plea bargain that would permit him to plead guilty to a gross misdemeanor and serve no jail time.

Time line: _____ X _____
                              —————————→
                         (action begun in the
                         past and continues
                         on into the present)

In contrast, the past perfect tense is used when one past action was completed before another past action. For example, a legal writer may find it useful to use the past perfect to distinguish the time sequence of the facts of the case from the time sequence of a court's actions, both of which occurred in the past.

Note that the past perfect tense is formed by adding "had" before the past participle.

EXAMPLE 1   **Past Perfect Tense**

The court <u>noted</u> that the defendant <u>had known</u> about the defective brakes for three months.

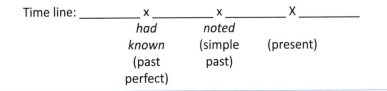

Time line: _____ x _____ x _____ X _____
                        had   noted
                        known   (simple   (present)
                        (past   past)
                        perfect)

The past perfect tense is also useful when discussing court proceedings at different levels. For example, a writer may use the simple past tense to describe the decisions of an appellate court and the past perfect to describe the decisions of the trial court.

EXAMPLE 2 **Past Perfect Tense**

The Court of Appeals <u>affirmed</u> the trial court, which <u>had ruled</u> that
              (simple past)   *(past perfect)*
the statute did not apply.

The future perfect tense is used when an action that started in the past ends at a certain time in the future. It is formed by adding "will have" before the past participle.

EXAMPLE **Future Perfect Tense**

By the time you finish dinner tonight, drunk drivers <u>will have claimed</u> five more victims on United States highways.

Time line: _____ X _____ x _____
           _____→
                          will have
                          claimed

Every verb can also be progressive, that is, it can show continuing action by adding "-ing."

Present progressive: is claiming
Past progressive: was claiming
Future progressive: will be claiming
Present perfect progressive: has been claiming
Past perfect progressive: had been claiming
Future perfect progressive: will have been claiming

One last word about verb tense: One common myth is that writers have to maintain a consistent verb tense. Although writers should avoid needless shifts in verb tense, shifts in verb tense are required when there is a shift in time. Such a shift in time may even occur within the same sentence.

EXAMPLES

Her landlord <u>knows</u> that she <u>will be</u> unable to pay her rent.
   (present)   *(future)*

Although Mr. Henderson <u>built</u> the shed on the property in 2014,
        (past)

he <u>admits</u> that Ms. Kyte <u>has owned</u> that corner since 2001.
 (present)   *(present perfect)*

Smith <u>will argue</u> that he <u>did</u> not knowingly or willingly <u>consent</u> to a
  (future)   *(past)*   *(past)*

search of his wallet.

§ 8.3.2 Mood

In grammar, the term "mood" refers to the approach the writer gives the verb. English has three moods: indicative, imperative, and subjunctive. The indicative mood is used for statements of fact or questions.

EXAMPLE **Indicative Mood**

The defendant <u>pleaded</u> "not guilty."

The imperative mood is used for sentences that are orders or commands. The subject of a sentence in the imperative mood is understood to be "you," the reader or listener.

EXAMPLE **Imperative Mood**

<u>Plead</u> "not guilty."

The subjunctive mood is the only mood that is a bit tricky. Although grammarians are constantly discussing its demise, the subjunctive mood is still used in a variety of situations.

1. The subjunctive is used to express ideas contrary to fact.

EXAMPLE

If I <u>were</u> the defendant, I would plead "not guilty."

2. The subjunctive is used to express a requirement.

The law requires that contracts <u>be signed</u> willingly, not under duress.

3. The subjunctive is used to express a suggestion or recommendation.

His attorney recommended that he <u>be allowed</u> to give his own closing argument.

4. The subjunctive is used to express a wish.

The clerk asked that the check <u>be postdated</u>.

Note that the contrary-to-fact clauses begin with "if"; the requirement, suggestion, recommendation, or wish clauses all begin with an expressed or elliptical "that."

The subjunctive mood is formed slightly differently depending on how it is used. For present conditions that are contrary to fact, it is formed from the past tense of the verb. For the verb "to be," it uses "were."

If the government inspector <u>took</u> a reading on the toxic particles being emitted right now, it would show that the factory has completely disregarded EPA guidelines.

If she <u>were</u> to testify, the defendant's sister would corroborate his story.

For past conditions that are contrary to fact, the subjunctive mood is formed from the past perfect.

<u>Had</u> the contract been signed, there would be no question that it is valid.

For requirements, recommendations, and suggestions, the subjunctive mood is formed from the infinitive form of the verb without the "to."

EXAMPLE

The law requires that the adverse possessor <u>prove</u> that the possession was open and notorious.

---

§ 8.4 Subject-Verb Agreement

Simply put, subject-verb agreement is matching the noun with the correct conjugation of the verb. Singular subjects take singular verbs, and plural subjects take plural verbs. For most native speakers of English, this kind of subject-verb agreement comes almost as naturally as breathing, as long as the sentence is short and simple.

EXAMPLES

The law requires that all drivers wear seat belts.

singular subject = law
singular verb = requires

The immigration laws require that all workers provide proof of citizenship before starting a job.

plural subject = laws
plural verb = require

In English, we often think that adding "s" makes the plural form of words. This is true for nouns but not for verbs. We add an "s" to the singular form of present tense verbs (except the verb "to be") when they are matched with a singular noun or the pronouns "he," "she," or "it." For example, we say "a client maintain<u>s</u>," "he reject<u>s</u>," "she allege<u>s</u>," or "it confirm<u>s</u>."

In simple sentences, a writer can usually make subjects and verbs agree by listening to the way the sentences sound. The writer's ear tells him or her what matches and what doesn't. In longer, more complicated sentences, like those that often occur in legal writing, the ear is more likely to be misled. The following rules cover those situations.

Rule 8.4(1)   A Subject and Its Verb Must Agree Even When They Are Separated by Other Words

When other words, particularly nouns, come between a subject and its verb, the writer may inadvertently match the verb to a word other than the subject.

EXAMPLE   **Incorrect**

Custom-made <u>towels</u> imprinted with the hotel's logo <u>satisfies</u> the
      (subject)   *(verb)*
requirement that the goods be specially manufactured.

The writer has mistakenly chosen the singular verb "satisfies" to match with the intervening noun "logo" when the verb should be the plural form "satisfy" to agree with the plural subject "towels." One way writers can check for this kind of agreement error is to read their subjects and verbs together without the intervening words. "Towels satisfy" will sound right to native speakers.

The number of the subject is not changed by adding intervening words that begin with expressions such as "accompanied by," "as well as," "in addition to," "with," "together with," or "along with." These expressions are considered prepositions and not coordinating conjunctions (see section 8.1), so they modify the subject. They do not change its number.

EXAMPLE   **Correct**

The defendant's <u>statement</u> to the police, as well as her testimony at trial, <u>suggests</u> that her actions were premeditated.

Rule 8.4(2)   **Two or More Subjects Joined by "and" Usually Take a Plural Verb**

Subjects joined by "and" are plural. This rule does not change even if one or all of the subjects are singular.

EXAMPLE

North Star Cinema and Highland Heights Theater question the validity of the admissions tax.

Unfortunately, writers sometimes hear only the second half of the subject with the verb and mistakenly select a singular verb ("Highland Heights Theater question<u>s</u>"). You may find it easier to mentally substitute the word "they" for plural subjects when using your hearing to find the correct form of the verb ("they question").

Exception

Occasionally two or more parts of the subject make up one idea or refer to one person or thing. In such cases, use a singular verb.

EXAMPLE

His wife and beneficiary was the only person mentioned in the will.

Rule 8.4(3)	**Subjects Joined by "or" or "nor" Take Verbs That Agree with the Part of the Subject Closest to the Verb**

To check subject-verb agreement in sentences with subjects joined by "or" or "nor," simply read only the second half of the subject with the verb and let your ear help you select the correct verb form. In the following examples, read "Lazar Television is" and "her older sisters have."

EXAMPLES

Neither Horizon Telecommunications nor Lazar Television is the type of enterprise that the bulk sales statutes seek to regulate.

The child's mother or her older sisters have been caring for her after school.

In a verb phrase such as "have been caring" in the preceding example, the helping, or auxiliary, verbs are the ones that change.

singular: has been caring
plural: have been caring

Rule 8.4(4)	**Most Indefinite Pronouns Take Singular Verbs**

Indefinite pronouns are ones that do not refer to any definite person or thing, or they do not specify definite limits. The following is a list of the most common indefinite pronouns:

all	each	everything	none
any	either	neither	somebody
anybody	everybody	nobody	someone
anyone	everyone	no one	something

See Quick Tip: Finding Indefinite Pronouns

Usually these pronouns refer to a single, indefinite person or thing, so they take singular verbs.

EXAMPLE

Everyone who ate in the restaurant is suffering the same symptoms.

A few indefinite pronouns—"none," "all," "most," "some," "any," and "half"—may take either a singular or a plural verb depending on the noun to which they refer.

EXAMPLES

All of the jewelry <u>was</u> recovered.

All of the rings <u>were</u> recovered.

Rule 8.4(5)	**Collective Nouns Take Singular Verbs When the Group Acts as One Unit; Collective Nouns Take Plural Verbs When the Members of the Group Act Separately**

Although it may seem like a jury is a group of individuals, a jury acts as one unit. Therefore, "jury" is singular. Similarly, when a court acts, it acts as one unit, so "court" also requires a singular verb. The following is a list of the most common collective nouns in legal writing:

jury	committee	board
audience	team	majority
family	crowd	number
Supreme Court	appellate court	fractions (when
names of companies/	prosecution	used as nouns)
corporations	defense	

The following examples all use collective nouns that are acting as one unit, so the verbs are singular.

EXAMPLES

The jury <u>has reached</u> its verdict.

The appellate court <u>has affirmed</u> the conviction.

Boeing <u>is concerned</u> about its liability.

Rule 8.4(6)	**Linking Verbs Agree with Their Subjects, Not Their Subject Complements**

In the following example, the linking verb "was" agrees with "testimony," not the subject complement "contradictory and intentionally misleading."

EXAMPLE

The defendant's testimony was contradictory and intentionally misleading.

In the next example, the linking verb "was" agrees with "reason," not "evaluations."

EXAMPLE

The reason for firing Jones was his low evaluations.

Rule 8.4(7)	**Verbs Agree with Their Subjects Even When the Subjects Come After the Verb**

Subjects follow verbs after expletive constructions such as "there is" and "there are."

EXAMPLES

There is a possibility that the defendant will plead "temporary insanity."

There are several options for ensuring that your loan is repaid.

Subjects may also follow verbs when normal word order is changed for emphasis.

EXAMPLES

At no time was Brown aware that his conversations were being tape recorded.

At no time were Brown and Smith aware that their conversations were being tape recorded.

Rule 8.4(8)	**The Title of a Work or a Word Used as a Word Takes a Singular Verb**

EXAMPLE

Tactics in Legal Reasoning is an excellent resource for both law students and practitioners.

When a word is used as a word, it is often enclosed in quotation marks or preceded by "the word."

EXAMPLES

"Premises" has at least three different meanings: (1) the introductory propositions to a syllogism, (2) the area of land surrounding a building, or (3) a building or part of a building.

The word "premises" has three different meanings.

Compare the two previous examples, both of which used the singular verb "has," with the following example, which requires the plural verb form "have."

EXAMPLE

The premises have been searched by the police.

Rule 8.4(9)	**Money, Distance, and Measurement Subjects Usually Take Singular Verbs**

EXAMPLE

Twenty thousand dollars is a reasonable fee for a case of this complexity.

§ 8.5 Pronouns

As we discuss in section 8.5.4, pronouns (I, me, he, him, she, her, they, them, their, it, its, etc.) are substitutes for nouns. Consequently, pronouns usually[4] refer back to a noun, and that noun is known as the antecedent.

EXAMPLE

<u>Marino</u> moved for reconsideration, but <u>her</u> motion was denied.
(antecedent)   *(pronoun)*

---

[4] Indefinite pronouns such as "someone," "anybody," "everything," and "neither" do not refer back to nouns. Also, some pronouns that are parts of idioms ("it is likely that . . ." "it is clear that . . ." "it is raining") do not have antecedents.

Pronouns allow us to have greater fluency in speech and writing because we can avoid using the same nouns repeatedly. This increase in fluency, however, comes at the expense of precision.

Pronouns are substitutes for nouns. They have no independent meanings. Consequently, they must refer to a noun and be consistent with that noun in gender, person, and number. Legal writers tend to have two kinds of problems with pronouns and their antecedents: (1) they use pronouns that have unclear or ambiguous antecedents; and (2) they use plural pronouns to refer back to singular antecedents.

§ 8.5.1 Each Pronoun Should Clearly Refer Back to Its Antecedent

Consider the following sentence:

EXAMPLE

Officer Robert O'Malley, who arrested Howard Davis, said that he was drunk at the time.

As it stands, the sentence has two possible readings because the pronoun "he" has two possible antecedents: Officer Robert O'Malley and Howard Davis. To clear up the ambiguity, do one of two things:

See Quick Tip: The Line Test for Pronouns ⊕

1. Repeat the noun rather than use a pronoun, or
2. Revise so that the pronoun is no longer ambiguous.

EXAMPLES   Possible Revisions

Officer Robert O'Malley, who arrested Howard Davis, said that Davis was drunk at the time.

Howard Davis was drunk when he was arrested by Officer O'Malley.

Officer O'Malley was drunk when he arrested Howard Davis.

According to the arresting officer, Robert O'Malley, Howard Davis was drunk at the time of the arrest.

See Quick Tip: The 5% Rule for Pronouns ⊕

Officer Robert O'Malley, who arrested Howard Davis, admitted being drunk at the time of the arrest.

§ 8.5.2 Avoid the Use of "It," "This," "That," "Such," and "Which" to Refer Broadly to a General Idea in a Preceding Sentence

Consider the following sentences:

EXAMPLE **Incorrect Pronoun**

Even if Mr. Huang's testimony about possible embarrassment caused by Acme is adequate to justify a damage award, emotional harm is difficult to quantify. This makes it unlikely that Mr. Huang will receive any substantial recovery.

To what does "this" in the second sentence refer? Because "this" does not seem to refer back to any specific noun in the preceding sentence, the reader is left to guess exactly how much or how little of the preceding discussion "this" is supposed to encompass.

The solution to many broad pronoun reference problems is often a rather simple one: Add a summarizing noun after the pronoun to show the limits of the reference.

EXAMPLE **Corrected**

<u>This difficulty</u> makes it unlikely that Mr. Huang will receive any substantial recovery.

The same technique often works well with "that" and "such."

EXAMPLE

Ms. Marquette has testified that Mr. Marquette has beaten her and their children on at least three occasions, that he has locked them out of their home twice, and that he has threatened to "cut their throats" if they told anyone. According to Mr. Marquette, that is a lie.

Corrected:

Ms. Marquette has testified that Mr. Marquette has beaten her and their children on at least three occasions, that he has locked them out of their home twice, and that he has threatened to "cut their throats" if they told anyone. According to Mr. Marquette, <u>that testimony</u> is a lie.

The use of the pronoun "which" to refer broadly to a preceding idea is a trickier problem to correct. Look at the following example and see if you can determine what the "which" stands for. Keep in mind the basic rule that a pronoun is a substitute for a noun.

> **EXAMPLE** **Incorrect Pronoun**
>
> In *Boone v. Mullendore*, Dr. Mullendore failed to remove Ms. Boone's fallopian tube, which resulted in the birth of a baby.

The only nouns that "which" could possibly refer to are the case name, "Dr. Mullendore," and "fallopian tube." Obviously, none of these nouns resulted in the birth of a baby. Instead, the writer seems to suggest that "which" is a substitute for the following idea: Dr. Mullendore's failure to remove Ms. Boone's fallopian tube. Notice that in expressing what the "which" referred to, we had to use the noun "failure" rather than the verb "failed." To correct the error, then, we must add the noun "failure" to the sentence.

> **EXAMPLE** **Corrected**
>
> In *Boone v. Mullendore*, Dr. Mullendore's failure to remove Ms. Boone's fallopian tube resulted in the birth of a baby.

Be sure to distinguish between the incorrect use of "which" to refer broadly to a previously stated idea and the correct use of "which" to introduce nonrestrictive clauses. (See Rule 9.1(4).)

§ 8.5.3 Pronouns Should Refer Back to Nouns, Not Adjectives

Occasionally a word that appears to be a noun is actually an adjective because it modifies a noun.

> **EXAMPLE**
>
> the <u>Rheams building</u>
>   *(adjective) (noun)*

Often the possessive form of a noun is used as an adjective in a sentence.

> **EXAMPLE**
>
> the <u>defendant's alibi</u>
>   *(adjective) (noun)*

But because a pronoun must always refer to a noun, adjectives that are noun look-alikes cannot serve as antecedents for pronouns.

EXAMPLES

Incorrect:

The Rheams building has undergone as many facelifts as he has.

Corrected:

The Rheams building has undergone as many facelifts as Rheams himself has.

Incorrect:

After hearing the defendant's alibi, the jurors seemed to change their opinion of him.

Corrected:

The jurors seemed to change their opinion of the defendant after they heard his alibi.

Admittedly, this rule is a grammatical technicality. Infractions rarely create ambiguity. Even so, because correctness and precision are required in legal writing, it is best to heed the rule.

§ 8.5.4 Pronoun-Antecedent Agreement

A pronoun must agree with its antecedent. The noun to which a pronoun refers is known as its antecedent.

Legal writers usually do not have problems making their pronouns and antecedents agree in gender or person. Agreement in number, however, can be a bit more difficult.

Rule 8.5.4(1)	**Singular Antecedents Require Singular Pronouns; Plural Antecedents Require Plural Pronouns**

EXAMPLES

William MacDonald may claim that his constitutional rights were
    (antecedent)   *(pronoun)*
violated.

<u>William MacDonald</u> and <u>Grace Yessler</u> may claim that <u>their</u>
   (antecedent)   *(antecedent)*   *(pronoun)*
constitutional rights were violated.

This rule, although simple on the surface, becomes a little trickier when the pronoun substitutes for a generic noun that is singular. Because English does not have a singular generic pronoun to fit these situations, writers are left with less-than-ideal choices. For example, in informal writing and oral language, you may frequently see or hear a plural pronoun used as a substitute for a singular generic noun, as in the ungrammatical example below. In fact, several authorities on grammar have adopted the use of the singular "they," including The American Dialect Society, psycholinguist and author Steven Pinker, and The Washington Post Style Guide.

In formal writing, such as legal writing, this practice is unacceptable.

EXAMPLE   Ungrammatical

A <u>defendant</u> may claim that <u>their</u> constitutional rights were violated.
(antecedent)   *(pronoun)*

Some writers try to solve the problem by resorting to the traditional masculine pronoun for all generic nouns. This practice is unacceptable to many modern writers who believe that language should be gender neutral. (See section 6.4.)

EXAMPLE   Poor Use of Masculine Pronoun

A <u>defendant</u> may claim that <u>his</u> constitutional rights were violated.
(antecedent)   *(pronoun)*

Occasionally, the problem can be solved by making the generic noun plural. Unfortunately, not all sentences will allow this quick fix.

EXAMPLE   Plural Noun

<u>Defendants</u> may claim that <u>their</u> constitutional rights were violated.
(antecedent)   *(pronoun)*

Even fewer sentences will allow a writer to remove the pronoun altogether without substantial revision or loss in meaning.

EXAMPLE   Removed Pronoun

A defendant may claim that constitutional rights were violated.

The example above avoids the grammatical problem but with a significant loss in meaning: The belief that one actually possesses constitutional rights is no longer included in the sentence's meaning.

What is left, then, is the option of using the slightly awkward "he or she," "his or her," "himself or herself."

EXAMPLE

A <u>defendant</u> may claim that <u>his or her</u> constitutional rights were
  (antecedent)   *(pronouns)*
violated.

While not perfect, this option seems to be the best choice, provided the writer doesn't put more than one "he or she," "his or her," or "himself or herself" in a sentence.

Exception to Rule 8.5.4(1)

Occasionally the word "each" or "every" precedes one or more of the parts of a plural antecedent. In such cases, use a singular pronoun.

EXAMPLE

Every girl and woman in the community feared for her safety.

Rule 8.5.4(2)	**When a Pronoun Refers to Two or More Antecedents Joined by "or" or "nor," the Pronoun Agrees in Number with the Nearer Antecedent**

EXAMPLE

Either <u>David Wilson</u> or <u>Donald Wilson</u> left <u>his</u> keys in the car.
     (antecedent)   *(antecedent)*   *(pronoun)*

When a singular and a plural antecedent are joined by "or" or "nor," place the plural antecedent last so that the pronoun can be plural.

EXAMPLE

Neither the <u>defendant</u> nor his <u>brothers</u> admit knowing where <u>their</u> neighbors keep items of value.

Rule 8.5.4(3)	When an Indefinite Pronoun Is the Antecedent, Use the Singular Pronoun

Indefinite pronouns are ones that do not refer to any definite person or thing, or they do not specify definite limits. The most common indefinite pronouns are "all," "any," "anybody," "anyone," "each," "either," "everybody," "everyone," "everything," "neither," "nobody," "no one," "none," "somebody," "someone," and "something."

EXAMPLE

<u>Anyone</u> would have noticed that <u>his</u> or <u>her</u> license plate had been removed.

As with Rule 8.5.4(1), writers must take care not to use the informal and ungrammatical plural pronoun or the generic "he" as a pronoun substitute for an indefinite pronoun.

EXAMPLES

Ungrammatical:

<u>Somebody</u> must have used <u>their</u> cell phone to call the police.

Poor Use of Masculine Pronoun:

<u>Somebody</u> must have used <u>his</u> cell phone to call the police.

Corrected:

<u>Somebody</u> must have used <u>his</u> or <u>her</u> cell phone to call the police.

OR

<u>Somebody</u> must have used a cell phone to call the police.

Rule 8.5.4(4)	When a Collective Noun Is the Antecedent, Use a Singular Pronoun If You Are Referring to the Group as One Unit and a Plural Pronoun If You Are Referring to the Individual Members of the Group

In professional and legal writing, the pronouns "they," "their," and "them" always refer to plural nouns. Singular nouns take singular pronouns. Some common collective nouns are "jury," "committee," "appellate court," "Supreme Court," "majority," "board," "team," "family," "audience," "crowd," "number," and the names of companies and corporations. These collective nouns should generally be referred to as

See Quick Tip:
Pronoun
Agreement ⊕

"it." For novice legal writers, the use of "it" to refer to a collective noun might sound awkward; however, with time, your ear will adjust.

The <u>jury</u> must not be misled about Jason Richardson's credibility when <u>it</u> is considering his testimony.

<u>Shopping Haven</u> discriminated against John Adams when <u>it</u> failed to issue him a new credit card for an existing account.

§ 8.6 Modifiers

Using modifiers correctly is simple. All one has to do is (1) remember to keep modifiers close to the word or words they modify and (2) make sure the words they modify are in the same sentence as the modifiers.

§ 8.6.1 Misplaced Modifiers

Forgetting to keep modifiers close to the word or words they modify leads to misplaced modifiers. Some words—"almost," "also," "even," "ever," "exactly," "hardly," "just," "merely," "nearly," "not," "only," "scarcely," "simply"—are particularly prone to being misplaced. Place these words immediately before the words they modify.

Notice, for example, how the placement of "only" changes the meaning in the following sentences.

<u>Only</u> the defendant thought that the car was rented.
No one but the defendant thought that.

The defendant <u>only</u> thought that the car was rented.
He did not know for sure.

The defendant thought <u>only</u> that the car was rented.
He thought one thing, nothing else.

The defendant thought that the <u>only</u> car was rented.
Only one car was available, and it was rented.

The defendant thought that the car was <u>only</u> rented.
He did not think it was leased or sold.

In speech, such single-word modifiers are often put before the verb even when the speaker does not intend them to modify the verb. Some authorities accept placing "only" immediately before the verb if it modifies the whole sentence.

Speech: He only drove ten miles.
Writing: He drove only ten miles.

Phrases, particularly prepositional phrases, can also be easily misplaced in sentences. The result can be imprecise writing, an awkward construction, and unintentional humor.

The writer of the following example was surprised to find out that because of a misplaced modifier he had inaccurately placed the brother instead of the cabin in New Hampshire.

EXAMPLE

The defendant owned a cabin with his brother in New Hampshire.

Corrected:

The defendant and his brother owned a cabin in New Hampshire.

The misplaced modifier in the following example gave the writer a meaning she never intended.

EXAMPLE

The witness to the events may be unavailable after the accident.

Although there are contexts in which this sentence is correctly written, the writer intended to say, "The witness to the events after the accident may be unavailable." Her version makes it sound like an intentional "accident" was being planned for the specific purpose of making the witness "unavailable"!

Take care to place a clause that begins with "who," "which," and "that" immediately after the noun it modifies.

EXAMPLE

The victim described her attacker as having a tattoo on his right buttock, which was shaped like a peace sign.

This sentence suggests that the attacker's right buttock, not his tattoo, was shaped like a peace sign.

EXAMPLE   Corrected

The victim described her attacker as having a tattoo that was shaped like a peace sign on his right buttock.

§ 8.6.2 Dangling Modifiers

Dangling modifiers are those modifiers that do not have a noun in the sentence that they can modify; hence, they are "dangling," or unattached to an appropriate noun. Legal writers tend to write dangling modifiers for one of two reasons: (1) the noun or pronoun the modifier is intended to modify is in the mind of the writer but inadvertently omitted from the sentence; or (2) the writer wanted to avoid the first-person pronouns "I" or "we"[5] and, in doing so, left a modifier dangling.

EXAMPLE **Dangling Modifier**

By calling attention to the defendant's post-arrest silence, the jury was allowed to make prejudicial and false inferences.

In the example above, the modifier "by calling attention to the defendant's post-arrest silence" should modify the noun "the prosecutor," which does not appear in the sentence. Unfortunately, it seems to be modifying the noun closest to it: "the jury."

EXAMPLE **Corrected**

By calling attention to the defendant's post-arrest silence, the prosecutor encouraged the jury to make prejudicial and false inferences.

Notice how in the following example the dangling modifier can be corrected by including the pronoun it modifies, "we," or by revising the sentence so that the dangling modifier is no longer a modifier.

EXAMPLE

In deciding whether to argue self-defense, more than the technical merits of the case have to be considered.

Corrected:

In deciding whether to argue self-defense, we must consider more than the technical merits of the case. *OR*

A decision about whether to argue self-defense must be based on more than the technical merits of the case.

---

[5] Many authorities in legal writing still advise legal writers to avoid using first-person references.

You can see that the majority of dangling modifiers occur at the beginnings of sentences. One way to avoid writing this type of dangling modifier is to remember to place the noun the modifier modifies right after the comma separating the modifier from the main clause.

> _____ Modifier,   Main Clause.
>   (noun)
> By calling attention . . . silence, the prosecutor . . .

If you are having difficulty deciding what noun the modifier should modify, ask yourself who or what is doing the action described in that modifier. Then place the answer to that question right after the comma separating the modifier from the main clause.

> In deciding . . . self-defense, we must consider . . . .

Some dangling modifiers can also be corrected by adding a subject to the modifier.

EXAMPLE

While petitioning for a permit, zoning regulations in the area were changed.

Corrected:

While the mental institution was petitioning for a permit, zoning regulations in the area were changed.

Subordinate clauses, such as the one in the revision above, are not dangling modifiers.

Dangling modifiers can also occur at the ends of sentences. Again, the problem is that the noun the modifier modifies does not appear in the sentence.

EXAMPLE   Dangling Modifier

This motion was denied in the interest of judicial economy, reasoning that there was evidence that raised a question regarding Anderson's knowledge of the relationship.

Who or what is doing the reasoning that there was evidence? Most certainly the court, but the noun "court" does not appear in the sentence.

EXAMPLE   Corrected

Reasoning that there was evidence that raised a question regarding Anderson's knowledge of the relationship, the court denied this motion in the interest of judicial economy.

It is also permissible to leave the modifier at the end of the sentence, as long as it modifies the subject of the sentence.

EXAMPLE   **Corrected**

The court denied this motion in the interest of judicial economy, reasoning that there was evidence that raised a question regarding Anderson's knowledge of the relationship.

---

§ 8.6.3 Squinting Modifiers

Squinting modifiers are labeled as such because they appear to be modifying both the word that precedes them and the word that follows them.

EXAMPLE

The bridge inspection that was done frequently suggested that the drawbridge's electrical system was beginning to fail.

This sentence has two possible interpretations: Are the inspections themselves done frequently, or are there frequent suggestions throughout the inspection report?

EXAMPLES   **Corrected**

The bridge inspection that was frequently done suggested that the drawbridge's electrical system was beginning to fail. *OR*

The bridge inspection that was done suggested frequently that the drawbridge's electrical system was beginning to fail.

---

§ 8.7 Parallelism

Consider the following pairs of sentences. What is it about version B of each pair that makes it easier to read?

EXAMPLES

1A. The defendant claims that on the day of the murder he was at home alone washing his car, he mowed his lawn, and his dog needed a bath so he gave him one.

1B. The defendant claims that on the day of the murder he was at home alone washing his car, mowing his lawn, and bathing his dog.

2A. Dr. Stewart is a competent surgeon with over 20 years of experience and who is respected in the local medical community.

2B. Dr. Stewart is a competent surgeon who has over 20 years of experience and who is respected in the local medical community.

3A. The defendant claimed the evidence was prejudicial and that it lacked relevance.

3B. The defendant claimed the evidence was prejudicial and irrelevant.

In all the preceding pairs, the version A sentences lack parallelism and, as a result, are grammatically incorrect, as well as clumsy. The version B sentences do not change the content significantly; they simply use the structure of the sentence to make that content more apparent and more accessible. Specifically, they use parallelism.

In grammar, parallelism is defined as "the use of similar grammatical form for coordinated elements." This definition may seem overly abstract or vague until it is broken into its components.

"Coordinated elements" are parts of a sentence joined by conjunctions, such as "and," "but," "or," "nor," and "yet." Sometimes they are pairs, but often they are a series or a list.

"Similar grammatical form" simply means that a noun is matched with other nouns, verbs are matched with other verbs, prepositional phrases are matched with other prepositional phrases, and so on.

For example, look at the poorly coordinated elements in sentence 1A above.

washing his car,
he mowed his lawn, and
his dog needed a bath so he gave him one

Even without analyzing exactly what kind of phrase or clause each one of these elements is, we can see that they do not have similar grammatical form. Now look at the coordinated elements of sentence 1B. Note how the "-ing" endings make the items parallel.

washing his car
mowing his lawn, and
bathing his dog

Matching endings of the first key word in each of the elements is one way to make elements parallel.

Now compare the coordinated elements in 2A and 2B.

2A. with over 20 years of experience and
     who is respected in the local medical community
2B. who has over 20 years of experience and
     who is respected in the local medical community

Again, without doing an analysis of the grammar of each element, we can see, or perhaps hear, that 2B is parallel, but this time the parallelism is signaled by using the same word, "who," to introduce each element.

In some cases, however, you will not be able to rely on matching endings to key words or matching introductory words; you will have to find the same grammatical form in order to make the elements parallel.

In 3A, for example, the writer has tried to match an adjective, "prejudicial," with a relative clause, "that it lacked relevance." The writer could have used the second tip—matching introductory words—and created the following parallel elements:

> that the evidence was prejudicial and
> that it lacked relevance

The more concise and better choice is to find the appropriate adjective to match "prejudicial."

> prejudicial and
> irrelevant

Because many sentences in legal writing are long and complicated, parallelism is critical for keeping the content and its presentation manageable. In the following sentence, for example, the defendant's two concessions are easier for the reader to see because they are set out using parallel constructions.

EXAMPLE

Counsel for the defendant conceded that she did assault Coachman and that a trial would determine only the degree of the assault.

> that she did assault Coachman
> . . . conceded <
> that a trial would determine only the degree
> of the assault.

Notice, too, in both the preceding and subsequent examples that by repeating the introductory word "that," the writer has made the parallelism more obvious, which, in turn, makes the sentence easier to read.

EXAMPLE

When questioned at the parole hearing, Robinson claimed that it was wrong to tell only one side of the story, that he had not received permission but felt he had a right to write what he wanted, and that people had a right to hear the other side of the story.

> that it was wrong to tell only one side of the story,
> . . . claimed <
> that he had not received permission but felt he had a right
> to write what he wanted, and
>
> that people had a right to hear the other side of the story.

Writing parallel elements is required for grammatical sentences; repeating an introductory word to heighten the parallelism is not required, but rather recommended for making the parallelism more obvious to the reader.

Issue statements, or questions presented, can also become much more manageable when the legally significant facts are laid out using parallel construction. The following example uses "when" as the introductory word to each element. Notice, too, how the legally significant facts are not only written using parallel construction but also grouped according to those that favor the defendant and those that favor the plaintiff. The conjunction "but" helps the reader see the two groupings.

EXAMPLE

Under Federal Rule of Civil Procedure 4(d)(1), is service of process valid when process was left with defendant's husband at his home in California, when defendant and her husband maintain separate residences, when defendant intends to maintain a separate residence from her husband, but when defendant regularly visits her husband in California, when defendant keeps some personal belongings in the California house, when defendant receives some mail in California, and when defendant received actual notice when her husband mailed the summons and complaint to her?

> when process was left with defendant's husband at his home in California
> when defendant and her husband maintain separate residences
> when defendant intends to maintain separate residence from her husband, BUT
> when defendant regularly visits her husband in California
> when the defendant keeps some personal belongings in the California house
> when defendant receives some mail in California
> when defendant received actual notice when her husband mailed the summons and complaint to her

Parallelism is also required when setting out lists.

EXAMPLE

Wilson challenges the admission of three photographs, which he claims are gruesome: (1) the photograph of Melissa Reed as she appeared when discovered at the crime scene; (2) the photograph of Melinda Reed as she appeared when discovered at the crime scene; and (3) a photograph of Wilson wearing dental retractors to hold his lips back while exposing his teeth.

Lists require parallelism when they are incorporated into the writer's text, as in the example above, and when they are indented and tabulated, as in the example below.

The school district will probably be liable for the following:

1. the cost of restoring the Archers' rose bushes, as well as the lost use value of their property during restoration;
2. the cost of replacing Mr. Baker's windows and the market value of his vase; and
3. compensation to the Carlisles for the annoyance and inconvenience they have experienced.

To create parallelism, match the *key* words in each element; the parallelism is not destroyed if all the modifying words and phrases do not match exactly.

In the following examples, the key words "received" and "released" match, and the key words "for . . . harm" and "for . . . expenses" match.

In *Pepper,* the injured plaintiff <u>received</u> medical treatment and <u>released</u> the defendant from liability.

The Bells are seeking damages <u>for severe emotional and financial harm</u> and <u>for substantial medical expenses related to the pregnancy</u>.

Parallelism is also required for elements joined by correlative conjunctions, which are conjunctions that come in pairs. The most common correlative conjunctions are "either . . . or," "neither . . . nor," "not only . . . but also," "both . . . and," "whether . . . or," and "as . . . as."

To make the elements joined by one of these pairs parallel, simply match what follows the first half with what follows the second half.

either _____   either <u>similar</u>
or _____   or <u>identical</u>

Campbell's prior convictions are either similar or identical.

neither _____   neither the <u>photographs</u>
nor _____   nor the <u>testimony</u>

Neither the photographs nor the testimony can prove who actually committed the alleged assault.

not only _____   not only <u>verbally</u>
but also _____   but also <u>physically</u>

EXAMPLE

The defendant admits that she not only verbally but also physically abused her children.

Take care when using these pairs. All too frequently legal writers lose the parallelism in their sentences by misplacing one of the words in these pairs.

EXAMPLE   **Lack of Parallelism**

The purpose of the rule is to ensure that actual notice is provided either by personal or constructive service.

either _____   either <u>by personal</u>
or _____   or <u>constructive</u>

Note that "by personal" is not parallel with "constructive."

EXAMPLE   **Corrected**

The purpose of the rule is to ensure that actual notice is provided either by personal or by constructive service. *OR*

The purpose of the rule is to ensure that actual notice is provided by either personal or constructive service.

Parallelism is also required when elements are compared or contrasted. Many of the comparing and contrasting expressions use "than." Notice in each of the following pairs where the blanks are for the parallel elements.

more _____   than _____
less _____   than _____
_____ rather than _____

EXAMPLES

Wilson's attention was centered more <u>on the assailant's gun</u> than <u>on his face</u>.

The court applied <u>the "clearly erroneous" standard</u> rather than <u>the arbitrary and capricious standard</u>.

CHAPTER

9

Punctuation

§ 9.1 The Comma

Commas are everywhere. They are the most frequently used punctuation mark and, unfortunately, the most frequently misused punctuation mark. They give most legal writers fits. Few writers seem to be able to control the little buzzards, and most seem to be more than a bit controlled by them. Many fairly good legal writers admit that they punctuate by feel, especially when it comes to commas. They rely on the "rule" that one should use a comma whenever the reader should pause—advice that works only about 70 percent of the time.

See Quick Tip: Poetic v. Technical Use of Commas ⊕

It is no wonder that few legal writers know and apply all the rules for commas. There are too many of them. In this section, we have no fewer than twelve rules, all designed to govern one little punctuation mark. Even so, these twelve rules don't cover every conceivable use of the comma, just the most frequent instances.

Commas are like the signs along the highway. They signal, usually subtly, how the sentence structure will unfold. The correct use of commas, like the correct highway sign, will prepare the reader for what's to come, whether it be another main clause, an explanatory appositive, or a shift from an introductory element to the main clause. Seasoned readers absorb the information they get from commas in much the same way seasoned

Chart 9.1   **Overview of the Comma Rules**

Rule 1: **Use a comma before a coordinating conjunction joining two main clauses.**

The prosecutor spoke about the defendant's motive, and the jury listened carefully.

Rule 2: **Use a comma to set off long introductory phrases or clauses from the main clause.**

Using their overhead lights and sirens, the police followed the defendant out of the area.

Rule 3: **Use a comma to prevent a possible misreading.**

At the time, the prosecution informed Jones that it would recommend a sentence of eighteen months.

Rule 4: **Use a comma to set off nonrestrictive phrases or clauses.**

Officer Bates, acting as a decoy, remained outside on the sidewalk.

Rule 5: **Set off nonrestrictive appositives with commas.**

A corrections officer called Diane Cummins, the defendant's girlfriend.

Rule 6: **Set off nonrestrictive participial phrases with a comma or commas.**

The trial court denied the motion, finding that the seizure fell under the plain view doctrine.

Rule 7: **Use a comma or commas to set off transitional or interrupting words and phrases.**

The trial court, however, imposed an exceptional sentence of 30 months.

Rule 8: **Use commas according to convention with quotation marks.**

Corbin said, "I never saw the other car."

Rule 9: **Use a comma or commas to set off phrases of contrast.**

Adams initially indicated that he, not Wilson, was involved in the robbery.

Rule 10: **Use commas between items in a series.**

Wong had no money, identification, or jewelry.

Rule 11: **Use a comma between coordinate adjectives not joined by a conjunction.**

The contract was written in concise, precise language.

Rule 12: **Use commas according to convention with dates, addresses, and names of geographical locations.**

The land in Roswell, New Mexico, was surveyed on October 4, 2001, and purchased less than a month later.

drivers absorb the information they get from highway signs. Sometimes it grabs their attention; more often than not, it works almost subconsciously.

> ### Rule 9.1(1) Use a Comma Before a Coordinating Conjunction Joining Two Main, or Independent, Clauses

There are seven coordinating conjunctions, which create the acronym FANBOYS: "for," "and," "nor," "but," "or," "yet," and "so."[1]

A main, or independent, clause has its own subject and verb, and it can stand alone as a sentence. The diagram below represents a sentence with a Rule 9.1(1) comma.

coordinating
_____, conjunction _____.
(main clause)   (main clause)

Brackets mark the main clauses in the following examples.

EXAMPLES

[The prosecutor spoke about the defendant's motive], and [the jury listened carefully.]

[The corrections officer contacted several other persons], but [none knew of Wilson's disappearance.]

When applying Rule 9.1(1), be sure that you are not mistakenly assuming that a comma must precede every coordinating conjunction. It precedes those coordinating conjunctions that join two main clauses.

In addition, be sure to distinguish between sentences with two main clauses (subject-verb, and subject-verb), which require a comma before the conjunction, and sentences with compound verbs (subject-verb and verb), which do not require a comma before the conjunction.

> See Quick Tip: When to Use a Comma Before "and" and "or" ⊕

EXAMPLES

Two Main Clauses (comma before conjunction):

The defendant's girlfriend denied that she knew where he was, and she refused to answer any more questions.

---

[1] Some writers prefer to use a semicolon before "yet" and "so." The semicolon signals a longer pause. While this usage is acceptable, it is not standard or common.

Compound Verbs (no comma before conjunction):

The defendant's girlfriend denied that she knew where he was and refused to answer any more questions.

See Quick Tip:
Finding and
Correcting
Comma Splices
and Fused
Sentences ⊕

If you omit either the coordinating conjunction or the comma joining two main clauses, you may miscue your readers. If you omit the coordinating conjunction, you have created a comma splice. If you omit the comma before a coordinating conjunction, you create a run-on sentence.[2] Legal readers will find these constructions disorienting and likely unacceptable.

EXAMPLES

Comma Splice:

The prosecutor spoke, the jury listened.

Run-on Sentence:

The defendant returned the watch and he apologized before police arrived.

Rule 9.1(2)   Use a Comma to Set Off Long Introductory Clauses or Phrases from the Main, or Independent, Clause

If a main, or independent, clause is preceded by introductory material, the reader needs a comma to signal where the introductory material ends and where the main clause begins. The diagram below represents a sentence with a Rule 9.1(2) comma.

$$\underline{\hspace{3cm}}, \underline{\hspace{4cm}}.$$

[*long introductory*   [*main clause*]
clause or phrase]

Long introductory clauses that must be set off with a comma are easy to spot. Because they are clauses, they will have a subject and a verb. Because they are subordinate, not main, clauses, they will also begin with a subordinating conjunction such as "after," "although," "as," "because," "before," "if," "unless," "until," "when," or "where." (See section 8.1 for more on subordinate clauses and subordinating conjunctions.)

---

[2] Some writers advocate that when the main clauses are short and closely related, the writer has the option to omit the comma before the coordinating conjunction. However, some readers will consider the resulting sentence a run-on, and you are never wrong to include both the comma and the coordinating conjunction between two independent clauses.

If the accident were unavoidable, Smith's intoxication was not "a cause . . . without which the death would not have occurred."

When Abbott failed to return to the work release facility, a corrections officer called his mother's home.

Of the many kinds of introductory phrases used in legal writing, the most common are prepositional phrases, infinitive phrases, and participial phrases. (Section 8.1 defines and explains prepositions, infinitives, and participles. It is not critical, however, to be able to identify the types of introductory phrases to punctuate them correctly.)

Introductory Prepositional Phrase:

In the present case, the record shows that Thompson initially assaulted Blevins.

Introductory Infinitive Phrase:

To support an argument that the trial court abused its discretion, a defendant must point to specific prejudice.

Introductory Participial Phrase:

Using their overhead lights and sirens, the police followed the defendant out of the area.

Notice that long introductory phrases are often made up of several prepositional phrases or a combination of prepositional, infinitive, and participial phrases.

Two Introductory Prepositional Phrases:

[On the evening] [of August 13, 2012], Larry Utter was robbed at gunpoint while making a deposit at a local bank.

Introductory Prepositional and Infinitive Phrases:

[At the hearing] [on McDonald's motion] [to dismiss], the parties stipulated to the admission of an incident report prepared by McDonald's probation officer.

Furthermore, there is no specific rule for what constitutes a "long" phrase or clause. An introductory phrase or clause of four or more words is usually set off with a comma, but writers have some discretion, particularly with introductory phrases. In general, there is no downside to using commas after every introductory phrase or clause, regardless of length.

Short prepositional phrases, for example, are often set off by a comma, especially when the writer wants to emphasize the information in the phrase, as with dates or case names.

EXAMPLES

In 2007, the Oltmans removed the fence separating their property from the farm.

In *Harris*, the defendant was charged with first degree robbery.

Short, introductory transitional expressions, such as "consequently," "for example," "therefore," "in addition," and "on the other hand," are almost always set off by a comma.

EXAMPLE

Consequently, unlawful restraint is invariably an element of the greater offense of attempted kidnapping.

Note that "although" and "because" are subordinating conjunctions, not transitional expressions, so they should not be set off by a comma.

EXAMPLE

Although the Dicksons purchased the home in 2006, they did not move in until fall of 2007.

Rule 9.1(3)   Use a Comma to Prevent a Possible Misreading

A reader should be able to read a sentence correctly the first time. If a comma can prevent a possible misreading, it should be included. Be warned, though, that this "rule" is more of an exception for very rare cases, not an excuse to punctuate however and wherever you please.

EXAMPLE

Confusing:

People who can usually hire their own lawyer.

Revised:

People who can, usually hire their own lawyer.

Revised to Avoid Comma:

People who are able to hire their own lawyer usually do.

Rule 9.1(4)	Use a Comma to Set Off Nonrestrictive Phrases or Clauses

Nonrestrictive phrases or clauses do not restrict or limit the words they modify. They give additional information. Commas in nonrestrictive phrases or clauses "set off" the material, much the way parentheses operate outside legal writing.

Restrictive phrases or clauses restrict or limit the words they modify. They add essential information.

EXAMPLES

Nonrestrictive Phrase:

Officer Bates, <u>acting as a decoy</u>, remained outside on the sidewalk.

Nonrestrictive Clause:

Officer Bates, <u>who acted as a decoy</u>, remained outside on the sidewalk.

In both of the examples above, "Officer Bates" is completely identified by her name. "Acting as a decoy" or "who acted as a decoy" does not give restricting or limiting information, so both are set off by commas.

If the name of the officer were unknown, the writer may need to use the phrase or clause as a way to identify the officer. The phrase or clause would then be restrictive because it would limit the meaning of "officer." When used as a restrictive phrase or clause, the same words are not set off by commas.

EXAMPLES

Restrictive Phrase:

An officer acting as a decoy remained outside on the sidewalk.

Restrictive Clause:

An officer who acted as a decoy remained outside on the sidewalk.

A few more examples may be helpful in learning to distinguish which phrases and clauses are nonrestrictive and therefore set off by commas.

EXAMPLE   Nonrestrictive Clause

The child's father, who is six months behind in his child support payments, has fled the state.

"The child's father" clearly identifies the individual in question; "who is six months behind in his child support payments" does not restrict or limit the meaning of "the child's father," even though it is important information for understanding the sentence.

EXAMPLE   Restrictive Clause

The uncle who lives in Oklahoma has agreed to care for the child until an appropriate foster home is found.

This sentence suggests that the child has more than one uncle. "Who lives in Oklahoma" restricts or limits the meaning of "the uncle." It is the uncle in Oklahoma, not the one in Arkansas, who has agreed to care for the child.

Notice that whether a phrase or clause is punctuated as restrictive or nonrestrictive can significantly change the meaning of a sentence.

EXAMPLE

Attorneys who intentionally prolong litigation for personal gain misuse the legal system.

The preceding sentence says that there is a restricted or limited group of attorneys—those who intentionally prolong litigation for personal gain—who misuse the legal system.

EXAMPLE

Attorneys, who intentionally prolong litigation for personal gain, misuse the legal system.

The preceding sentence does not refer to a restricted or limited group of attorneys. It says that all attorneys misuse the legal system and that all attorneys intentionally prolong litigation for personal gain.

The tricky issue with restrictive and nonrestrictive clauses is that both examples above are grammatical, but each means something very different.

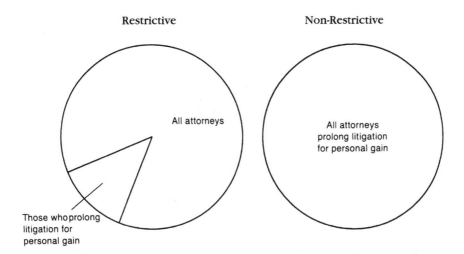

Restrictive   Non-Restrictive

All attorneys

All attorneys
prolong litigation
for personal gain

Those who prolong
litigation for
personal gain

Restrictive and nonrestrictive clauses that modify people begin with "who" or "whom." Careful writers still observe the usage rule that restrictive clauses that modify things or objects use "that" and nonrestrictive clauses that modify things or objects use "which."

See Quick Tip:
That vs. Which

That	Which	Who
Restrictive	Nonrestrictive	Either
No Commas	Uses Commas	Either
Used for Things	Used for Things	Used for People

EXAMPLES

Incorrect Usage:

The instruction which is unchallenged is an accomplice instruction that includes the "ready to assist" language.

Corrected:

The instruction that is unchallenged is an accomplice instruction that includes the "ready to assist" language. *OR*

Instruction 21, which is unchallenged, is an accomplice instruction that includes the "ready to assist" language.

Rule 9.1(5)   Set Off Nonrestrictive Appositives with Commas

Appositives are nouns or noun substitutes that follow another noun to identify it or further describe it.

EXAMPLE

A corrections officer called <u>Diane Cummins</u>, the <u>defendant's girlfriend</u>.
(noun)   *(appositive)*

Because most appositives are nonrestrictive, they need to be set off with commas. However, restrictive appositives, like the restrictive phrases and clauses in Rule 9.1(4), add information that restricts or limits the preceding noun; therefore, restrictive appositives are not set off with commas.

EXAMPLE   Nonrestrictive Appositive

The court sentenced the defendant, a juvenile, to a term outside the standard range.

There is only one defendant; "a juvenile" adds information but does not restrict or limit the meaning of "defendant."

EXAMPLE   Restrictive Appositive

The defendant's brother Joseph contradicted the story another brother Daniel told to the police.

The defendant has more than one brother, so the noun phrases "defendant's brother" and "another brother" must be restricted or limited by the brothers' names.

Some appositives are introduced by the word "or." Be sure to distinguish between the appositional "or," which is a restatement of or explanation for the preceding noun, and the disjunctive "or," which introduces an alternative to the preceding noun.

EXAMPLES

Appositional "or":

You may designate an attorney-in-fact, or agent, to make your health care decisions in the event you are unable to do so. *("Attorney-in-fact" and "agent" are the same thing.)*

Disjunctive "or":

The girl's father or uncle always accompanied her on dates. *("Father" and "uncle" are alternatives.)*

Rule 9.1(6)	**Set Off Nonrestrictive Participial Phrases with a Comma or Commas**

Participles, which are formed from verbs, can serve as adjectives. Present participles have an "-ing" ending; past participles have a variety of endings, depending on whether the verb is regular or irregular. Common past participle endings include "-d," "-ed," "-t," "-n," and "-en."

verb	present participle	past participle
reason	reasoning	reasoned
find	finding	found

Many sentences in legal writing use a beginning or an ending participial phrase to describe the rationale for the action expressed in the main verb. Such participial phrases are not dangling or misplaced (see section 8.6.2) if, as in the following examples, they modify the subject of the sentence.

_____ , _____

(participial phrase)   (main clause)

_____ , _____

(main clause)   (participial phrase)

EXAMPLES

__Reasoning that the sentence imposed was disproportionate to the gravity of the offense__, the State Supreme Court reversed and remanded for resentencing.

The State Supreme Court reversed and remanded for resentencing, __reasoning that the sentence imposed was disproportionate to the gravity of the offense__.

__Finding that the seizure fell under the plain view doctrine__, the trial court denied the motion.

The trial court denied the motion, __finding that the seizure fell under the plain view doctrine__.

Rule 9.1(7)	**Use a Comma or Commas to Set Off Transitional or Interrupting Words and Phrases**

Legal writers frequently break the flow of a sentence intentionally by inserting a word or phrase in the middle of a main clause. Readers have no trouble understanding what the main clause is and what the transitional or interrupting word or phrase is as long as those transitions or interrupters are set off with commas. The diagram below represents a sentence with an interrupter.

_____, interrupter, _____.
          (main)   *(clause)*

EXAMPLES

The trial court, <u>however</u>, imposed an exceptional sentence of 30 months.

The Court of Appeals held that Wells, <u>through her own fault and connivance</u>, caused the delay between the time the State filed the information and the time of Wells's arraignment.

Note, however, that many of the same transitional words and phrases ("however," "therefore," "on the other hand") that interrupt a main clause can also be used between two main clauses. Be sure to distinguish between the two and punctuate accordingly.

EXAMPLES

Interrupter:

His vision, <u>therefore</u>, was blurred.

Transition Between Two Main Clauses:

The driver lost his contact lenses; <u>therefore</u>, his vision was blurred.

Rule 9.1(8)   Use Commas According to Convention with Quotation Marks

Commas are frequently used to separate short or informal quotations from words in the same sentence that introduce, interrupt, or follow the quotation.

EXAMPLES

Corbin said, "I never saw the other car."

"I never saw the other car," Corbin said, "until it was right on top of me."

"I never saw the other car," said Corbin.

Commas are placed inside closing quotation marks[3] and outside closing parentheses or brackets.

Inside Closing Quotation Marks:

Identification searches are valid if limited to wallets or other "common repositories of identification papers," and the examination is confined to locating a driver's license or similar document. 4 Wayne LaFave, *Search and Seizure* § 9.6(g), at 695 (4th ed. 2004).

A 24-month sentence does not appear to be "clearly excessive," especially when the presumptive range of 12-14 months could have been increased by 12 months under Wash. Rev. Code § 9.94A.510 (2001).

Outside Closing Parentheses:

Both of the defendants are young (19 and 20), and both of them are first-time offenders.

Quotations that are immediately preceded by "that" do not have a comma between the quotation and "that."

In *Herron v. King*, the court stated that "actual malice can be inferred from circumstantial evidence including . . . the reporter's knowledge that his sources are hostile to the plaintiff . . . ." 109 Wash. 2d at 524, 746 P.2d at 302.

Rule 9.1(9) Use a Comma or Commas to Set Off Phrases of Contrast

Phrases of contrast usually begin with "not," "but," or "yet."

Adams initially indicated that he, <u>not Wilson</u>, was involved in the robbery.

Some writers occasionally omit commas with phrases of contrast that begin with "but." Either way is correct, but you are always allowed

---

[3] Most countries apply a different rule. For example, in the United Kingdom, India, Australia, Canada, and South Africa, the comma goes outside the quotation marks unless it is part of the quotation, in which case, it goes inside the closing quotation mark.

to use the commas. In addition, commas are usually omitted between elements joined by the paired conjunctions "not only . . . but also . . . ."

EXAMPLE

The trial court not only overruled defense counsel's repeated objections but also accused the defendant's attorney of intentionally delaying the proceedings.

Rule 9.1(10)   Use Commas Between Items in a Series

A series is three or more items that are grouped together and that are in the same grammatical form. Each item may be as short as one word or as long as a clause.

EXAMPLES

Series of Single Words:

Wong had no money, identification, or jewelry.

Series of Verb Phrases:

Mason moved at least twice during the period of his escape, changed his name and his appearance, and held four or five jobs.

Series of Clauses:

Koenig could not remember who he was, where he lived, what he did for a living, or what he had done during the last two weeks.

Even a series composed of short main clauses can use commas to separate the items.

EXAMPLE

Matthews pulled a knife on O'Hara, she screamed, and he turned and ran away.

Although the comma before the final "and" in a series is sometimes described as "optional,"[4] legal writers should make it a habit to include it because some sentences become ambiguous when that comma is omitted.

---

[4] In journalism, and therefore in most newspapers and popular magazines, the comma before the final "and" or "or" is omitted. Likewise, in many English-speaking countries outside of the United States, the comma before the final "and" or "or" is also omitted.

EXAMPLE   **Ambiguous Meaning**

Mrs. Corsini wants her property divided equally among the following relatives: Michael Corsini, Glenda Corsini, Ralph Meyers, Joanna Mitchem, Louis Mitchem, Donna Mitchem and Donald Mitchem.

Should the property be divided six or seven ways? Assume Donna Mitchem and Donald Mitchem are married. Did Grandmother Corsini intend for the couple to get one-sixth of her property, or did she intend for each of them to receive one-seventh?

Adding a comma before the final "and" tells the reader that the property should be divided seven ways. Adding another "and" before "Donna Mitchem" says that it should be divided six ways and that Donna and Donald should, as a couple, receive a one-sixth share.

Remember that the rule to add the comma applies to a <u>series</u>, which is <u>three</u> or more items. Ordinarily, commas are not used to separate <u>pairs</u> of words, phrases, or clauses that are joined by coordinating conjunctions.

> **See Quick Tip: When to Use a Comma Before "and" and "or"** 🌐

EXAMPLES

Pair of Words:

Lundquist was <u>arrested</u> and <u>charged</u> with negligent homicide.

Pair of Phrases:

The Supreme Court is remarkably free <u>to emphasize certain issues of the case over others</u> or <u>to stress completely new issues</u>.

Pair of Clauses:

The trial court asked the defendant <u>whether he understood his right to a jury trial</u> and <u>whether he received any promises of better treatment if he waived that right</u>.

Commas are not used between items in a series when all the items are joined by coordinating conjunctions. As a stylistic technique, joining all the items in a series with conjunctions has the effect of slowing down a series, which may be desirable on rare occasions when the writer wants the reader to focus special attention on each of the individual items in the series. (See section 7.2.2 on cadence.)

EXAMPLE

> **See Quick Tip: Serial Commas** 🌐

There is no indication that the delay was negligent or deliberate or unusual.

Rule 9.1(11)	Use a Comma Between Coordinate Adjectives Not Joined by a Conjunction

Coordinate adjectives are two or more adjectives that independently modify the same noun.

concise, precise language
(adj.)   (adj.)   (noun)

The test for whether adjectives are coordinate is simple: (1) reverse the order of the adjectives; or (2) add an "and" between the adjectives. If the adjectives are modifying the noun independently, then changing their order or adding an "and" will not change the meaning.

1. precise, concise language
2. concise, precise language
3. precise and concise language

The following example does not have a comma because it does not contain coordinate adjectives. Instead, "black" modifies "leather" and "leather" modifies "briefcase." Notice that you can tell that the adjectives are not coordinate by applying either part of the test. Both create awkward constructions.

EXAMPLE

black leather briefcase

Reverse Order:

leather, black briefcase *(does not retain meaning)*

Add "and":

black and leather briefcase *(does not retain meaning)*

Rule 9.1(12)	Use Commas According to Convention with Dates, Addresses, and Names of Geographical Locations

When a full date is written out in the month-day-year order, use a comma after the day.

July 4, 1776

Dates in this order also require a comma (or other punctuation) after the year when the sentence continues after the date.

The land was surveyed on October 4, 2014, and purchased less than a month later.

If the day is omitted or if the full date has the month and date reversed, omit commas because there are no adjacent groupings of digits.

See Quick Tip:
Commas with
Dates ⊕

July 1776   4 July 1776

Use commas to set off individual elements in addresses and geographical names. Note that the state and zip code are considered one element and therefore are not separated by a comma. When addresses or geographical names are followed by the remainder of a sentence, they should be followed by a comma.

Chicago, Illinois   Ontario, Canada

The string of robberies began in San Diego, California, and ended in Oakland, California, after the police arrested the defendant.

When possible, rephrase a date or geographical name used as a modifier when the date or geographical name will have to be followed by a comma.

Awkward:

the June 21, 2016, meeting

Revised:

the meeting on June 21, 2016

§ 9.2 The Semicolon

The semicolon is one of the easiest punctuation marks to learn how to use. Unfortunately, some legal writers avoid using semicolons because they believe semicolons are quite complicated and will require learning numerous rules. Exactly the opposite is true. There are only two general rules for using semicolons; all other uses are variations of or exceptions to these two rules.

| Rule 9.2(1) | Use a Semicolon to Separate Main, or Independent, Clauses Not Joined by a Coordinating Conjunction |

The diagram below represents a sentence with a Rule 9.2(1) semicolon.

main clause ____ ; ____ main clause.

Main clauses contain a subject and verb. They can stand alone as a sentence. There are only seven coordinating conjunctions: "and," "but," "or," "for," "nor," "yet," and "so."[5]

EXAMPLES

Officer Thompson administered the breathalyzer test; the results showed that the defendant's blood alcohol level was over the maximum allowed by the state.

The plaintiff is a Nevada resident; the defendant is a California resident.

If you use a comma or no punctuation between main clauses, you will produce a comma splice or run-on sentence.

Main clauses joined by a semicolon should be closely related in meaning. Often the semicolon suggests that the ideas in the connected main clauses work together as a larger idea. (See the first example above.) The semicolon can also be used to balance one idea against another. (See the second example above.) In all cases, the semicolon signals to the reader to pause slightly longer than a comma but shorter than a period.

Variation on Rule 9.2(1)

To show the relationship between the main clauses, a conjunctive adverb frequently follows the semicolon separating main clauses. The conjunctive adverb is usually followed by a comma. The most commonly used conjunctive adverbs are "accordingly," "also," "besides," "consequently," "furthermore," "hence," "however," "indeed," "instead," "likewise," "meanwhile," "moreover," "nevertheless," "still," "then," "therefore," and "thus." (See section 8.1.) The diagram below represents a sentence with a Rule 9.2(1) semicolon followed by a conjunctive adverb.

---

[5] As mentioned in Rule 9.1(1), some writers prefer to use a semicolon rather than a comma before the coordinating conjunctions, especially "yet" and "so," when they join two main clauses. This usage is permissible, but not necessarily recommended, when you want to signal a longer pause before the conjunction or when the main clauses are grammatically complicated or have internal commas.

<u>   main clause </u> ; *therefore,*<u>   main clause </u> .
[conjunctive
adverb]

The summons was not delivered to his usual place of abode; therefore, service was not effected in the manner prescribed by law.

The elements of the test have not been completely defined; however, the court has clarified the policies underlying the rule.

Conjunctive adverbs may also occur in the middle of main clauses. In such cases, they are preceded and followed by a comma, and no semicolon is used. (See comma Rule 9.1(7).)

<u>   main   </u> , *therefore,*<u>   clause   </u> .

EXAMPLE

The motor was not running, however, because of a problem with the distributor cap.

See Quick Tip: Avoid Semicolon Overuse ⊕

Compare the preceding example and the following example.

EXAMPLE

The motor was not running because of a problem with the distributor cap; however, the inoperability of the vehicle was irrelevant.

Rule 9.2(2)	**Use Semicolons to Separate Items in a Series If the Items Are Long or If One or More of the Items Has Internal Commas**

A series is three or more items of equal importance. If the items in a series are relatively short or if they do not have internal commas, then the items can be separated by commas.

<u>item 1</u>, <u>item 2</u>, <u>and item 3</u>
Typical series with items separated by commas

<u>item 1   </u>;<u>   item 2   </u>;<u>   and item 3</u>
Long items separated by semicolons

<u>item 1   </u>,<u>   </u>;<u>   item 2   </u>,<u>   </u>; <u>and item 3</u>
Internal commas in one or more items separated by semicolons

Long Items:

The Montana court has applied these definitions to cases with the following fact patterns: the driver was asleep and intoxicated; the driver was positioned behind the steering wheel; the vehicle's motor was running; and the vehicle was parked.

Long Items:

The court must determine the following issues to resolve your claim:

1. whether your ex-landlord sent you a written statement within 30 days of termination;
2. whether your ex-landlord withheld your deposit in bad faith; and
3. whether the court wishes to include attorneys' fees as part of a possible damage award.

Internal Commas:

The prosecutor called the following witnesses: Linda Hastings, an advertising executive; Samuel Hedges, an accountant; and Timothy Lessor, president of the company.

Internal Commas:

The defendant claims to reside in Maryland, even though (1) his car is registered in California; (2) he is registered to vote in California; and (3) all of his financial assets, including stocks, bonds, and a savings and checking account, are in a California bank.

Note that if the individual items are numbered, the items are invariably separated by semicolons, even in two-item lists.

§ 9.3 The Colon

Colons are useful to legal writers for a number of reasons. They are regularly used to introduce quotations or lists, and they are often the best way to set up explanations or elaborations.

Rule 9.3(1)   Use a Colon to Introduce Quotations

The main function of a colon is to introduce what will follow. For this reason, a colon requires a lead-in main clause that is grammatically complete. The following diagram represents a sentence with a colon.

grammatically complete main clause: _____.

In the example that follows, "the subsections that do not apply are" is not grammatically complete; therefore, the colon is used incorrectly.

EXAMPLE   **Incorrect**

The subsections that do not apply are: 201-1, 201-1(3)(b), and 201-1(3)(c).

One way to correct the example above is to omit the colon.

EXAMPLE   **Corrected**

The subsections that do not apply are 201-1, 201-1(3)(b), and 201-1(3)(c).

Another option is to add filler expressions, such as "the following" or "as follows," to make the lead-in main clause grammatically complete.

EXAMPLE   **Corrected**

The subsections that do not apply are the following: 201-1, 201-1(3)(b), and 201-1(3)(c).

What follows the colon may or may not be a main clause. If a complete sentence follows a colon, the writer has the option of capitalizing the first word of that sentence.

Quotations that are integrated into the writer's own sentences are not introduced by a colon.

EXAMPLE

The first letter the Guptas received stated that "permits are issued subject to existing water rights."

Because colons set up the endings of sentences, they can be used effectively to create emphasis. (See section 5.6.4.)

EXAMPLES

Orlando's trial was originally scheduled for May 15, 2012: 93 days after his arraignment.

Gibson claimed that his intent was to do a lawful act: administer parental discipline.

Traditionally colons were followed by two spaces, but in typeset material, one space is often used after colons.

In support of this result, the court noted that the limitation on the use of the *corpus delicti* rule is based on the "suspect nature" of out-of-court confessions: "Corroboration of the confession is required as a safeguard against the conviction of the innocent persons through the use of a false confession of guilt." *Id.* at 419.

Rule 9.3(2)   Use a Colon to Introduce Lists

There are three ways to measure a plaintiff's recovery for personal property damage: (1) if the destroyed personal property has a market value, the measure is that market value; (2) if the destroyed property has no market value but can be replaced, then the measure is the replacement cost; or (3) if the destroyed property has no market value and cannot be replaced, then the measure is the property's intrinsic value.

Rule 9.3(3)   Use a Colon to Set Up Explanations and Elaborations

The periodic polygraph examinations are arguably connected logically to the ultimate goal of Nyles's rehabilitation: to deter him from molesting children.

Mr. Baker has sustained personal property damage: his picture windows and valuable vase were smashed.

§ 9.4 The Apostrophe

Apostrophes determine who owns what. If you and your clients care about whether ownership is stated correctly, then apostrophes are worth the few minutes it takes to learn how to use them correctly.

All the apostrophe rules are important, but take special note of Rules 9.4(5) and 9.4(6). Misusing these two rules can create either ambiguity or the appearance of incompetence.

Rule 9.4(1)	**Use 's to Form the Possessive of Singular or Plural Nouns or Indefinite Pronouns Not Ending in -s**

defendant's alibi   children's guardian
a day's wages   everyone's concern

Rule 9.4(2)	**Use 's to Form the Possessive of Singular Nouns Ending in -s as Long as the Resulting Word Is Not Difficult to Pronounce**

James's contract   Congress's authority
business's license   witness's testimony

Three or more s sounds together are difficult to pronounce. When necessary, avoid three s sounds together by dropping the s after the apostrophe. In general, you are still correct to include the s. Using the s after the apostrophe can prevent the occasional misreading.

In the examples above, the double s ending in "business" or "witness" makes only one s sound, so when the 's is added, as in "business's" and "witness's," only two *s* sounds are required. However, when these same words are followed by words that begin with s, then you can elect to drop the s after the apostrophe for ease in pronunciation.

business' sales   witness' signature

For the same reason, many idioms that include the word "sake" drop the s after the apostrophe.

for goodness' sake   for appearance' sake

Although almost all singular proper names follow the standard rule and form their possessive by adding 's, those few proper names with internal and ending s sounds also drop the s after the apostrophe for ease in pronunciation. Note that the s sound may be made by a z or an x as well as an s.

Jesus' teaching   Alexis' prior conviction
Velasquez' hearing   Kansas' case law

But Arkansas's case law (because the final s in Arkansas is silent)

Rule 9.4(3)   Use Only an Apostrophe to Form the Possessive of Plural Nouns Ending in -s

framers' intent   workers' rights
ten dollars' worth   30 days' notice

Plural proper nouns follow the same rule.

the Smiths' attorney   the Thomases' dog

It is easier to form plural possessives correctly if you form the plural first and then apply the rules for possessives.

Singular	Plural	Plural Possessive
day→	days→	two days' labor
family→	families→	families' petition
Jones→	Joneses→	Joneses' prenuptial agreement

Occasionally a singular idea is expressed in words that are technically plural, for example, "United States," or "General Motors." In such cases, apply the rule for forming plural possessives and add just an apostrophe.

United States' commitment   General Motors' lobbyists

Rule 9.4(4)   Use 's After the Last Word to Form the Possessive of a Compound Word or Word Group

mother-in-law's statement   district manager's idea
attorney general's office   somebody else's problem
the Governor of Florida's
    recommendation

Rule 9.4(5)   To Show Joint Possession, Use 's Only After the Last Noun in a Group of Two or More Nouns; to Show Individual Possession, Use 's After Each of the Nouns in a Group of Two or More Nouns

John and Mary's stocks →   stocks are jointly owned
John's and Mary's stocks →   some stocks are owned by John;
                             some are owned by Mary

> **Rule 9.4(6)**   **To Form the Possessive of Personal Pronouns, Do Not Use an Apostrophe**

hers   its   ours   theirs   yours

Many writers confuse the contractions "it's," "they're," and "who's" with the possessive of the personal pronouns "its," "their," and "whose."

it's = it is	its = possessive of "it"
they're = they are	their = possessive of "they"
who's = who is	whose = possessive of "who"

See Quick Tip: Apostrophes (Forming the Possessive) ⊕

Besides showing possession, the apostrophe has a few other uses, including the formation of contractions and some plurals.

> **Rule 9.4(7)**   **To Form Contractions, Use an Apostrophe to Substitute for One or More Omitted Letters or Numbers**

it's = it is	ma'am = madam
they're = they are	class of '98 = class of 1998

Note that contractions are used rarely in formal writing, including most legal writing.

> **Rule 9.4(8)**   **To Form the Plural of Numbers, Letters, or Words Referred to as Words, Add 's**

seven 0's	cross all the t's and dot all the i's
1950's	replace all the and's with or's
two Boeing 787's	

Some authorities recommend adding just *s* to make numbers plural: 1950s, two Boeing 767s.

§ 9.5 Other Marks of Punctuation

§ 9.5.1 Quotation Marks

a. Identification of Another's Written or Spoken Words

There is nothing mysterious about quotation marks; they do just what their name suggests: They mark where something is quoted.

As we mentioned in section 6.2.3, many legal writers have a problem with excessive quoting. However, there are still several occasions, most notably statutes and memorable phrasing, where quoting is necessary or appropriate. For these occasions, use quotation marks around those words that are not your own and that you have taken from the cited source.

EXAMPLE 1

The relationship between Southwestern Insurers and each of its agents is governed by an agreement that includes the following statement: "The location of the agent's office cannot unduly interfere with the business established by another agent."

EXAMPLE 2

In *Ryan*, the Court of Appeals ruled that the plaintiff's choice in not swerving was "prudent under the circumstances." *Id.* at 508.

Take care to quote the source's words exactly: use the ellipsis (see section 9.5.2) to indicate any omissions you have made to the wording, and use brackets (see section 9.5.3) to indicate changes in capitalization and additions for clarity and readability.

EXAMPLE 3

In his *Roviaro* dissent, Justice Clark observed that "[e]xperience teaches that once this policy [of confidentiality] is relaxed . . . its effectiveness is destroyed. Once an informant is known, the drug traffickers are quick to retaliate." *Id.* at 67.

Notice that in Examples 2 and 3, the quotation is integrated into the writer's own sentence. When you integrate a quotation into one of your own sentences, be sure that the parts fit. The grammar of your sentence must be compatible with the grammar of the quotation.

EXAMPLE 4

Incorrect:

An actionable nuisance is "an obstruction to the free use of property, so as to essentially interfere with the comfortable enjoyment of life and property, is a nuisance and the subject of an action for damages and other further relief." Wash. Rev. Code § 7.48.010 (2016).

Revised:

An actionable nuisance is "an obstruction to the free use of property, so as to essentially interfere with the comfortable enjoyment of life and property . . . ." Wash. Rev. Code § 7.48.010 (2016).

b. Block Quotations

Do not use quotation marks around quotations of 50 words or more. A quotation of this length should be set up as a block quotation, that is, single-spaced, indented left and right, and without quotation marks.

Unfortunately, some court rules require quotation marks for block quotations. As a writer, then, determine which method your reader prefers and then apply it. Know, too, that the trend seems to be toward using block quotations for long quotations that are not quite 50 words. The rationale seems to be that it is easier for the reader to see where the quotation begins and ends.

EXAMPLE 5

Davis argues that the trial court erred in giving instruction 19, which read as follows:

> Evidence has been introduced in this case regarding the fact that stop signs were installed in the neighborhood of Ohio and Texas Streets approximately one and one-half years after the accident of December 24, 2016. You are not to consider this evidence as proof of negligence nor as an admission of negligence on the part of the City.

Block quotations also tend to highlight the quoted material; consequently, some writers use them for persuasive reasons even when the quotation is fairly short.

c. Effective Lead-ins for Quotations

In Examples 1 and 5 above, the quotations are not integrated into the writer's own sentences; instead, they are formally introduced and set up as separate statements. Notice that the language in the lead-ins prepares the reader for the quotation, sometimes by summarizing or paraphrasing the quotation, sometimes by explaining in advance why the quotation is significant.

Compare the lead-ins in the following pairs of examples. The ineffective lead-ins do little more than indicate that a quotation will follow; the effective lead-ins guide the reader into the quotation and suggest what the reader should look for in it.

EXAMPLES

Ineffective Lead-in:

The court found the following:

> The juvenile has an extensive record of adjudications and diver-sions for a variety of criminal offenses. . . . The court concludes that a sentence within the standard range would constitute a manifest

> injustice. . . . [C]ommitment . . . for a period of fifty-two (52) weeks is a more appropriate and reasonable sentence, taking into consideration the age of the defendant, his level of criminal sophistication and lack of success in rehabilitation . . . .

Effective Lead-in:

The court found a "manifest injustice" and increased Boyd's sentence because of his criminal history:

> The juvenile has an extensive record of adjudications and diversions for a variety of criminal offenses. . . . The court concludes that a sentence within the standard range would constitute a manifest injustice. . . . [C]ommitment . . . for a period of fifty-two (52) weeks is a more appropriate and reasonable sentence, taking into consideration the age of the defendant, his level of criminal sophistication and lack of success in rehabilitation . . . .

Ineffective Lead-in:

In *Curtis v. Blacklaw*, the court said the following:

Effective Lead-in:

In *Curtis v. Blacklaw*, the court explained the relationship between the standard of ordinary care and the emergency doctrine:

> [T]he existence of a legally defined emergency does not alter or diminish the standards of care imposed by law upon the actors . . . . With or without an emergency instruction, the jury must determine what choice a reasonably prudent and careful person would have made in the same situation.

Id. at 363.

Notice, too, that when a quotation is formally introduced and preceded by a colon, the portion of the sentence before the colon—the lead-in—should be grammatically complete. (See section 9.3.)

d. Quotations Within Quotations

Occasionally, something you want to quote will already have quotation marks in it, either because your source quoted someone else or because your source used a term in a special way. For a quotation within a quotation, use single quotation marks (an apostrophe on most keyboards).

EXAMPLE

"Police must discover incriminating evidence 'inadvertently,' which is to say, they may not 'know in advance the location of [certain] evidence and intend to seize it,' relying on the plain view doctrine as a pretext." *Texas v. Brown*, 460 U.S. 730, 743 (1983) (quoting *Coolidge*, 403 U.S. at 370).

e. Quotation Marks with Other Marks of Punctuation

Periods and commas go inside closing quotation marks; semicolons and colons go outside closing quotation marks. Dashes, question marks, and exclamation points go inside closing quotation marks when they are part of the quotation and outside closing quotation marks when they are part of the larger sentence.

EXAMPLES

Davis's employer described him as a "street-smart youngster who knew what not to get involved with."

The jury could have arguably considered Wilson's insulting remarks to Harris as "unlawful," thereby depriving Harris of her self-defense claim.

Parole is a "variation on imprisonment"; therefore, parole and its possible revocation are a continuing form of custody relating back to the criminal act.

The defendant asked the officer, "May I have a glass of water?"

Does Williams have standing for her claim of wrongful death when she is the person "to whom the estate of the deceased would pass under the laws of intestate succession"?

f. Other Uses for Quotation Marks

Quotation marks may also indicate that a word is being used in some special way.

EXAMPLES

Mrs. Hartley claims that her husband played "mind games" with her to get her to sign the agreement.

The Court of Appeals held that the attorney's phrasing was calculated to imply that Morris was a "hired gun" for insurance carriers.

Special terms are often introduced by phrases such as "the word" or "the term." Put the words that follow these phrases in quotation marks, but do not use quotation marks around words that follow "so-called."

EXAMPLE

The words "beyond a reasonable doubt" in the constitutional error test created confusion in the Arizona courts for some time.

Quotation marks should also be used around words that follow the terms "signed," "endorsed," or "entitled."

EXAMPLE

The contract was signed "Miss Cathryn Smith," not "Ms. Kathryn Smith."

Do not use quotation marks around the single words "yes" and "no"; do not use quotation marks around a paraphrase.

EXAMPLE

When the officer asked her if she needed a ride home, she said yes.

§ 9.5.2 Ellipses

Use the ellipsis (three spaced periods) to indicate an omission in a quotation. The ellipsis allows you to trim quotations down and focus the reader's attention on the parts of the quotation that are relevant to your case.

EXAMPLE

Helen signed a quitclaim deed to Richard, disclaiming "an interest in the . . . property."

Retain the space before the first period and after the last period in an ellipsis.

When the omission occurs in the middle of a quoted sentence, retain any necessary punctuation. Notice, for example, that the comma after "union" is retained in the following quotation because it is necessary punctuation for the sentence as it is quoted.

EXAMPLE

"We the people of the United States, in order to form a more perfect union, . . . do ordain and establish this Constitution for the United States of America."

When the omission occurs at the end of a quoted sentence, use the ellipsis to indicate that omission and then space and add a fourth period for the punctuation to end the sentence.

EXAMPLE

"We the people of the United States, in order to form a more perfect union, . . . do ordain and establish this Constitution . . . ."

When the omission occurs after the end of a quoted sentence, punctuate the quoted sentence and then insert the ellipsis. In such a case, the sentence period is closed up to the last word in the sentence.

This is demonstrated in the next two examples, both of which are quotations from the following original material.

EXAMPLES

Original Material:

The hostility/claim of right element of adverse possession requires only that the claimant treat the land as his own as against the world throughout the statutory period. The nature of his possession will be determined solely on the basis of the manner in which he treats the property. His subjective belief regarding his true interest in the land and his intent to dispossess or not dispossess another is irrelevant to this determination.

Id. at 860–61.

Quotation from the Original Material:

The hostility/claim of right element of adverse possession requires only that the claimant treat the land as his own as against the world throughout the statutory period. . . . His subjective belief regarding his true interest in the land and his intent to dispossess or not dispossess another is irrelevant to this determination.

Id. at 860–61.

Another Quotation from the Same Original:

"The hostility/claim of right element of adverse possession requires only that the claimant treat the land as his own as against the world throughout the statutory period. . . . [H]is intent to dispossess or not dispossess another is irrelevant to this determination." *Id.* at 860–61.

When the omission occurs at the beginning of the quotation, do not use an ellipsis. The reader will be able to tell that the original quotation did not begin at that point because the quotation begins with a lowercase letter.

Incorrect:

In 1995, King granted to the State a ". . . permanent easement assignable in whole or in part" over King's property. CP 106.

Correct:

In 1995, King granted to the State a "permanent easement assignable in whole or in part" over King's property. CP 106.

When the quoted material is just a phrase or clause, no ellipsis is needed before or after the quoted material.

Courts weigh the cost against the need of the other party, which must be "substantial" in order to prevail. *Doe*, 232 F.3d at 1267.

When a paragraph or more is omitted, indent and use the ellipsis plus the fourth period for the end punctuation.

The Safe Drivers' Insurance policy contains the following relevant provisions:

Definitions

> . . . .

> A car is a 4-wheel motor vehicle licensed for use on public roads. It includes any motor home that is not used for business purposes and any utility trailer.

> . . . .

> A motor vehicle is a land motor vehicle designed for use on public roads. It includes cars and trailers. It also includes any other land motor vehicle while used on public roads.

Like all good things, ellipses can be misused. Never use the ellipsis to change the original intent in the quotation. Also, take care not to overuse the ellipsis in any one quotation. Too many omissions make the quotation difficult to read.

§ 9.5.3 Brackets

Brackets are used to show changes in quotations. The most common are additions of clarifying material and changes in capitalization and verb tense.

Addition of Clarifying Material:

The defendant can emphasize that asylum seekers are in a unique position of desperate need for relief, that denial of her claim is "replete with danger . . . that [she] will be subject to death or persecution if forced to return to [her] home country." *INS v. Cardoza-Fonseca*, 480 U.S. at 449.

Capitalization Change:

The Fifth Amendment states that "[n]o person . . . shall be compelled in any criminal case to be a witness against himself." U.S. Const. amend. V.

Change in Verb Tense:

The Council authorized the construction of a 12-story tower, finding that reducing the tower to this height "substantially mitigate[s] adverse impacts on the land use pattern in the vicinity."

Use empty brackets ("[ ]") to indicate that a single letter has been omitted.

In some cases, a pronoun in a quotation may be ambiguous in the new context, so for clarity the writer substitutes the appropriate noun in brackets. In such cases, the omission of the pronoun does not need to be indicated.

At the time of her medical release, Wainwright made the following admission: "I did continue to have some pain and discomfort in my back, neck, and arms, but [Dr. Rodgers] felt this was normal pain and discomfort and that it would go away."

Occasionally, something that you want to quote has a significant error in it. In such cases, use a bracketed "*sic*" immediately after the error to indicate that the error was in the original and not inadvertently added.

On the day after the union vote was held, the shop foreman issued a memo to all machinists stating that how they voted "would not effect [*sic*] their performance reviews."

§ 9.5.4 Parentheses

In everyday writing, parentheses are used to add additional information to sentences. They are one way to signal that that information is of lesser importance or a qualification of something previously stated.

EXAMPLE

Newcombe wrested one-eighth ounce of marijuana (worth $40) from Tyson's pocket.

Because conciseness is a cardinal virtue in legal writing, legal writers usually edit out any information that is of lesser importance. Consequently, parenthetical inserts are not common in legal writing.

This does not mean that parentheses themselves do not appear anywhere in legal documents. They are frequently used in the following ways.

a. To Enclose Short Explanations of Cases Within Citations

EXAMPLES

Washington courts have held the emergency doctrine inapplicable when the actor is already in a position of peril. *Mills v. Park*, 409 P.2d 646 (Wash. 1966) (in which the defendant's vision in a snowstorm was already obscured and a snowplow throwing snow on defendant's car did not constitute a sudden emergency); *see also Hinkel v. Weyerhaeuser Co.*, 494 P.2d 1008 (Wash. Ct. App. 1972) (in which dense smoke did not constitute application of the emergency doctrine because the defendant was warned of the smoke ahead).

The costs of asserting one's Fifth Amendment right against self-incrimination that are held to be too high are often economic or proprietary costs. *See, e.g., Slochower v. Bd. of Higher Educ. of N.Y.C.*, 350 U.S. 551, 559 (1956) (holding termination of state-employed professor based on adverse inference of guilt from refusal to answer violated due process); *Spevak v. Klein*, 385 U.S. 511, 518 (1967) (holding disbarment of lawyer for asserting the privilege violated Fifth Amendment).

b. To Refer Readers to Attached or Appended Documents

EXAMPLE

Before signing the agreement, Miller crossed out the language "at time of closing" in paragraph 12 and inserted the language "pro ratio as received by sellers" in paragraph 24. (See appendix 1.)

c. To Confirm Numbers

EXAMPLE

In 2007, Patrick and Rose Milton borrowed five thousand dollars ($5,000) from Southern Security Company.

d. To Enclose Numerals or Letters That Introduce the Individual Items in a List

EXAMPLE

The company's regulations list seven circumstances under which an employee may be separated from his or her job: (1) resignation, (2) release, (3) death, (4) retirement, (5) failure to return from a leave of absence, (6) failure to return from a layoff, and (7) discharge or suspension for cause.

e. To Announce Changes to a Quotation That Cannot Be Shown by Ellipses or Brackets

EXAMPLES

"[I]solated incidents are normally insufficient to establish supervisory inaction upon which to predicate § 1983 liability." *Wellington*, 717 F.2d at 936 (footnote omitted).

The court held that "[a]n instruction, *when requested,* defining intent is required when intent is an element of the crime charged." *Id.* (emphasis added).

f. To Introduce Abbreviations After a Full Name Is Given

EXAMPLE

Beaver Custom Carpets (BCC) has been in business for one year.

§ 9.5.5 The Hyphen

Hyphens combine words to form compound modifiers or compound nouns. The trick is knowing when a pair or grouping of modifiers or nouns should be joined by hyphens to show that they are acting as one unit.

For modifiers, the first step is a simple one: If the modifiers do not precede the noun they modify, then they are usually not hyphenated.

EXAMPLES

Owens's argument ignores other rules of statutory construction that are <u>well established</u>.

Owens's argument ignores other <u>well-established</u> rules of statutory construction.

Notice that legal writers use many compound modifiers that begin with "well." As long as these modifiers precede the noun they modify, they are hyphenated.

> a well-reasoned opinion   a well-defined test
> a well-known fact   a well-founded argument

Obviously, though, not all compound modifiers begin with "well," and, unfortunately, often the only way to know whether to hyphenate is to consult a good dictionary with a recent publication date. The recent publication date is important because our language changes: What was once two or more separate words may later be hyphenated and eventually combined into one word.

$$air\ plane \rightarrow air\text{-}plane \rightarrow airplane$$

Separate

> trier of fact   prima facie case
> leave of absence

Hyphenated

> price-fixing contract   take-home pay
> out-of-pocket expenses   stop-limit order
> sudden-emergency doctrine   court-martial
> cross-examination   hit-and-run accident
>   family-car doctrine

Combined

> wraparound mortgage   quitclaim deed
> counterclaim   online
> ongoing   layoffs

Our changing language also gives us new hyphenated nouns.

> frame-up   split-off   squeeze-out

Many words are in transition. For example, you may notice that "line-up" is spelled with a hyphen in some cases and as the combined word "lineup" in others. The same is true for "pre-trial" and "pretrial" and "e-mail" and "email." In such instances, consult your most recent authority and try to be consistent within the document you are writing.

In addition to using the dictionary as a guide to hyphen use, there are a few general rules about when to use hyphens.

Rule 9.5.5(1)   Always Hyphenate Modifiers and Nouns That Begin with the Prefixes "All," "Ex," and "Self"

> all-American   all-purpose
> ex-partner   ex-employee
> self-defense   self-incrimination

Rule 9.5.5(2)	Generally Speaking, Do not Use a Hyphen with Other Prefixes, Including "Anti," "Co," "De," "Inter," "Intra," "Multi," "Non," "Para," "Pro," "Re," "Semi," and "Super"

antitrust	nonpayment
codefendant	paralegal
degenerate	prorate
interagency	reallocate
intrastate	semiannual
multinational	supersede

Unfortunately, however, there are enough exceptions to this general rule that you may often have to look up the word you need. The following exceptions apply to larger categories of words:

   a. Use the hyphen when it is needed for clarity ("re-create," not "recreate");
   b. Use the hyphen when it is needed to prevent a doubled vowel ("re-enact," "de-emphasize") or a tripled consonant;
   c. Use the hyphen when it is needed because the second element is capitalized ("post-World War II," "un-American," or "anti-Semitic").

Rule 9.5.5(3)	Use a Hyphen Before "Elect," the One Suffix That Usually Requires a Hyphen

governor-elect   president-elect

Rule 9.5.5(4)	Use Hyphens to Form Compound Numbers from Twenty-one to Ninety-nine and with Fractions Functioning as Adjectives, but Not with Fractions Functioning as Nouns

the seventy-second Congress
one-half acre *but*
   one half of the employees
two-thirds majority *but*
   two thirds of the board

Rule 9.5.5(5)	Use Hyphens to Join a Number and a Noun to Make a Compound Modifier

20-year-old appellant	ten-year lease
three-mile limit	ten-acre tract
nine-year-old conviction	first-year student

Rule 9.5.5(6)	Do Not Use a Hyphen with Certain Modifiers

Do not use a hyphen in the following instances:

    a. when the first word in a two-word modifier is an adverb ending in "-ly" ("previously taxed income," "jointly acquired property");

    b. when the compound modifier contains a foreign phrase ("bona fide purchaser," "per se violation");

    c. when a civil or military title denotes one office ("justice of the peace" but "secretary-treasurer").

Sometimes two or more compound modifiers share the same second element. In such cases, use hyphens after each first element and do not use the second element twice.

high- and low-test gasoline
nine- and ten-acre parcels

Rule 9.5.5(7)	Use Hyphens to Combine Two Parties into One Modifier

    attorney-client privilege   husband-wife tort actions

Rule 9.5.5(8)	Use a Hyphen in "Afro-American" but Not in Other Terms That Combine Races or Nationalities

Initially hyphens were common in terms such as "Mexican-American" and "Asian-American." Recently, however, the trend seems to be to drop the hyphen. The exception is "Afro-American." (See section 6.5.2.)

Rule 9.5.5(9)	In Most Cases, Use a Hyphen After "E" to Abbreviate "Electronic" Before Another Word

Most new words that have abbreviated "electronic" with an "e" before another word retain the hyphen, but both "e-mail" and "email" are now common usage.

    e-book   e-commerce

§ 9.5.6 The Dash

The traditional dash, now known as the em dash, is rarely used in legal writing. The consensus seems to be that dashes are too informal for the serious work of law.

Still, there are a few occasions when the dash is useful. For example, in sentences in which a list is an appositive, a pair of dashes can be used to signal the beginning and end of the list.

EXAMPLES

By 1996, the defendant had opened up bank accounts in several foreign countries—Switzerland, Brazil, South Africa, and Spain—all under different names.

The conservative bloc—Rehnquist, O'Connor, Scalia, and Kennedy—controlled the major cases of the 1988–1989 term.

Similarly, a dash is needed to set off an introductory list containing commas.

EXAMPLE

Name-calling, threats, and repeated beatings—these were the ways Wilson gave attention to his son.

When used with discretion, dashes can also be an effective way to create emphasis. Notice how in the following sentences, the dashes do more than the commas to highlight what they enclose.

EXAMPLES

Commas:

The victim's age, 18 months, made him particularly vulnerable.

Dashes:

The victim's age—18 months—made him particularly vulnerable.

Dashes can also be used to show abrupt shifts or to cue the reader that the words that follow are shocking or surprising.

EXAMPLE

Several witnesses—including the defendant's mother—testified that they believed Willie was capable of committing such a heinous crime.

With typesetting and increasingly sophisticated software programs, writers should distinguish between the en dash ("–"), which is slightly longer than a hyphen and found in the "symbol" or "special characters" pull-down menus, and the em dash ("—"), which is longer than an en dash.

The en dash means "to" and is used to connect numbers and occasionally words.

The advertised salary, $120,000–$140,000, was significantly more than her previous salary.

The Dallas–Chicago flight was cancelled.

Note that the en dash should not be used if the word "from" or "between" precedes the first number or word. In such instances, the words "to" and "and," respectively, should be used instead of the en dash.

The advertised salary range from $120,000 to $140,000 was significantly more than her previous salary.

The flight between Dallas and Chicago was cancelled.

PART

III

A Guide to Legal Writing for English-as-a-Second-Language[1] Writers

Legal writing is challenging for native speakers of English who have spent their lives immersed in a culture heavily influenced by the United States legal system. Even for law students raised speaking English, some of the terminology of legal prose is new, and many of the conventions are unfamiliar.

If you are an English-as-a-second-language (ESL) legal writer, you have two additional language-related challenges. First, there are numerous grammatical rules that native speakers have internalized but that non-native speakers must still learn. The first half of Chapter 10 focuses on three grammatical areas that many ESL legal writers find difficult: articles, verbs, and prepositions.

Second, if you are an ESL legal writer who was raised in a different culture, you will have naturally internalized your native culture's approach to writing. Consequently, as an ESL legal writer, you will face a second challenge: learning how native speakers of English, particularly those in the United States legal culture, approach writing. These different approaches to writing, or what we will call "rhetorical preferences," tend to affect the

---

[1] In this chapter we have used the term "English-as-a-Second-Language" and the acronym "ESL" to apply to persons who are living in the United States but whose first language is not English, as well as to persons who studied English as a foreign language when living in their home country.

whole piece of writing and include such things as what is assumed about the writer-reader relationship, how direct and explicit writers are when they explain and support their arguments, and what writing patterns are commonplace and expected. The second half of Chapter 10 addresses how the rhetorical preferences in the United States and particularly in the legal culture may differ from the rhetorical preferences of other cultures.

Legal Writing for English-as-a-Second-Language Writers

§ 10.1 Grammar Rules for Non-native Speakers of English

§ 10.1.1 Articles

Errors in the use of articles ("a," "an," and "the") are distracting to many readers. Too many missing or incorrect articles draw attention away from content and toward the errors. Consequently, most ESL legal writers find that if they want their writing to be considered professional, they must devote time and energy to mastering the use of articles in English.

One of the simplest and most effective strategies for learning the correct use of articles is to note how they are used in judicial opinions and other writing about law. Many ESL legal writers simply memorize phrases and law terminology, including how articles are used in these phrases and with these terms, from the writing of capable native speakers.

A second strategy is to learn the rules governing the use of articles in English. Unfortunately for most ESL legal writers, many of their native languages do not use articles, and others use articles in ways that are different from English. As a result, most ESL legal writers cannot rely on their native languages to help them with the rules of English articles. Instead they must learn the general rules and then be aware that there are still many exceptions.

Exhibit 10.1, on page 253, is a *decision tree* that summarizes the discussion about how to use articles with common nouns in English.

Rule 10.1.1(1)	Use the Indefinite Articles "a" and "an"[1] with Count Nouns When the Noun Is Singular and When the Reader Does Not Know the Specific Identity of the Noun

Count nouns[2] refer to persons, places, or things that can be counted. Count nouns have both a singular and plural form.

EXAMPLES

Singular Form of Count Nouns:

a contract   an easement   a trial court   an appellate court
one juror

Plural Form of Count Nouns:

contracts   easements   trial courts   appellate courts
twelve jurors

Non-count Nouns:

anger   equipment   pollution   science   testimony[3]   wealth

Remember that "a" and "an" are used only (1) with the singular form of a count noun (2) when the reader does not know the specific identity of that noun. The second part of the rule usually applies when a particular noun is mentioned for the first time in the writing because at that point the reader does not know the specific identity of the noun.

---

[1] "A" is used before consonant sounds; "an" is used before vowel sounds. Examples: "A jury," "a contract," "an assault," "an incident," "an unusual request," "an alleged victim," "an hour," "an honest man," ("h" is silent in "hour" and "honest") "a unique opportunity," "a university," "a unit," "a unanimous jury," ("u" has consonant "y" sound in "unique," "university," "unit," and "unanimous") and "a one-hour delay" ("o" has "w" sound in "one"). See **A/An** in the Glossary of Usage.

[2] Many nouns such as "paper" can be used as count or non-count nouns depending upon the particular sense in which they are used. Most ESL dictionaries indicate whether a noun is a count or non-count noun and, for nouns that can be both, under which meanings the noun is a count or non-count noun.

[3] Although the online Merriam Webster dictionary (http://www.merriam-webster.com/dictionary/testimony) includes a plural form of "testimony," United States attorneys and judges continue to treat it as a non-count noun.

(Assume "truck" is being mentioned for the first time.)
<u>A</u> truck slowly approached.

Rule 10.1.1(1) also applies when the specific identity of the noun is unknown to the writer or when the writer intends to name a general member of a class or group.

(The writer does not know the specific identity of the officer.)
<u>An</u> officer observed a truck slowly approach.

(The writer intends a general member of the class of cell phones.)
A cell phone is often a good safety precaution.

Rule 10.1.1(1) Exception	Do Not Use "a" or "an" with a Singular Count Noun That Is Preceded by Another Noun Marker

Noun markers include possessive nouns such as "Kelly's" or "Florida's," numbers, and pronouns such as "his," "her," "its," "their," "this," "that," "these," "those," "every," "few," "many," "more," "most," "much," "either," "neither," "each," "any," "all," "no," "several," and "some."

Incorrect Examples:

A this officer observed a truck slowly approach.
("This" is a noun marker, so "a" should be omitted.)

An one officer observed a truck slowly approach.
("One" is a noun marker, so "an" should be omitted.)

Corrected Examples:

This officer observed a truck slowly approach.

One officer observed a truck slowly approach.

Other common exceptions to Rule 10.1.1(1) include many prepositional phrases that are idiomatic expressions.

on vacation	by plane	by car	at home	in school
to bed	to college	in class	at night	at school
in bed				

EXAMPLE

The defendant testified that he was <u>at home</u> by 8:00 p.m. and <u>in bed</u> by 8:30 p.m.

Rule 10.1.1(2)	**Do Not Use "a" or "an" with Non-Count Nouns**

Non-count nouns refer to abstractions that cannot be counted. Non-count nouns do not have a plural form.

EXAMPLES

negligence	evidence	violence	arson	discretion

However, if an amount of a non-count noun is expressed by adding a quantifier, then an article is used before the quantifier.

a piece of evidence   an act of violence

In most instances, the following words are non-count nouns.

Nouns naming drinks and food:

water, milk, coffee, tea, wine, juice,
fruit, fish, beef, chicken, meat

Nouns naming generalized objects:

ammunition, clothing, equipment, freight, furniture, jewelry, luggage, lumber, machinery, mail, money, propaganda, scenery, stationery, traffic, vegetation

Nouns naming substances, matter, or material:

(Asterisks indicate the substance, not an object.)
air, coal, dirt, electricity, gasoline, gold, grass, hair, ice, iron*, oil, oxygen, paper*, plastic, steel, wood

Nouns related to weather:

fog, ice, rain, snow

Nouns naming subject matter:

architecture, art, chemistry, civics, economics, engineering, geology, grammar, history, literature, mathematics, music, philosophy, physics, science, and all names of languages *(Arabic, Chinese, English, French, German, Italian, Japanese, etc.)* when they are used as nouns

Nouns related to games, sports, and recreation:

(Asterisks indicate the game, not an object.)
baseball*, basketball*, bowling, bridge, camping, chess, dancing, football*, golf, hiking, hockey, hunting, opera, sailing, singing, soccer, swimming, tennis, television*, volleyball*

Abstract nouns:

advice, anger, beauty, capitalism, communism, confidence, democracy, education, employment, energy, fun, happiness, health, help, homework, honesty, ignorance, information, intelligence, justice, kindness, knowledge, laughter, liberty, life, love, merchandise, nature, news, pollution, poverty, recreation, research, satisfaction, society *(in the sense of people in general)*, strength, technology, transportation, trouble, truth, violence, virtue, wealth, wisdom, work

Some law-related nouns:

abandonment, abatement, access, acquiescence, adultery, alimony, arson, authentication, capital (in the sense of money or property), commerce, conduct, depreciation, discretion, duress, evidence, extortion, harassment, housing, insolvency, insurance, intent, land, malice, negligence, privacy, real estate, testimony

EXAMPLES

The detective found a weapon and ammunition in the defendant's trunk.
(No article before non-count noun "ammunition.")

Magistrates must exercise discretion when determining whether to authorize hidden recording devices.
(No article before non-count noun "discretion.")

Gerunds[4] and gerund phrases are non-count nouns and therefore do not require "a" or "an."

---

[4] Gerunds are verbals that end in "-ing" and that function as nouns. Gerunds with modifying phrases fall under Rule 10.1.1(3) and are preceded by "the." Example: "The drowning of her second child raised the prosecutor's suspicions."

<u>Drowning</u> was the cause of death.
(gerund)

Most attorneys enjoy <u>making arguments</u>.
(gerund phrase)

Rule 10.1.1(3)	Use the Definite Article "the" with Count[5] and Non-count Nouns When the Specific Identity of the Noun Is Clear to the Reader

The specific identity of a noun can be clear to the reader for a number of reasons.

Reason #1: Readers know the specific identity of a noun after it has already been used once in a given context.

EXAMPLE

<u>A</u> truck slowly approached. An officer noticed <u>the</u> truck contained several garbage cans.
(Use "a" before "truck" when it is first mentioned; use "the" before "truck" for subsequent references.)

Reason #2: Readers know the specific identity of a noun when it is followed by a phrase or clause that restricts or limits its identity.

EXAMPLE

<u>The</u> driver of the truck appeared nervous.
(Use "the" before "driver" because "of the truck" is a phrase that restricts or limits the meaning of "driver.")

Many but not all modifying phrases and clauses that follow a noun restrict or limit the noun's identity, thereby making it specific. You can determine which "of" prepositional phrases restrict or limit the identity of a noun by testing to see if they can be changed to the possessive form. If they can be changed to the possessive form, they are restricting or limiting the noun, so "the" should precede the noun.

---

[5] Notice that this rule applies to both singular and plural count nouns.

EXAMPLES

the driver of the truck → the truck's driver
the cost of a trial → the trial's cost
the length of the skidmarks → the skidmarks' length

Other "of" phrases, however, do not restrict or limit the identity of a noun; they show that only a part or a measured amount of the noun is intended. These "of" phrases cannot be changed to the possessive form. Use "a" or "an" before these nouns.

EXAMPLES

a pound of marijuana　　　a third of her salary
a slice of bread　　　　　a gallon of gasoline

Similarly, when a noun is followed by a phrase or clause that defines rather than restricts or limits, use "a" or "an" before the noun.

EXAMPLE

A contract that has all of its terms in writing is a formal contract.
(An "a" is used before "contract" because "that has all of its terms in writing" defines it.)

Reason #3: Readers know the specific identity of a noun when it is preceded by a superlative[6] or ranking adjective.[7]

EXAMPLES

The best example of a public figure is a film star.
(Use "the" because "example" is preceded by the superlative "best.")

The defendant was the tallest man in the line-up.
(Use "the" because "man" is preceded by the superlative "tallest.")

The plaintiff will be unable to satisfy the third element.
(Use "the" before the ranking adjective "third.")

---

[6] Superlatives compare the thing modified with two or more things. Superlatives include "best," "worst," words ending in "est" ("biggest," "smallest," "tallest," "shortest," "wisest," "fastest," "slowest," "luckiest," "loudest"), and comparisons that use "most" or "least" ("the most beautiful," "the most egregious," "the least responsible," "the least humiliating"). Be sure not to use comparative or superlative forms with things that cannot be compared ("perfect," "unique," "pregnant," "dead," "impossible," and "infinite").

[7] Ranking adjectives include sequential adjectives such as "first," "second," "third," and "next" and adjectives that show the noun is one of a kind ("unique").

Reason #4: Readers know the specific identity of a noun when both the writer and the reader have shared knowledge about the identity of the noun. Shared knowledge can be universal, such as knowledge of the sun, and it can be local, such as knowledge of a local landmark.

<u>The</u> moon provided enough light for the officers to see the defendant open his trunk.
(Use "the" before "moon" because the writer and the reader have shared knowledge about its identity.)

Numerous gang-related activities have occurred at <u>the</u> shopping mall.
(Use "the" before "shopping mall" if the writer and reader have shared knowledge about its identity as a local landmark.)

One way to determine whether a noun is specific is to ask "which one (or ones)?" For specific nouns, you will have a specific answer. When you have a specific answer, use "the." For example, if the test is applied to some of the earlier example sentences, the questions and answers are as follows:

Question: Which driver?   Answer: The driver of the truck
Question: Which example?   Answer: The best example
Question: Which element?   Answer: The third element
Question: Which moon?   Answer: The moon we all know
                                       about
Question: Which shopping   Answer: The shopping mall that is
    mall?   a local landmark

If the answer to the "which one (or ones)?" question is "any one" or "all" or "I don't know which one" or "one that has not been mentioned before," then the noun is general.

Rule 10.1.1(4)	**Do Not Use "the" Before Plural Nouns Meaning All in a Class, All of a Group, or "in General"**

Defendants have the right to an attorney.
(No "the" before "defendants" because it is plural and all defendants are intended, but "an" before "attorney" because it is singular and no specific attorney is intended.)

Appellate courts do not re-try the facts of a case.
(No "the" before "appellate courts" because it is plural and the intended meaning is appellate courts "in general"; "the" before "facts" because the

restricting phrase "of a case" makes it specific, and "a" before "case" because it is singular and no specific case is intended.)

Rule 10.1.1(5)	Do Not Use "the" Before Most Singular Proper Nouns, Including Names of Persons, Streets, Parks, Cities, States, Continents, and Most Countries

EXAMPLES

Navarro was last seen in Yellowstone National Park.

Tam offered trips to New York City, Florida, Germany, and Africa as sales incentives.

The possessive form of a singular name is also not preceded by "the."

EXAMPLE

Mr. Hempstead learned of the affair by reading Carol's email.
(No "the" before possessive "Carol's.")

Notice, however, that the plural form of proper nouns that are family names is preceded by "the." (See Rule 10.1.1(7).)

EXAMPLE

The Navarros were last seen in Yellowstone National Park.

Rule 10.1.1(6)	Use "the" with Proper Nouns Containing the Word "of"; a Political Word Such as "Kingdom," "Union," or "Republic"; or Organizational Words Such as "Institute," "Foundation," or "Corporation"

EXAMPLES

the city[8] of Los Angeles	the Republic of Korea
the University of Notre Dame	the Ford Foundation
the Intel Corporation	the Commonwealth of Virginia

---

[8] Words such as "city" are usually, but not always, written in lowercase when they precede the noun and when they appear in text. In citations, however, capitalize geographic terms such as "city." See Rule 10.2.1(f) in *The Bluebook*.

Notice that many things have two proper noun names and that "the" is only used with the form containing "of" or the political or organizational word.

the city of Los Angeles	*but*	Los Angeles
the Republic of Korea	*but*	Korea
the University of Notre Dame	*but*	Notre Dame
the Ford Foundation	*but*	Ford
the Intel Corporation	*but*	Intel
the Commonwealth of Virginia	*but*	Virginia

Do not use "the" with names of universities, colleges, or schools unless the name is written with an "of."

EXAMPLES

Harvard University Law School	the School of Law
Smith College	the College of Engineering

Rule 10.1.1(7) Use "the" Before Most Plural Proper Nouns, Including the Plural Form of a Family Name

EXAMPLES

the United States	the United Nations	the Bahamas
the Rockies	the Philippines	the Cayman Islands
the Smiths	the Joneses	the Nguyens

Rule 10.1.1(8) Use "the" Before the Names of Most Bodies of Water and the Names of Specific Geographic Regions

EXAMPLES

the Atlantic Ocean	the Mississippi River	the Persian Gulf
the Southwest	the Midwest	the Middle East

Exhibit 10.1 — Decision Tree and General Definitions for Articles in English

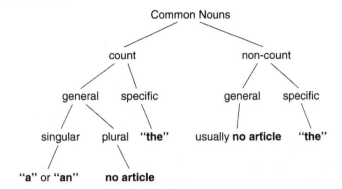

Step 1: Decide if the noun is a count or non-count noun.

Step 2: If the noun is a count noun, decide if the use of the noun is general or specific. If the use is specific, usually "the" is the correct article. Rule 10.1.1(3).

Step 3: If the use of a count noun is general, decide if the noun is singular or plural. If the noun is singular, usually "a" or "an" is the correct article. If the noun is plural, usually no article is needed. *Rule 10.1.1(4).*

Step 4: If the noun is a non-count noun, decide if its use is general or specific. If the use is general, usually no article is needed. If the use is specific, use "the." *Rule 10.1.1(3).*

Count nouns refer to persons, places, or things that can be counted. Count nouns have both a singular and plural form.

a contract	contracts	an appellate court	appellate courts
an easement	easements	one juror	twelve jurors
a trial court	trial courts		

Non-count nouns refer to entities or abstractions that cannot be counted.

negligence   evidence   violence   arson   discretion   harassment

General use of a noun usually occurs the first time a noun is used in a given context. General use of a noun also occurs when the writer intends any one of a group or class.

Specific use of a noun usually occurs for any one of the following reasons:

1. The noun has already been used once in a given context;
2. The noun is followed by a phrase or clause that restricts its identity;
3. The noun is preceded by a superlative or a ranking adjective;
4. The writer and the reader have shared knowledge about the identity of the noun.

Specific nouns will have a specific answer to the question "which one (or ones)?"

Rule 10.1.1(9)	Do Not Use "a," "an," or "the" Before Non-count Nouns Used in a General Sense or Plural Common Nouns Used in a General Sense

EXAMPLES

Information can lead to justice.
(No article before non-count nouns "information" and "justice" when used in a general sense.)

Expert witnesses have become common in courtrooms.
(No article before plural nouns "expert witnesses" or "courtrooms" when used in a general sense.)

§ 10.1.2 Verbs

Verbs present many challenges to both native and non-native speakers of English. Some of these challenges are addressed in other chapters. (Sections 8.3.1 and 8.3.2 discuss verb tense and mood, section 8.4 discusses subject-verb agreement, section 5.1 discusses active and passive voice, and sections 5.3 and 5.4 discuss action verbs and the distance between subjects and verbs.)

As an ESL legal writer, you also need to pay special attention to verb phrases that contain auxiliary, or helping, verbs and verb tenses in conditional and speculative sentences. In addition, you will need to learn which verbs commonly used in legal writing are followed by gerunds, infinitives, and objects.

a. Verbs with Auxiliary (Helping) Verbs

Unlike article errors, errors in verbs often change the meaning and are therefore much more serious. Fortunately, few ESL legal writers have difficulty with the main verbs in English verb phrases. The challenge is to learn the subtle yet often significant differences in meanings that auxiliary, or helping, verbs add to the main part of the verb phrase.

For example, "can" (or "cannot") before a verb shows ability or knowledge.

EXAMPLE

Despite his back injury, the plaintiff <u>can</u> still drive a semi-truck.
("Can" indicates the ability to drive.)

"Can" is also used to suggest that the action is a possibility or an option.

EXAMPLE   **EXAMPLE**

The defendant <u>can</u> argue that *Smith* applies.
("Can" indicates the possibility of the defendant arguing that Smith *applies.)*

Chart 10.1 lists the most common meanings for many auxiliary, or helping, verbs.

In addition to learning how meanings change based on auxiliary, or helping, verbs, ESL legal writers have to master which form of the verb is used with various helping verbs.

<u>Auxiliary, or helping, verbs that are followed by the base form</u>

Use the base form of a verb after the following auxiliary, or helping, verbs: "can," "could," "did," "do," "does," "may," "might," "must," "shall," "should," "will," and "would."

EXAMPLES

can argue	could deny	did object	may plead
might consider	must rely	should admit	will determine

<u>Auxiliary, or helping, verbs that are followed by objects and then the base form</u>

A few verbs ("make," "let," and "have") must be followed by a noun or pronoun object and then by the base form of a verb.

EXAMPLES

The children's father lets <u>them</u> <u>leave</u> for school without eating breakfast.
(pronoun)(base form)

The mother makes the <u>children</u> <u>do</u> their homework.
(noun) (base form)

The verb "help" can be followed by a noun or pronoun and then a base form or the infinitive form of a verb.

EXAMPLES

Both parents helped the children <u>learn</u> different sports.
(base form)

Both parents helped the children <u>to learn</u> different sports.
(infinitive)

Chart 10.1   Common Meanings for Auxiliary, or Helping, Verbs

Auxiliary Verb	Meanings	Example Sentences
can	shows ability or knowledge	Despite his back injury, the plaintiff can still drive a semi-truck.
	suggests possibility	The defendant can argue that *Smith* applies.
	gives an option	The prosecutor can charge the defendant with first- or second-degree murder.
could	shows past ability	Before his back injury, the plaintiff could drive a semi-truck.
	shows possibility	The defendant could argue that *Smith* applies.
could have	suggests past opportunity that was missed	The plaintiff could have learned to drive a semi-truck, but he cannot now because of his back injury.
may	asks or gives permission	Students may leave the campus during the lunch hour.
	shows possibility	The court may grant a motion to dismiss.
might	shows possibility	The court might grant a motion to dismiss.
must	shows requirement	The court must ask the defendant how she pleads.
	shows probability	The defendant must be considering a plea bargain.
must not	shows prohibition	The prosecution must not suggest that the defendant's post-arrest silence implies guilt.
should	shows advisability or expectation	The court should grant a motion to continue when the State amends a charge the day before trial.
	shows obligation	The court should instruct the jury to disregard that remark.
	shows expectation	You should receive the signed agreement in tomorrow's mail.
should have	shows obligation that was not met	The court should have instructed the jury to disregard that remark, but it failed to do so.
	shows expectation that was not met	You should have already received the signed agreement in the mail; I do not know why it is late.
	shows advisability after the fact	The officer should have handcuffed the suspect, but he did not.
ought to	shows advisability or expectation	The court ought to grant a motion to continue when the State amends a charge the day before trial.

	shows obligation	The court ought to instruct the jury to disregard that remark.
	shows expectation	You ought to receive the signed agreement in tomorrow's mail.
ought to have	shows obligation that was not met	The court ought to have instructed the jury to disregard that remark, but it failed to do so.
	shows expectation that was not met	You ought to have received the signed agreement in yesterday's mail; I do not know why it is late.
	shows advisability after the fact	The officer ought to have handcuffed the suspect, but he did not.
will	shows future time	The verdict will be announced after the parties return to the courtroom.
	shows a promise or willingness	Acme will clean up the toxic waste site.
would	indicates a repeated past action	The arsonist would often warn his victims.
	indicates a future act in a past tense sentence	The arsonist warned his victims that he would set fire to the building.

Auxiliary, or helping, verbs that are followed by the past participle of the verb

Use the past participle of a verb with "have," "has," or "had."

EXAMPLES

have determined   has begun   had stolen   has written

Auxiliary, or helping, verbs that are followed by the present participle of the verb

Use the present participle of a verb after forms of "be," including "am," "are," "is," "was," "were," "have been," and "had been."

EXAMPLES

are relying   is considering   was driving

b. Verb Tense in Conditional Sentences

Lawyers frequently use conditional sentences to express possibilities or to suggest what might happen in the future. "If" and "unless" clauses are commonly used either before or after the main clause. Use present tense in the "if" or "unless" clause and future tense in the main clause.

EXAMPLES

If the court <u>applies</u> the *Reed* test, it <u>will find</u> that the element is met.
    (present tense)   *(future tense)*

The prosecutor <u>will charge</u> the defendant with arson unless she <u>has</u> an
    (future tense)   *(present tense)*
alibi.

c. Verb Tense in Speculative Sentences

To show that an outcome is possible but unlikely, use past tense in an "if" clause and "would," "could," or "might" as the auxiliary, or helping, verb in the main clause.

EXAMPLES

If the witness <u>saw</u> the defendant's car at the accident scene, he would
    (past tense)
have also seen the defendant.

The jury might ignore its instructions if it <u>believed</u> the police fabricated
        (past tense)
the evidence.

To speculate about something that did not happen, use the past perfect tense in an "if" clause and "would have," "could have," or "might have" as auxiliary, or helping, verbs with the past participle. Remember that "had" is the helping verb that creates the past perfect tense.

EXAMPLES

If the defendant had spoken to Mr. Torres, he would have apologized to him, not threatened him.

The tenants could have complained to the building superintendent if he had been available.

To express conditions that are contrary to fact, use "were" in an "if" clause and "would," "could," or "might" in the main clause.

EXAMPLES

If I were you, I might try apologizing to the plaintiff.

If Mrs. Henderson were alive, she would not want the jury to find the defendant guilty of manslaughter.

d. Verbs + Gerunds, Infinitives, or Objects

Some verbs should be followed by gerunds (a verb form ending in "-ing" and used as a noun); other verbs should be followed by infinitives (a verb form made up of "to" plus the base form of the verb); others require objects (nouns or pronouns); and some verbs can be followed by either a gerund or an infinitive.[9] Some ESL legal writers may find that the most effective strategy for determining whether to use an infinitive or gerund after a certain verb is to apply the "Bolinger principle," which is to use infinitives to express something "hypothetical, future, unfulfilled" and to use gerunds to express something "real, vivid, fulfilled."[10]

EXAMPLES

The defendant wants <u>to enter</u> a plea of not guilty.
(The sentence expresses an as yet unfulfilled action so the infinitive is used.)

The defendant admits <u>hitting</u> the pedestrian.
(The sentence expresses a past action so the gerund is used.)

The neighbors hope <u>to obtain</u> an easement.
(The sentence expresses a future action so the infinitive is used.)

His responsibilities include <u>hiring</u> employees.
(The sentence expresses a real, not a hypothetical action.)

Exceptions

Unfortunately, the Bolinger principle does not apply to approximately one-fourth of the verbs in question, including the following verbs:

---

[9] Most verbs can also be followed by "that" clauses, e.g., "The parties agreed that the picket fence was a sufficient barrier."

[10] Dwight Bolinger, Aspects of Language (1st ed. 1968).

<u>Verbs that are exceptions to the Bolinger principle and use gerunds</u>

anticipate, consider, delay, envision, imagine, keep, mind, postpone, recommend, risk, suggest, understand

<u>Verbs that are exceptions to the Bolinger principle and use infinitives</u>

claim, continue, fail, get, have, hire, manage, teach, tell

EXAMPLES

Her attorney will recommend <u>accepting</u> the offer.
(gerund)
(The sentence expresses a future action but still uses a gerund after the verb.)

The officer managed <u>to distract</u> the gunman.
(infinitive)
(The sentence expresses a past action but still uses an infinitive after the verb.)

Consequently, many ESL legal writers may prefer using lists that group verbs according to what must follow them. Below are lists of verbs commonly used in law grouped by what follows them. The patterns for each combination are in boldface type.

<u>Verbs that are usually followed by a gerund rather than an infinitive[11]</u>

(<u>verb</u> + _____-ing)

acknowledge	disclaim
admit	discuss
advocate	dislike
anticipate	enjoy
appreciate	entail
approve	escape
avoid	evade
begrudge	facilitate
cannot help	finish
complete	get through
condemn	give up
consider	imagine
contemplate	involve
defend	justify
defer	keep
delay	keep on
deny	mention
detest	mind

---

[11] Although gerunds rather than infinitives often follow these verbs, using a gerund is not required. Many of these verbs are often followed by "that" clauses.

miss	resent
necessitate	resist
postpone	resume
practice	risk
put off	sanction
quit	shirk
recall	suggest
recollect	tolerate
recommend	understand
relinquish	visualize
relish	withhold
renounce	witness
report	

EXAMPLE

The defendant admits <u>knowing</u> the victim, but he denies <u>killing</u> him.
              (gerund)   *(gerund)*

Some verbs can be immediately followed by an infinitive; others are followed by an object and then an infinitive; still other verbs can be followed by either an object or an infinitive. When an object is between the verb and the infinitive, the object performs the action of the infinitive.

Verbs that can be followed by either an infinitive or a "that" clause with little or no change in meaning are indicated by an asterisk below.

<u>Verbs that are usually followed by an infinitive rather than a gerund</u>

(**verb + to** _____)

agree*	know how
appear	learn
arrange	manage
ask	need
attempt	offer
bother	plan
care	prepare
claim	pretend*
condescend	promise*
consent	refuse
decide*	say
demand	seem
deserve	struggle
desire	swear
endeavor	tend
expect	threaten
fall	venture
happen	volunteer
have	want
hesitate	wait
hope*	wish

The workers expect <u>to reconcile</u> their differences with management.
(infinitive)

Management plans <u>to offer</u> them a contract with a 5 percent salary
(infinitive)
increase.

The mediator hoped <u>to extend</u> the negotiation deadline.
(verb followed by infinitive "to extend")

The mediator <u>hoped that</u> the negotiation deadline would be extended.
(verb followed by "that" clause)

Verbs that can be followed by either a gerund or an infinitive

A few verbs can be followed by either a gerund or infinitive with little change in meaning.

<u>(verb</u> + _____-ing OR <u>verb</u> + to _____)

abhor	disdain
afford	dread
attempt	endure
bear	go
begin	hate
cannot bear	intend
cannot stand	like
cease	love
choose	neglect
commence	propose
continue	scorn
decline	start

Landowners continue <u>to assert</u> their rights.
(infinitive)

Landowners continue <u>asserting</u> their rights.
(gerund)

A few verbs can be followed by a gerund or infinitive but with a significant change in meaning. One common pattern, which is supported by the Bolinger principle (infinitive expresses unfulfilled action, gerund expresses fulfilled action), is that when the verb is followed by a gerund, past time is indicated; when the verb is followed by an infinitive, future time is indicated.

forget   prefer   regret   remember   sense   stop   try

Mrs. Warren remembered <u>locking</u> the safe.
(gerund)
(She has a past memory of locking the safe.)

Mrs. Warren remembered <u>to lock</u> the safe.
(infinitive)
(She did not forget to lock the safe.)

Mrs. Warren must remember <u>to lock</u> the safe.
(infinitive)
(She must remember this for the future.)

Verbs usually followed by objects, then infinitives (except in passive voice[12])

(<u>verb</u> + (object) + to _____)

advise	oblige
allow	order
appoint	permit
authorize	persuade
cause	remind
challenge	request
command	require
convince	select
encourage	teach
forbid	tell
force	tempt
get	train
hire	trust
instruct	urge
invite	warn

---

[12] In passive voice, the action of the verb is done to the subject. Example: "The motion was denied." In the example, "was denied" is done to "the motion." In active voice, the subject performs the action in the verb. Example: "The judge denied the motion." In this example, the judge is doing the denying. See section 5.1 for an extensive discussion of passive and active voice.

Opposing counsel <u>will advise</u> her <u>client</u> <u>to settle</u>.
                    (verb)   (object)(infinitive)

The judge <u>permitted</u> the <u>prosecutor</u> <u>to ask</u> questions about prior
            (verb)   (object) (infinitive)
convictions.

Acme <u>encouraged</u> its <u>employees</u> <u>to participate</u> in the political campaign.
        (verb)   (object)   (infinitive)

Acme <u>instructed</u> <u>them</u> <u>to use</u> their lunch hour stuffing envelopes.
        (verb) (object)(infinitive)

Employees <u>were permitted</u> <u>to attend</u> the rally.
              (passive verb) (infinitive)
(No noun or pronoun before infinitive because verb is in passive voice.)

Verbs that can be followed by either an object or an infinitive

(<u>verb</u> + (object)) *OR* **(<u>verb</u> + to _____)**

ask	need
beg	prefer
choose	prepare
dare	promise
expect	want
help	wish
intend	would like
like	

The landlord expected the tenants to check the batteries in the smoke
detectors.
(Object "the tenants" follows "expected.")

The landlord expected to hear tenants complain about the rent increase.
(Infinitive "to hear" follows "expected.")

Verbs followed by "too," "enough," and "how" expressions and an infinitive

Use infinitives when expressions with "too," "enough," or "how" follow
a verb.

The police arrived too late to apprehend the burglar.
("too" expression followed by infinitive "to apprehend")

The defendant is not strong enough to kick that door down.
("enough" expression followed by infinitive "to kick")

A 20-year-old woman knows how to protect herself.
("how" expression followed by infinitive "to protect")

e. Two- or Three-Word Verbs

Learning which prepositions[13] to use in two- or three-word verbs, or phrasal verbs, is crucial because the prepositions in these verbs often completely change the meaning of the verb.

One-Word Verb	*Meaning of One-Word Verb*
catch	find and stop
Two-Word Verb	*Meaning of Two-Word Verb*
catch up	to improve and reach the same standard
Three-Word Verb	*Meaning of Three-Word Verb*
catch up with	to come from behind and reach OR to find someone doing something illegal and punish that person

Because there are so many two- or three-word verbs in English and because several of them (such as "catch up with") have different meanings for different contexts, the best strategy for learning them is to note how they are used in native speakers' oral and written language. In addition, note that most of these verbs have more formal synonyms that are preferred in legal writing.

The brief must be *turned in* by 5:00 p.m. → The brief must be *submitted* by 5:00 p.m.

---

[13] The prepositions in phrasal verbs are often called "particles."

The protester *handed out* leaflets. → The protester *distributed* leaflets.

The attorney *put off* the meeting. → The attorney *postponed* the meeting.

Firefighters *put out* the blaze. → Firefighters *extinguished* the blaze.

§ 10.1.3 Prepositions

The preceding section discussed two- or three-word verbs in which the addition of one or more prepositions made a significant change to the base verb's meaning. Other English verbs, adjectives, and nouns must also be followed by specific prepositions. Unfortunately, the use of prepositions is idiomatic; it is not based on rules. Consequently, we have resorted to alphabetical lists of verbs, adjectives, and nouns commonly used in legal writing and their correct prepositions. When more than one preposition can be used with a given verb, adjective, or noun, the different preposition choices are separated by slash (/) marks. Parentheses show the types of words that may follow a given preposition. Brackets indicate meaning. Some verbs are in their present tense form; others are in their past tense form.

a. Prepositions That Follow Verbs Commonly Used in Law

absolved from (wrongdoing)
absolved of (financial liability)
accompanied by
accused of
acquainted with
acquiesced in/to
adhered to
affected by
agree on (a contract, a date)
agree to [means "to acquiesce"]
agree with [means "to be in accord with" or "have the same opinion"]
allude to
appeal from
apply for (a position)
apply to
approve of [means to "find something good or suitable"]
attribute to
based on/upon
blamed for
caused by

charge at/into/toward
charge with (murder)
comment on
commit to
communicate to [means "to express thoughts or feelings"]
communicate with [used when two people understand thoughts or feelings]
compare to [used with similarities]
compare with [used with similarities and differences]
compensate for
compete against/for
compete with
composed of
confined to
consent to
contrast with [used with differences]
convicted of (crimes)
convicted on (counts)
cooperate with

covered with

decide against/for (the plaintiff)

decide in favor of (the plaintiff)

decide on (a date)

derived from

discriminate against

distinguish between/from

divided into

divorced from

experiment with (drugs)

fill in (a crack or hole)

filled out (an application)

filled up (a tank)

filled with (emotion, light, sound)

finished with

founded by (a person)

founded in (a date)

founded on [means the main idea
that something else develops
from]

free from/to

gain access to

impressed by/with

informed about/of [means to give
information]

informed on [used when information is given to police or an
enemy]

interfere with

object to

participate in

prevent from

prohibit from

protect against/from

questioned about/concerning

reach (a conclusion) about

reach for (a gun)

recover from

refer to

rely on/upon

rescue from

resigned from

respond to

save for [means "to keep money to
use for a specific purpose"]

save from (harm or danger)

steal from

suffer from

suspected of

worry about

b. Prepositions That Follow Adjectives Commonly Used in Law

accustomed to

afraid of

amazed at

angry about/at/over/with

anxious about

appreciative of

appropriate for

ashamed of

averse to

aware of

bad at

bored with

capable of

careful about/with

certain about/of

clever at

comparable to/with

concerned about/with

confident about

confused about

conscious of

consistent with

critical of/to

dedicated to

delighted at/by/with

dependent on/upon

different from

eager for/to

enthusiastic about

excited about/by

experienced in

familiar to/with

famous for

far above/below/from

fearful of

fond of

glad about

good at/for

grateful for

guilty of

happy about/with

hopeful about/of

inconsistent with

innocent of

interested in

jealous of

known for

liable for (damages) [means "to be legally responsible for"]

liable to [means "to be likely to"]

married to

nervous about

oblivious of/to (danger)

opposed to

proud of

qualified for

quick to

regardless of

related to

responsible for

satisfied with

sensitive about/to

similar to

sorry about/for

suitable for

tired of

tolerant of

upset about/by/over

used to

c. Prepositions That Follow Nouns Commonly Used in Law

access to

amendment to

approval of

attempt at

authority on (area of expertise)

belief in

choice between/of

commitment to

complaint about/against

concern about/for/over

confidence in

confusion about/as to/over

dedication of/to

difference among (three or more)

difference between (two)

division between/of

doubt about/as to

effect of/on

experience in/of/with

explanation for/of

fear for/of

idea about/for/of

knowledge about/of

liability for

means of

need for

in need of

objection to

opposition to

participation in

possibility for/of

preference for

prevention of

process of

protection against/from

reason for

reference to

reliance on

respect for/of

response to

responsibility for

satisfaction from/in/of

search for

skill at/in

success as/in

d. Prepositions in Idioms

during the course of (his employment)

in circumstances like (those in this case)

in contrast
in favor of
in light of
on the contrary

§ 10.1.4 Sentence Patterns in Legal Writing

When lawyers write, they rely heavily on many of the same sentence patterns that all writers in English use: (1) addition; (2) cause/effect; (3) condition/result; (4) comparison; and (5) contrast. Recognizing these common sentence patterns, or templates, and learning how to use them is an important foundation for any legal writer.

In addition, lawyers tend to draw upon another set of sentence patterns that help them express some of the particular points that come up frequently in law: (6) juxtaposition; (7) concession; (8) resumption after concession; (9) sequencing for emphasis; and (10) speculation. These sentence patterns help convey some of the more nuanced and sophisticated lines of reasoning and argument that lawyers employ.

These sentence patterns build upon the basic sentence patterns we introduced in Chapters 8 and 9 in our discussion of basic sentence grammar and punctuation. The patterns act as templates or patterns to guide you, but you will need to supply the necessary language to fill in the appropriate content, use the appropriate verb tense, and know how to punctuate correctly.

a. Addition Sentence Patterns

There isn't anything simpler than just adding one idea to another. The most common sentence patterns that convey adding one idea to another are combining two main clauses with either a comma and a coordinating conjunction (*and, but, or*) or a semicolon and a conjunctive adverb or phrase (e.g., *in addition, furthermore, moreover*).

_____, and _____.
      (main clause)   *(main clause)*

EXAMPLE

Eyewitnesses said Ms. Wood looked confused, and she admitted she felt lost.

_____; in addition, _____.
      (main clause)   *(main clause)*

EXAMPLE

Eyewitnesses said Ms. Wood looked confused; in addition, she admitted she felt lost.

Notice that words or phrases like "and" or "in addition" suggest simply a second point added to the first one. Writers who want to suggest that the second point may be a stronger point might choose conjunctive adverbs or transitional phrases like "furthermore" or even "moreover."

_____; furthermore, _____.
      (main clause)   *(main clause)*

EXAMPLES

Eyewitnesses said Ms. Wood looked confused; furthermore, she admitted she felt lost.

Eyewitnesses said Ms. Wood looked confused; moreover, she admitted she felt lost.

In other words, writers can take a simple sentence pattern like the one for addition and create subtle nuances by choosing different connecting words

"and"/"in addition"	=	adding two equal points
"furthermore	=	the second point might be slightly stronger than the first
"moreover"	=	the second point is stronger than the first

With all these variations of the addition sentence pattern, the key to correct punctuation is noting whether the two main clauses are joined by a coordinating conjunction *(and, or, but, nor, for, yet, so)* or whether the two main clauses are joined by a conjunctive adverb or phrase. If the main clauses are joined by a coordinating conjunction, use a comma before the coordinating conjunction (see Rule 9.1(1)); if the main clauses are joined by a conjunctive adverb or phrase, use a semicolon before the conjunctive adverb or transitional phrase and a comma after it (see Rule 9.2(1)).

b. Cause/Effect Sentence Patterns

As you will see in the diagram below, one of the most commonly used versions of the cause/effect sentence pattern in legal writing is the same as that shown above for a conjunctive adverb or phrase. The difference, of course, is that the writer chooses from the conjunctive adverbs or phrases that signal the cause/effect relationship (e.g., *consequently, therefore, thus, as a consequence*).

_____; therefore, _____.
     (main clause—   *(main clause—*
    describes cause)   *describes effect)*

The Zaires failed to get a permit; therefore, <u>they violated a key section of</u>
          (main clause—   *(main clause—*
          describes cause)   *describes effect)*
<u>the Residential Building Code.</u>

Writers can also set up a cause/effect sentence by putting the "cause" part
of the content in a subordinate, or dependent, clause introduced by a word
like "because." Note in the diagrams that follow, when the subordinate clause
comes first, it is set off with a comma; when the subordinate clause comes
after the main clause, the comma is frequently omitted (see Rule 9.1(2)).

Because _____, _____.
          (subordinate clause—   *(main clause—*
          describes cause)   *describes effect)*

<u>Because the Zaires failed to get a building permit,</u> <u>they violated a key section</u>
<u>of the code.</u>

_____ because _____.
          (main clause—   *(subordinate clause—*
          describes effect)   *describes cause)*

<u>The Zaires violated a key section of the code because they failed to get a</u>
<u>building permit.</u>

One more subtle and sophisticated version of the cause/effect pattern
is used when the writer wants to convey that the "cause" was a given and
the "effect" was an automatic result.

The position required a CPA license; as a result, Mr. Drew did not qualify for it.

Note: Instead of "as a result" above, you could substitute "accordingly" or
"consequently."

Given that _____, _____.
          (subordinate clause—   *(main clause—*
          describes condition)   *describes result)*

The phrase "given that" itself is one way to set up this kind of cause → automatic result sentence.

<u>Given that the position required a CPA license</u>, <u>Mr. Drew did not qualify for it</u>.

A "cause" that is agreed upon, specified, or a certainty can also be introduced by "considering," "inasmuch as," "in light of," "in view of the fact that," "as a result of," or "owing to."

<u>Considering the serious injuries to the victim</u>, <u>the prosecutor will charge the defendant with first degree robbery.</u>

<u>In light of this new evidence</u>, <u>the defendant wishes to change his plea.</u>

c. Condition/Result Sentence Pattern

The most common condition/result sentences use an if/then structure (see Rule 9.1(2)).

If _____, then _____.
          (condition)   *(result)*

<u>If the court hears Mr. Singh's testimony</u>, <u>then it will find the defendant guilty</u>.
     (condition)   *(result)*

_____ if _____.
          (result)   *(condition)*

<u>The court will find the defendant guilty if it hears Mr. Singh's testimony</u>.
     (result)   *(condition)*

Note that an "if" subordinate clause that follows the main clause is always restrictive. Therefore, do not put a comma before the "if" (see Rule 9.1(4)).

d. Comparison Sentence Patterns

The diagram in subpoint a. showing two main clauses joined by a semicolon and a conjunctive adverb or phrase also works for the comparison sentence pattern. Given how frequently legal writers need to make comparisons and argue analogously, this sentence pattern is particularly useful.

_____; similarly, _____.
    (main clause—describes   *(main clause—*
    first half of comparison)   *describes second half)*

Note: In place of "similarly," you can also use "likewise."

EXAMPLE

In *Smith*, the driver was temporarily blinded by oncoming headlights; similarly, in our case, the driver was temporarily blinded by the loss of his contact lens.

Another sentence pattern that is effective in showing a comparison is mirroring the first half of a sentence with the second half. This sentence pattern allows a writer to present specifics from an analogous case and then mirror them with similar specifics from the case at hand.

_____, _____.
    (common features   *(common features*
    1a, 2a, 3a, etc.)   *1b, 2b, 3b, etc.)*

EXAMPLES

Like the driver in *Smith*, who was temporarily blinded by oncoming headlights,
     1a   *2a*   *3a*
in our case the driver was temporarily blinded by the loss of his contact lens.
       1b   *2b*   *3b*

As in *Smith*, in which the driver was temporarily blinded by oncoming headlights,
    1a   *2a*   *3a*
in our case the driver was temporarily blinded by the loss of his contact lens.
 1b   *2b*   *3b*

Notice that this second comparison pattern requires opening the sentence with "like" or "as in" or "similar to" to signal that a comparison is coming. Notice, too, that the sentences are more effective when the analogous case is discussed first.

e. Contrast Sentence Patterns

Just as lawyers often lay out the similarities between an analogous case and their case, they also distinguish cases by showing how the facts in the analogous case are different from the facts in their case. A number of sentence patterns work well for highlighting distinctions, some of which we have already seen used for other purposes. The difference, of course, is the use of a coordinating conjunction *(but),* conjunctive adverb (e.g., *however*), or transitional phrase (e.g., *on the other hand*) that signals contrast.

_____ , but _____ .
    (main clause)   *(main clause)*

_____ ; however, _____ .
    (main clause)   *(main clause)*

EXAMPLES

The accused claims he did not set the fire, but the witnesses saw him at the scene just minutes before they saw the flames and called the fire department.

The accused claims he did not set the fire; however, the witnesses saw him at the scene just minutes before they saw the flames and called the fire department.

Another pattern that is useful for contrast is one that was used for comparison. However, instead of comparing the facts in the analogous case to the facts in his or her case, the writer distinguishes the cases, using words like "unlike" rather than "like."

_____ , _____ .
   (distinguishing features   *(distinguishing features*
     1a, 2a, 3a, etc.)   *1b, 2b, 3b, etc.)*

EXAMPLE

Unlike the driver in *Smith*, who was temporarily blinded by oncoming headlights,
       1a   *2a*
the driver in our case could easily see the accident up ahead.
  1b   *2b*

Yet another pattern that conveys a subtly different contrast can be used to show that one half of a contrast is weaker, or stronger, than the other half. To signal the weaker half, the writer can introduce that half with "although" or "even though."

Although _____ , _____ .
            (weaker half)   *(stronger half)*

   Although Chu's father had told his daughter he would leave the farm to her, in his will he left the farm to his son.

_____ although _____.
        (stronger half)   *(weaker half)*

   In his will Chu left the farm to his son although he had told his daughter he would leave it to her.

f. Juxtaposition Sentence Patterns

Juxtaposition is a sophisticated form of contrast. Placing two things side by side forces comparison and highlights differences.

   One of the simplest ways of creating juxtaposition is to have two sentences, one after the other, mirror the same sentence structure. Points 1, 2, 3, and so forth in sentence 1 are mirrored in sentence 2. In the example below, the juxtaposed age and gender help to create the desired contrast.

_____, _____, _____, _____.   _____, _____, _____, _____.
     (points 1a, 2a, 3a, etc.)   *(points 1b, 2b, 3b, etc.)*

   The victim in *Lee* was a 22-year-old male. The victim in this case is a
     (1a)   *(2a)*   *(3a)*   *(1b)*
   6-year-old female.
     (2b)   *(3b)*

Juxtaposition can also be created by using two main clauses joined by a semicolon. Once again, the points should be arranged as mirror images of each other. To achieve this effect, use the same grammatical structure in the two main clauses.

_____; _____.
     (main clause)   *(main clause)*

   The victim in *Lee* was 22-year-old male; the victim in this case is a 6-year-old female.

g. Concession Sentence Pattern

Conceding a point can be a tricky business. Done well, a concession can result in the reader's finding the writer more credible. Done poorly, a concession can hurt your case and help your opponent.

One way of setting up a concession is to use words or phrases like "granted," "of course," "to be sure," or "admittedly."

Of course _____.
                (conceded point)

EXAMPLE

Of course the younger employees were paid a lower wage.

h. Resumption After a Concession Sentence Pattern

Although every lawyer will have to concede a point from time to time, the most effective advocates will have a strategy for de-emphasizing the concession and resuming their most persuasive line of argument. One approach is to pivot from the concession back to their argument or their response.

Of course _____; _____.
              (concession)   *(rebuttal)*

EXAMPLE

Of course the younger employees were paid a lower wage; they had less
                (concession)   *(rebuttal)*
experience.

Another approach for setting up the rebuttal after a concession is to use terms that signal resumption of the argument *("still," "nevertheless," "nonetheless," "even so," "all the same," "that being said,")* at the beginning of the second main clause.

_____; nevertheless, _____.
(concession main clause)   *(resumption main clause)*

EXAMPLE

The younger employees were paid a lower wage; nevertheless, they were paid a fair wage given their experience.

i. Sequencing for Emphasis Sentence Patterns

As you may recall from the discussion in section 5.6.2 on positions of emphasis, the end position in a sentence is usually the most emphatic position. Using this insight about natural emphasis, writers can create a sequence, or series, that builds to a climax.

_____, _____, _____, and _____.
    (item 1)   *(item 2)*   *(item 3)*   *(item 4)*

EXAMPLE

Before awarding custody, the judge must consider <u>the mental and physical health of all individuals involved</u>, <u>the child's adjustment to home and school</u>, <u>the wishes of the parents</u>, <u>the wishes of the child</u>, and <u>the relationship of the child with the parents</u>.

To get more out of this strategy, writers can also use an emphasizer (e.g., *"especially," "most importantly," "particularly,"*) right before the last item in the series.

_____, _____, _____, and most importantly, _____.
   (item 1)   *(item 2)*   *(item 3)*   *(emphasizer)*   *(item 4)*

EXAMPLE

Before awarding custody, the judge must consider the mental and physical health of all individuals involved, the child's adjustment to home and school, the wishes of the parents, the wishes of the child, and <u>most importantly</u>, the relationship of the child with the parents.

---

j. Speculation Sentence Patterns

In subpoint c., we discussed a common condition/result sentence pattern that uses an "if/then" structure. One important variation on the basic if/then sentence structure can be used when the writer wants to indicate speculation. To create speculation, the "if" clause in the sentence should be written in the past tense, and the "then" or result clause should use "would," "could," or "might" as an auxiliary, or helping, verb.

<u>If + past tense verb</u>_____, _____<u>"would"</u>_____.
(speculative condition)   *(possible result)*

EXAMPLE

If the witness <u>saw</u> the defendant's car at the accident scene, he <u>would</u> have also seen the defendant.

As was true with the simple version of the if/then condition/result sentence pattern, the speculation sentence pattern can also have the speculation/result precede the condition.

| _____"might"_____ | if | + past tense verb. |
| *(possible result)* | | *(speculative condition)* |

EXAMPLE

The judge <u>might</u> be sympathetic <u>if</u> she <u>believed</u> the accused was remorseful.

Occasionally lawyers will want to speculate about something that did not happen and the possible result had it happened. To do so, they use the past perfect verb tense (with "had" as the marker for past perfect) in the "if" clause and "would have," "could have, or "might have" as auxiliary, or helping, verbs in the result clause.

| If   + "had" for past perfect tense verb   , | "would have"   . |
| *(speculation about what did not happen)* | *(result that did not happen)* |

EXAMPLE

If the defendant <u>had spoken</u> to Mr. Torres, he <u>would have apologized</u> to him, not threatened him.

To show speculation, writers can also flip the speculation and result and begin the sentence with the result that did not happen.

| _____"could have"_____ | if | + "had" for past perfect tense verb   . |
| *(result that did not happen)* | *(speculation about what did not happen)* |

EXAMPLE

The tenants <u>could have complained</u> to the building manager <u>if</u> he <u>had been</u> available.

§ 10.2 Rhetorical Preferences in Writing[14]

Discourse patterns vary from language to language and from culture to culture. The way an expert writer makes a point in one culture is often quite different from the way an expert writer in another culture would make the same point. Indeed, what one culture may consider a good point in a given context, another culture might consider irrelevant in the same context.

What is particularly fascinating about this phenomenon, though, is that it often goes unnoticed. In fact, most writers have internalized their own culture's rhetorical preferences to the point that these preferences are subconscious choices. Most people seem to assume that their culture's world view and how it is expressed in writing is the way all human beings "naturally" think and write.

Because these cultural differences in discourse are so deeply embedded in language and in our subconscious, they are rarely taught to English language learners. Most ESL law students report that their foreign language classes concentrated only on vocabulary and sentence grammar; they stopped short of addressing the larger cultural issues that affect the overall approach to writing. If this was true of your language classes, you may be unconsciously assuming that what was appropriate and conventional when writing in your native language is also appropriate and conventional when writing in English. The specific preferences of legal English add even more complications.

This section examines the rhetorical preferences in expository and argumentative writing in the United States culture, with a particular emphasis on how those preferences are manifested in legal writing. The section also compares and contrasts these preferences with some of the more common rhetorical preferences from other cultures in hopes of giving ESL legal writers insights about writing in English.

Remember, however, that this is a discussion of what is generally true about writing in the discourse community of United States lawyers and judges, and that in certain instances, the generalizations will not apply. For example, while it is generally true that writing that is direct is preferred in the United States legal culture, there are occasions when vagueness or indirection better serves the writer's purposes. The discussion makes similar generalizations about writing preferences in other cultures based on the research done by contrastive, or intercultural, rhetoricians.[15] Again, like all generalizations, they may not be true in every instance, and unfortunately, the research available on rhetorical preferences in other cultures is somewhat incomplete. Even more important to remember is that language,

---

[14] This section concerns expository and argumentative writing, not literary prose.

[15] The sources for the information in the following section are in the Bibliography for ESL Law Students, which begins on page 299, and one for legal writing professors at the end of the Teaching Notes for Chapter 10 in the Teacher's Manual. Students who are interested in reading the source material that applies to their specific native language and culture should consult the Bibliography for ESL Law Students.

including rhetorical preferences, does not stand still. The information that follows will need constant updating as the rhetorical preferences of various cultures evolve.

§ 10.2.1 Cultural Assumptions About Readers and the Purposes for Writing

All cultures treat writing as an act of communication, but they differ widely in their assumptions about that communication. Some operate under the assumption that the reader bears the heavier responsibility; it is the reader who must strive to understand the writer. Other cultures operate under the assumption that the writer has the heavier responsibility; it is the writer who must strive to be understood by the reader.[16] In reader-responsible cultures, writers may intentionally obscure meaning. Good writing often has an element of mystery to it. Readers are expected to work at understanding what is written. If they fail to understand, it is their fault.

In writer-responsible cultures, writers are expected to work at being clear. Good writing is not mysterious. Writers are expected to present their ideas in ways that can be easily understood. If the reader has trouble understanding, it is the writer's fault. See Chart 10.2.

a. Assumptions and Expectations in the United States and in the United States Legal Culture

Because English is a writer-responsible language, the primary responsibility for successful communication lies with the writer. Writing clear sentences that can be understood the first time they are read is expected.[17] Being able to make a complicated topic easy for a reader to understand is admired.

The Reader's Time Is Valuable

An underlying assumption of the United States legal culture is that the reader's time is more valuable than the writer's time. Legal readers—including judges and partners in law firms—tend to have positions of power over the writers of legal prose: lawyers writing briefs for the court; interns and associates writing memoranda for supervising attorneys. Consequently, writers are expected to expend their time and energy writing clearly so that readers do not have to spend extra time and energy understanding.

In addition, United States readers tend to be far less patient than readers from other cultures. Consequently, the beginning of a piece of writing in

---

[16] John Hinds, Reader versus Writer Responsibility: A New Typology in Writing Across Languages: Analysis of L2 Text (Ulla Connor & Robert B. Kaplan eds., 1987).

[17] Clarity has not always been a top priority in legal writing. In the past, consumer contracts and statutes were often written in long, complex sentences that were difficult to understand because they were filled with abstractions and other legalese. See section 6.3.

Chart 10.2	**Writer-Responsible vs. Reader-Responsible Languages and Cultures**

English ⇩ Writer-Responsible	Most East Asian and Middle Eastern Languages ⇩ Reader-Responsible
• Primary responsibility for successful communication lies with the writer	• Primary responsibility for successful communication lies with the reader
• If the reader has trouble understanding, it is the writer's fault	• If the reader has trouble understanding, it is the reader's fault
• Writers are expected to work at being clear	• Writers may intentionally obscure meaning; good writing often has an element of mystery to it
• Writers are expected to present their ideas in ways that can be easily understood	• Readers are expected to work at understanding what is written
• Writing clear sentences that can be understood the first time they are read is expected	• Readers do not expect sentences that can be readily understood the first time they are read
• Being able to make a complicated topic easy for a reader to understand is admired	• Not fully grasping a writer's intended meaning does not frustrate these readers

the United States tends to get to the point quickly. It answers the question, "What is this about?"

Legal readers in the United States tend to expect a quick overview at the beginning of a piece of writing that sets out its content and structure. Many prefer statements of facts with an overview paragraph that introduces the parties, the legal problem, and the source of the facts. Discussion sections in legal memoranda are almost always begun by giving an overview of the law and a roadmap to its application. Even when a writer must describe how the law developed over a period of time, such historical discussion tends to be brief. The writer hits only the high points and moves rapidly toward the current state of the law. Giving some background and context for understanding the policy underlying the law is also common, but these discussions tend to be short and to the point. In general, United States legal readers want only enough background and context for the law to deal with the case before them.

As a rule, judges are even more impatient than other United States legal readers. They are eager for brief writers to get to the application of the law to the facts. Long-winded introductions or treatises on the applicable law are likely to irritate judges who are already knowledgeable about the law and who are reading the brief with the primary purpose of thinking through how that law applies to the case before them.

Introductory paragraphs in letters to clients also tend to have some features of an overview. They may include a short, polite beginning that helps establish or reinforce the relationship between the writer and reader, but then they usually move rather quickly to stating the purpose of the letter. In many cases, that means stating the legal question the client brought to the attorney and, particularly when the answer to that question is one the client will like, introducing the answer the attorney found after researching the problem.

The Reader Wants to Know What You Are Thinking: Be Direct and Explicit

To ensure that their meaning is clearly conveyed to their readers throughout a document, attorneys use two common features of the prose style used in the United States: directness and explicitness. For example, in office memoranda, which are typically in-house documents that are read only by members of the firm, writers are expected to be direct and candid with their readers. Writers should lay out the facts, the rules, the relevant cases, and the arguments each side is likely to make. Writers should tell their readers when, in the writer's opinion, the court will probably find an argument weak or persuasive. Unfavorable facts, rules, analogous cases, and weaknesses in the client's case are dealt with openly. A key objective of the office memorandum is a frank and honest assessment of the case. Some firms also want office memoranda to include some candid strategic advice, such as whether the firm should take the case or whether settling out of court might be the client's best option.

Directness manifests itself in a brief when the writer tells the court exactly what he or she wants from the court (for example, denial of summary judgment or admission of some evidence). Directness may lead a brief writer to concede a point, but it does not mean that a brief writer should be neutral or lay out the opponent's arguments in a favorable light.

Keep in mind: it is possible, of course, to be too direct with a court. Some judges and justices admit that they do not like being told by an attorney that they "must" do something even when that something is required by law. Using "should" rather than "must" in sentences such as "The court should grant the motion to suppress . . ." or "This court should find that the trial court abused its discretion . . ." allows the writer to be direct without seeming to be ordering the court around. Passive voice is another way to avoid sounding like the writer is bossing the court around. Revising "The court must grant the motion . . ." to "The motion should be granted . . ." is less likely to elicit a negative reaction from a judge. Yet another way of being direct without seeming to boss the court is to make the law the subject of the sentence—"Section 409 requires that . . . ."

In letters to clients, directness tends to be most obvious when an attorney writer is telling the client about his or her options. Attorneys writing to clients also find that it is effective to be direct about any instructions or deadlines they must convey to the client, even though these instructions and deadlines may be softened a bit with a word such as "please" (for example, "Please sign and return the enclosed documents to my office by Tuesday, December 18, 2016"). Attorney writers are also invariably direct in pointing out that their predictions are their professional opinions and not guarantees of a certain outcome. On the other hand, attorneys writing to clients tend to be slightly less direct about conveying bad or disappointing news. While the writer may save unhappy news for the end of a letter or soften the blow with an empathetic word like "unfortunately," the attorney writer will still be clear about what the bad news is.

Despite the preference for directness, most attorneys avoid first and second person references ("I" and "you") in both legal memoranda and briefs. Rather than write "I think the court will find the first element is met" in an office memorandum, most attorneys write "the court will probably find that the first element is met." Rather than write "you should consider" when addressing the court, virtually all attorneys write "the court should consider." Use of "I" and "you" is more common in letters to clients, but even there many attorneys prefer "in my opinion" to "I think" or "I believe." Even though the use of "you" is commonplace in letters to clients, indiscriminate use of "you" can make a letter seem bossy or too informal. Many attorneys prefer using "we" in letters to clients to mean both the client and the attorney. "We" conveys the impression that the two are or will be working together as a team.

Explicitness is most evident when legal memorandum and brief writers construct their arguments. Facts are analogized and distinguished explicitly. Little is left to the imagination as the writer makes explicit connections between points and draws explicit conclusions from the points he or she has made. Summaries that synthesize and repeat earlier points are admired. Indeed, explicitly drawn conclusions are hallmarks of United States legal writing.

The Writing Has to Get a Job Done

Another assumption of the United States legal culture is that writing is primarily functional; it has a job to do—explain, persuade, or both—and its value is judged almost exclusively by whether it accomplishes its purpose. Legal writers would not create prose that is aesthetically pleasing for its own sake. Eloquence is admired only when it serves the underlying purposes of explaining or persuading. Further, excessive elaboration is not considered eloquent writing; rather, it is treated as unwanted fluff or padding.

The Writer Should State and Support a Position

Writing is assumed to be the writer's own view or opinion. Readers in the United States expect writers to state a position and then defend it. Other people's writing is considered "fair game"—that is, it is completely acceptable to challenge, disagree with, or criticize the writing and analysis of another, including an expert in the field or even a court, as long as the challenge, disagreement, or criticism is well supported and directed at the ideas and arguments and not at the individual. Attacking the arguments of one's opponents is expected, but once again the criticism should address the weaknesses in the arguments and not become personal.

Support for one's ideas can take a number of forms. In United States writing in general, facts, statistics, and other "hard data" are favorite forms of support. Readers expect concrete support for most of a writer's points. The use of detail as evidence supporting one's position is considered persuasive. Simple assertions that are not backed up by supporting evidence are widely criticized as unpersuasive.

In the United States legal culture, support for one's ideas or arguments generally falls into four categories: plain language arguments, analogous case arguments, framers' intent arguments, and policy arguments. United States legal readers expect that most of a legal writer's points will be supported by cited authority. A plain language argument relies on the authority of the law and a common sense reading of it. An analogous case argument relies on the authority of another court and how it ruled in a similar case. Policy arguments often cite legislative history as the authority for statements about the policy underlying a rule. Citing to the record and using detailed facts from the case to support one's arguments are all considered effective advocacy. Conversely, assertions without support are considered poor advocacy.

When an attorney uses facts and cases to support an argument, the expectation is that attorneys will be meticulously accurate. If an attorney is caught misrepresenting a fact or a case, he or she loses credibility. Legal readers would become suspicious of that attorney's other representations of fact and law. What is also expected in the United States legal culture, however, is that attorneys writing as advocates will "characterize" the facts and case law in a light that is favorable to their client. Attorneys disagree about where the line is drawn between characterizing and misstating facts. Most agree that characterization includes emphasis. For example, favorable facts are highlighted and discussed in detail; unfavorable facts are downplayed and only mentioned briefly. Most agree that omitting key facts or cases that are unfavorable is not only dishonest and ineffective advocacy, but also a probable violation of the ABA Model Rules of Professional Conduct (2016). Virtually all agree that misstating key facts or cases is totally unacceptable and possibly even malpractice.

One way to determine whether a given way of expressing a fact or discussing a case is just a favorable characterization or an outright misstatement is to ask what the opponent would say in response. If an opponent would be inclined to say something like "I wouldn't put it that way," then the attorney can assume he or she has stayed within the legitimate boundaries of characterization. If an opponent would say "that's not true," then the attorney can assume he or she has stepped over the line into misstatement.

Assuming then that misstatement is not an option, what is still confusing is whether it is better to err on the side of understatement or on the side of overstatement. Many lawyers would argue that understatement is safer and better for building one's reputation with other attorneys and judges.

Even so, a quick survey of writing in the profession would probably show that, if an attorney is erring on one side or the other, most err on the side of overstatement.

Writing Is Like Personal Property: Avoid Plagiarism

An added complication to the United States culture's views about writing and support for ideas is its notion of plagiarism.[18] See Chart 10.3. Because people in the United States place a high value on originality, an original idea or an original expression in words is considered a valuable possession. Consequently, people in the United States culture tend to think that a writer's ideas, and especially the words a writer uses to express those ideas, are that writer's personal property. Using someone's ideas or words *without attribution* is treated like stealing that person's ideas or words. Using someone's ideas or words *with attribution*,[19] however, is a commonplace and respectable form of supporting one's own points. In fact, use of attributed quotations from experts and other authorities is considered effective support as long as the writer is selective about what he or she quotes. Overquoting, while not nearly as serious a mistake as plagiarism, is frowned upon because it suggests the writer has borrowed too heavily from other sources and has not contributed any original thinking.

Concerns about plagiarism also appear in legal writing, but they are somewhat overshadowed by the heavy emphasis on having authority for one's arguments. Citing cases, statutes, books, law review articles, and other secondary sources is considered of paramount importance. These citations show that the writer has the support of the law, other courts, and other legal minds behind his or her arguments. There is universal agreement about not only the need for citations to authority but also the use of quotation marks[20] to show that a writer has set out the exact language of a rule.[21]

There is a difference of opinion, however, in the United States legal culture about whether legal writers need to use quotation marks as well as the citation when they are using the exact language of a court. Some legal writers and readers seem to feel that court opinions are almost like public property. Others continue to be careful to use quotation marks around exact language from another court. The safe choice is to apply the same standards in legal writing as in other writing in the United States and use quotation marks around another's words.

---

[18] The Legal Writing Institute defines plagiarism as follows: "Taking the literary property of another, passing it off as one's own without appropriate attribution, and reaping from its use any benefit from an academic institution." Legal Writing Inst., Law School Plagiarism v. Proper Attribution (2003), http://lwionline.org/publications/plagiarism/policy.pdf.

[19] In some instances, writers also need the original author's express permission.

[20] Long quotations of 50 words or more are written as block quotations. No quotation marks are used with block quotations even though the wording is exactly the same as the original. See section 9.5.1b in this book, Rule 38.5(a) in the *ALWD Guide to Legal Citation,* and Rule 5.1 in *The Bluebook.*

[21] Using ellipses to omit parts of the rule that are not applicable to the matter at hand is completely acceptable.

Chart 10.3	United States Concept of Plagiarism

- People in the United States culture tend to think that a writer's ideas, and especially the words a writer uses to express those ideas, are that writer's personal property.
- Using someone's ideas or words without attribution is treated like stealing that person's ideas or words.
- When using someone else's ideas, include citations to the source; when using someone else's words, include citations to the source and use quotation marks around that person's words.

An additional important point concerns plagiarism in law school settings: In all United States law schools, plagiarizing is considered a serious ethical offense. Despite the recent shift to encouraging some limited collaboration in legal writing classes, virtually every United States law school has a student code of conduct that strictly forbids copying another student's work and representing it as one's own. Plagiarizing the words, ideas, or even the key organizational features of another student's writing has serious consequences, often including expulsion from law school. Similarly, law students writing seminar papers and law review articles must be conscientious about citing their sources and using quotation marks when they are using the language of an authority. The penalties for plagiarizing the work of a published author are usually identical to the penalties for plagiarizing the work of another student.

In United States law firms, however, very different standards apply. Attorneys who are members of the same firm often share sample forms, in-house memoranda, and even rule sections from briefs. Using the writing of another member of the firm as a model is common. Some firms even have memorandum and brief "banks," which are copies of office memoranda and briefs written by firm members that other firm members can use when they are writing about similar legal problems. This sharing within a firm is not considered plagiarism; rather, it is considered a practical way to save time and resources.

b. Assumptions and Expectations in Other Cultures

Most East Asian and Middle Eastern languages are reader-responsible languages. Consequently, not fully grasping a writer's intended meaning does not frustrate these readers. They do not expect sentences that can be automatically understood the first time they are read. Japanese readers, for example, assume that the writer may have deliberately hidden some of the meaning. Even though a Japanese writer may continually return to the theme of an article, the theme may not be stated explicitly. Similarly, Hebrew and Arabic readers expect to "read between the lines" and draw the appropriate conclusion on their own.

The tradition in Russian academic writing is for writers to show their intelligence and the importance of their ideas by being intentionally complex. Long sentences, long paragraphs, and even long paragraphs that are made up of one long sentence are admired. Writers achieve some of the complexity by using subordination, parallelism, and parenthetical comments. Using technical terms, sometimes without even defining them, adds to the complexity.

A few cultures and their written languages seem to be in a transition period. Experts in intercultural rhetoric believe, for example, that modern Chinese (Mandarin) is in the process of changing from a reader-responsible to a writer-responsible approach.

In some cultures, the best way to begin a piece of expository writing is with an appropriate proverb, parable, or anecdote. This sets a tone for the discussion that follows and also underscores the "truth" of what will be said. Thai writing, for example, tends to begin with an anecdote, is followed by specific detail, and then ends with an overall statement of the main point in the very last sentence. In Haitian Creole, or Kreyòl, essays begin with flowery and philosophical introductions and then may go on to include numerous proverbs. In Japanese prose, *ki*, which is comparable to the introduction, does not include the thesis. German writers are also taught not to state a thesis before they have set out the evidence that supports it. Other cultures favor a personal approach to beginnings; relating how the topic is connected to the writer is a common way to introduce a topic. Still others rely heavily on beginnings that develop a historical context. Arabic speakers tend to set the stage for their topics by broad statements about the general state of affairs.

The length of the introduction or how much of the total piece of writing should be taken up by the introduction also varies greatly from culture to culture. Lengthy introductions are a noteworthy feature of Spanish writing. An introduction that takes up to a third of the total pages would not be uncommon.

Rather than introducing the main point quickly, Chinese writers use a "brush clearing" or "clearing the terrain" approach. In this approach, the writer begins by discussing all the ideas related to his or her main idea. Once this is done (the brush is cleared), the main idea is ready to be explored.

As a general rule, writers in East Asian languages prefer indirectness to directness and implying meaning rather than writing explicitly. Stating one's point baldly is equated with a lack of sophistication. Chinese writers, for example, may give concrete examples, but the cultural preference is to stop after listing the examples and allow the reader to make the connections and draw the inevitable conclusion. Explicit conclusions are considered repetitious and possibly even insulting to educated readers.

Japanese writers may, as a general rule, be even more indirect than Chinese writers. Good Japanese writing implies or alludes to rather than explicitly states its points. Making a point indirectly, or hinting at meaning is regarded as a sign of intelligence and sensitivity. Directness is equated with brashness. Korean writers rarely use direct persuasion and explicit description. Arguing directly or explicitly is apt to have a negative effect on readers. The more common approach is to hide criticisms in metaphors.

The preference to be indirect is not limited, however, to writers of Asian languages. Finnish writers also tend to leave unsaid things that seem obvious.

In many cultures, writing is treated as received wisdom. Writers strive to pass along the insights of the past; consequently, readers do not assume that a writer is expressing his or her own opinion. Instead, students are encouraged first to memorize and later to repeat in their own writing the words of the respected authorities from the past. The purpose of writing in these cultures is to create harmony between writer and reader, not to debate or explicate a point of view. In China, for example, being a writer is equated with being a scholar and therefore one who knows and writes the truth.

Other cultures, by contrast, have developed a long history of skepticism about their governments and the so-called expert opinion that may be based on officially sanctioned "truth." As a result, writers in these cultures tend not to support their arguments by quoting other authorities, citing statistics that come from governmental agencies, or offering concrete proof. Polish writers, for example, tend not to refer to the work of others; instead, the dominant rhetorical techniques in their tradition are comparing and contrasting and defining and redefining.

In Japanese writing, there is a tendency to use a mix of arguments for and against a position. Japanese writers also may end an argument by taking a different position from their beginning position. Even in argumentative essays, Japanese writers tend to be somewhat tentative and use more hedges and qualifiers than do writers from other cultures.

Korean writers may use a formulaic expression like "some people say" as a way to introduce their own point of view, particularly when the position they are taking is a controversial one. The formulaic expression allows the writer to avoid being too direct and to suggest that there is other support for the position the writer states.

Other cultures treat writing more as an art than as a functional skill. Japanese writers, for example, tend to be very concerned about the aesthetics of their writing. Writers of Romance languages like Spanish or French pride themselves in using the language beautifully. Writers in Arabic also tend to place a stronger emphasis on the form of language. They prefer richness in language, particularly in the form of metaphors and other figurative language, over conciseness.

The best support for one's points varies from culture to culture. Some cultures support points through analogies, appeals to intuition, beautiful language, or references to sages from the past. Chinese writers prefer elaborate metaphors and literary references. They also use numerous references to historical events. Rather than using different pieces of evidence as support, some cultures prefer to argue the same point in many different ways. Different cultures also disagree about what is understatement and overstatement. Middle Eastern law students, particularly those who were educated in classical Arabic, may consider a supporting statement as neutral that a typical person from the United States would consider an exaggeration. What native speakers of English would consider neutral, a classical Arabic speaker would tend to view as examples of understatement.

§ 10.2.2 Culturally Determined Patterns in Writing

a. Preferences in the United States

As a general rule, students in the United States receive more direct instruction in rhetorical patterns in writing than do students in most other school systems. Composition textbooks stress paragraphs that use a general topic sentence, specific supporting sentences, and a general concluding sentence. The five-paragraph essay taught in junior high and high school expands this same general → specific → general structure over a slightly longer piece of prose. The typical term paper or research paper with its thesis statement expands the structure over a still longer piece of writing.

In other words, United States students internalize a hierarchical approach with numerous levels of subordination as the appropriate way to present ideas. In fact, the degree to which a writer uses a hierarchical approach to writing is often the basis for judging whether that writer's work is mature. Conversely, frequent use of coordination (this point "and" this point "and" this point "and" this point) is considered a sign of an immature prose style. One-sentence paragraphs are also generally frowned upon and thought to be the mark of undeveloped ideas.

Writing in the United States legal culture emulates this same hierarchical approach. An effective prose style in law typically uses an overview → analysis → synthesis organizational strategy. In fact, successful attorney writers deliberately use topic sentences, signposts, and enumeration to reveal the hierarchical organization of their line of reasoning.

Writing that is deemed "coherent" prose in the United States usually has very explicit language links to guide readers across the levels of generality and specificity. Indeed, lexical ties are the primary ways native speakers of English create coherence in their prose. These sentence-to-sentence connections result in a linear prose style. Narratives in English also tend to be linear because speakers of English perceive time as linear. Temporal-causal sequencing is typical.

English sentences tend to be written in an old information → new information pattern. Topics tend to be in the first half of sentences.

b. Preferences in Other Cultures

The traditional United States formula for writing (introduction, body, conclusion) with roadmaps and signposts along the way is considered mechanical, unsophisticated, and even childish in many other cultures. French writing, for example, uses more of a meandering approach. The writer might touch on the topic initially and then circle back to it later in the writing. Topic sentences are not part of the French writing tradition, primarily because they are deemed too obvious and condescending to readers. Contrary to the English tradition of conclusions simply summarizing what has already been said, French writers often conclude an essay by introducing a new but related topic.

The Japanese formula for prose, *ki-shoo-ten-ketsu*, is as predictable as the traditional United States structure of introduction, body, and conclusion, but the Japanese version has distinct differences. *Ki*, which is roughly comparable to the introduction, will not typically include the thesis; *shoo* will develop the argument; *ten* will abruptly shift and introduce a new sub-theme, which is often an examination of the thesis from a new angle; and *ketsu*, which is the conclusion, may state the thesis, but rather than just summarize the earlier ideas, *ketsu* may introduce some new ideas. *Ketsu* need not have the closure expected from a United States conclusion. It may end with a question or otherwise express some lingering doubt.

Korean expository essays also tend to be organized from specific to general. Like the Japanese *ketsu*, Korean conclusions may contain the thesis but only in an indirect form.

The Slavic countries such as Poland use yet another form of organization known as "circumvoluted discourse."[22] In this approach, the writer tackles a point from numerous perspectives and works toward a thesis, which is finally revealed near the end. Like the Japanese *ten*, the circumvoluted approach may seem to English readers to take the writing off course when in fact the technique is more about tackling a topic from many points of view.

Several cultures, particularly Arabic-speaking cultures, do not particularly value hierarchy and subordination in ideas. As a rule, Arabic writers are inclined to restate their positions, often with warnings, rather than support them with examples. In fact, the Arabic language has relatively few markers for subordination. Instead, parallelism is a key ingredient in Arabic for conveying a rich array of parallel ideas. Coordination and balance are the hallmarks of sophisticated Arabic prose. Unlike in English, where excessive coordination is treated as "unsophisticated," mature Arabic writers tend to join many of their ideas together with "*wa*," the Arabic word for "and." Writers in many other languages, including Chinese, also favor additive conjunctions to connect ideas.

Unlike United States writers, who tend to move from the general to the specific, Japanese writers prefer to move from the specific to the general. This tradition is reinforced in Japanese journalistic writing, which begins with details and saves the lead until much later in the story. Chinese writers also tend to use an inductive approach.

Many other cultures prefer to hide the underlying organization of a piece of writing. Numbering one's points or reasons is not favored. In general, writers in most other cultures use fewer language links than do their United States counterparts. In a few languages, most notably Puerto Rican Spanish, one- or two-sentence paragraphs are common.

Native speakers of Chinese tend to use centrifugal organizational patterns, and native speakers of Spanish tend to use linear organizational patterns but with tangential breaks. Spanish writers do not tend to use signposts or transitional words and phrases to guide readers through the text.

---

[22] Leslie Kosel Eckstein et al., Understanding Your International Students: An Educational, Cultural, and Linguistic Guide (Jeffra Flaitz ed., 2003).

Because both Chinese and Japanese are languages that rely heavily on the concept of topic, the typical sentence structure in these languages is a topic-comment structure. Consequently, ESL legal writers who have Chinese or Japanese as their first language may be inclined to replicate this sentence structure preference in English and produce what native speakers of English would consider too many sentences that begin with "as for," "in regard to," "there is," or "there are."

§ 10.2.3 Conciseness vs. Repetition

a. Preferences in the United States

In all types of expository prose in the United States, conciseness is heralded as a writing virtue. Saying a great deal in a few words is considered a sign of the writer's intelligence and respect for his or her readers. In the United States legal culture, conciseness is even more highly prized as lawyers fight to keep their heads about the paper blizzard created by complex litigation. Courts require lawyers to write within page limits. Judges warn attorneys "to be brief." Supervising attorneys chastise young lawyers to "get to the point."

In the United States legal culture, writers are expected to be concise in two different ways: They are expected to edit their sentences of all excess verbiage (see section 6.2), and they are expected to stay on track and focused on points that are central to developing a line of reasoning. Straying, even slightly, from the point puzzles and irritates legal readers in the United States, who are likely to view writing with digressions as disorganized, unfocused, and a waste of their time. In fact, one of the strongest condemnations of any part of a piece of legal writing is to label it "irrelevant."

Only in law review articles is exploration of a related side issue encouraged. However, even in law review articles, this type of digression must be done in footnotes and not in the main body of the text. A few writers have borrowed the law review footnote system as a means for exploring tangential points in memoranda and briefs, but this practice is the exception, not the norm. Many more memoranda and brief writers use appendices when they believe that some but not all of their readers might appreciate extensive supporting, background, or related information. In any case, the virtually unanimous view is that anything in the body of the text of any memorandum or brief must be directly "on point."

Although writing textbooks, including legal writing textbooks, often advise writers to be concise and denounce "needless" repetition, at least two kinds of repetition are favored in legal prose style. First, legal writers tend to repeat their conclusions. In legal memoranda, the overall conclusion may appear in both the brief answer and in the separate conclusion section. In addition, legal writers often state mini-conclusions after an extended discussion of a significant point and then draw these mini-conclusions together into an overall conclusion.

Second, when writing as advocates, lawyers tend to repeat points, albeit subtly, that are favorable to their case. In fact, many effective advocates expend a great deal of effort finding slightly different ways to emphasize essentially the same point. Brief writers who write an argumentative point heading and then open the next section with a positive assertion are often making exactly the same point but choosing a different sentence structure and slightly different words. The net effect of deliberate but subtle repetition is to create an overall theme, or theory of the case, that the writer hopes the reader will adopt. Lawyers in the United States who use subtle repetition as a form of advocacy generally know that they must use this technique selectively and carefully because they are aware that they risk annoying legal readers, particularly judges, if the repetition becomes too obvious.

b. Preferences in Other Cultures

In many other cultures, elaborate and extended prose is greatly admired. In most Romance languages, for example, sophisticated writers use frills and flourishes to embellish their points. The very kinds of digressions that United States legal readers find irritating and irrelevant are admired in many other cultures. Spanish readers, for example, consider the exploration of side points a sign that the writer is highly intelligent and well versed in the topic. French writers also have much more freedom to digress and introduce related material. Earlier we saw how Japanese writers use an organizational framework called *ki-shoo-ten-ketsu*. They shift the topic and look at it from a new angle when they are in the *ten* element.

Many cultures prefer to argue the same point in many different ways. Paragraph after paragraph says essentially the same thing with only modest additions or changes. Arabic writers, for example, pride themselves in saying the same thing in many different ways. Polish writers have a tradition of restating the same idea. Chinese writers return several times to a main idea before moving on. Their readers expect repetition; indeed, they expect Chinese writers to use and re-use stock phrases. Naturally, the repetition in all these rhetorical traditions lengthens a typical piece of writing.

See Chart 10.4, contrasting rhetorical preferences.

Chart 10.4 — Contrasting Rhetorical Preferences[1]

	U.S. Legal Writing	Chinese	Japanese	Korean	French	Spanish	Arabic	Russian
Introductions	• U.S. legal writers tend to give a quick overview at the beginning of a piece of writing that sets out its content and structure. • Beginnings in writing tend to get to the point quickly, answering the question, "What is this about?"	• Chinese writers often use a "clearing the terrain" approach, discussing all of the ideas related to the main idea before exploring the main idea.	• Japanese writers using the organizational framework called *ki-shoo-ten-ketsu*, do not typically include the thesis in *ki*, which is roughly comparable to the introduction.			• Spanish writers tend to compose lengthy introductions that may take up to a third of the total pages.	• Arabic writers tend to set the stage for topics by broad statements about the general state of affairs.	• Russian writers tend to use shorter introductions that are generally brief and dedicated to defining the significance of the topic.
Conciseness	• Conciseness—saying a great deal in a few words—is considered a sign of the writer's intelligence and respect for his or her readers. • Writers are expected to be concise by (1) editing their sentences of all excess verbiage and (2) staying on track and focusing on points that are central to developing a line of reasoning.	• Chinese writers return several times to the main idea before moving on. • Chinese readers expect repetition. • Chinese readers expect writers to use and re-use stock phrases.					• Arabic writers prefer richness in language, particularly in the form of metaphors and other figurative language, over conciseness. • Arabic writers pride themselves in making the same point in many different ways.	• Russian is an expressive language with rich grammatical variation and synonyms. Chekhov wrote, "Brevity is the sister of talent," expressing the fondness among Russian writers of looking for the perfect word and the perfect phrasing. • Russian legal writing tends to be dense and concise.

	U.S. Legal Writing	Chinese	Japanese	Korean	French	Spanish	Arabic	Russian
Directness	• Writers are generally expected to be direct and candid with their readers. • Writers should lay out the facts, the rules, the relevant cases, and the arguments each side is likely to make. • Unfavorable facts, rules, analogous cases, and weaknesses in the client's case are dealt with openly. • Although brief writers should be direct by telling a court exactly what they want, writers do not want to sound like they are ordering the court around. • Despite the preference for directness, most attorneys avoid first and second person references ("I" and "you") in both legal memoranda and briefs.	• Chinese writers may give concrete examples but the cultural preference is to stop after listing the examples and allow the reader to make the connection and draw the inevitable conclusion.	• Japanese writers may continually return to the theme of an article, although the theme may not be stated explicitly. • Making a point indirectly or hinting at meaning is regarded as a sign of intelligence and sensitivity. • Good writing implies or alludes to rather than explicitly states its points. • Directness is equated with brashness.	• Korean writers rarely use direct persuasion and explicit description. • Arguing directly or explicitly is apt to have a negative effect on Korean readers. • It is common to hide criticisms in metaphors.			• Arabic writers expect readers to "read between the lines" and draw appropriate conclusions on their own.	• Russian writers tend to show their intelligence and the importance of their ideas by being intentionally complex. • The tone of Russian legal writing is sometimes intentionally formal and official.

	U.S. Legal Writing	Chinese	Japanese	Korean	French	Spanish	Arabic	Russian
Digressions	• U.S. legal readers are likely to view writing with digressions as disorganized, unfocused, and a waste of their time. • Only in law review articles is exploration of a related side issue encouraged, and even in law review articles, this type of digression must be done in footnotes, not in the main body of the text.	• Chinese writers have much more freedom to digress and introduce related material.	• Japanese writers, using the organizational framework called *ki-shoo-ten-ketsu*, shift the topic and look at it from a new angle when they are in the *ten* element.		• French writers have much more freedom to digress and introduce related material.	• Spanish readers consider the exploration of side points a sign that the writer is highly intelligent and well versed in the topic.		• Russian literary language is full of digression. However, in academic and legal writing, digressions are avoided. Scholars and lawyers prefer to be brief, precise, and objective and avoid personal opinions.
Writer's Opinion	• Writers are assumed to be expressing their own view or opinion. • Readers in the United States expect writers to state a position and stick to it. • It is acceptable to challenge, disagree with, or criticize the writing of another, including an expert in the field or even a court, as long as the challenge, disagreement, or criticism is well supported and directed at the ideas and arguments and not at the individual.	• Writers are equated with scholars and therefore people who know and write the truth.	• Japanese writers tend to be more tentative and use more qualifiers than writers from other cultures.	• Korean writers may use a formulaic expression like "some people say" as a way to introduce their view, particularly when they are taking a controversial position.				• In Russian academic and legal writing, writers are expected to provide opinions, but those opinions must be supported by rigorous background research. • Russian writers often use the pronoun "we" instead of "I," even when the writing has a single author.

U.S. Legal Writing	Chinese	Japanese	Korean	French	Spanish	Arabic	Russian
• Writers use facts, statistics, and other "hard data" as forms of support. • Legal writers are expected to be meticulously accurate when using facts and cases to support an argument. • In the U.S. legal culture, it is also expected that attorneys, writing as advocates, will "characterize" the facts and case law in a light that is favorable to their client. • Citing cases, statutes, books, law review articles, and other secondary sources is important to show that the writer has the support of the law, other courts, and other legal minds behind his or her arguments.	• Chinese writers prefer to support their points through elaborate metaphors and literary references. • Chinese writers also use numerous references to historical events.	• Japanese writers tend to use a mix of arguments for and against a position. • Japanese writers may also end an argument by taking a different position from their beginning position.				• Arabic writers are inclined to restate their positions, often with warnings, rather than support them with examples.	• Russian writers prefer verifiable facts, research, data, statistics, and other forms of concrete support.

Support

	U.S. Legal Writing	Chinese	Japanese	Korean	French	Spanish	Arabic	Russian
Rhetorical Patterns/Organizational Strategies	• U.S. writers use a linear prose style that moves from the general to the specific. • Writers generally use a hierarchical approach with numerous levels of subordination to express their ideas. • Frequent use of coordination is considered a sign of an immature prose style. • One-sentence paragraphs are generally disfavored. • An effective prose style in law typically uses an overview analysis synthesis organizational strategy. • Successful writers use topic sentences, signposts, and enumeration to reveal the hierarchical organization of their line of reasoning.	• Chinese writers tend to use an inductive approach, moving from the specific to the general. • Native Chinese speakers tend to use centrifugal rather than linear organizational patterns. • Chinese writers favor additive conjunctions to connect ideas. • The typical sentence structure in Chinese is a topic-comment structure.	• Japanese writers move from the specific to the general. • The Japanese formula for prose, ki-shoo-ten-ketsu, is as predictable as the traditional American structure of introduction, body, and conclusion, but the Japanese version has distinct differences. • The typical sentence structure in Japanese is a topic-comment structure. • Japanese writers tend to be very concerned about the aesthetics of their writing.	• Korean expository essays tend to be organized from specific to general.	• French writing uses more of a meandering approach; the writer might touch on the topic initially and then circle back to it later in the writing. • Topic sentences are not used because they are deemed too obvious and condescending to readers. • Writers of Romance languages, like French, pride themselves in using the language beautifully.	• Spanish writers tend to use linear organizational patterns but with tangential breaks. • Spanish writers do not tend to use signposts or transitional words and phrases to guide readers through the text. • One- or two-sentence paragraphs are common. • Writers of Romance languages, like Spanish, pride themselves in using the language beautifully.	• Arabic writers do not particularly value hierarchy and subordination in ideas. • Parallelism is a key ingredient for conveying a rich array of parallel ideas. • Coordination and balance are signs of sophisticated Arabic prose. • Arabic writers tend to join many of their ideas together with "wa," the Arabic word for "and." • Arabic writers tend to place a strong emphasis on the form of language.	• Russian writers are intentionally complex, using subordination, parallelism, parenthetical comments, and technical terms, sometimes without defining them. • Long sentences, long paragraphs, and even long paragraphs that are made up of one long sentence are admired. • Russian legal writers favor a linear prose style that moves from general to specific information.

		U.S. Legal Writing	Chinese	Japanese	Korean	French	Spanish	Arabic	Russian
Conclusions		• Summaries that synthesize and repeat earlier points are admired. • Explicitly drawn conclusions are hallmarks of U.S. legal writing. • Legal writers tend to repeat their conclusions. • The overall conclusion may appear in more than one place, such as in office memoranda, where the overall conclusion may appear in both the brief answer and in the separate conclusion section.	• Explicit conclusions are considered repetitious and possibly even insulting to educated readers.	• *Ketsu*, which is roughly comparable to the conclusion, may state the thesis, but rather than just summarize the earlier ideas, *ketsu* may introduce some new ideas. • *Ketsu* need not have the closure expected from an American English conclusion. • It may end with a question or otherwise express some lingering doubt.	• Korean conclusions may contain the thesis but only in an indirect form.	• French writers often conclude an essay by introducing a new but related topic.			• Russian writers value formal conclusion sections, even when the information has been revealed before the conclusion. • The conclusion is considered a key feature of the analysis.

¹ The many empty boxes in the chart highlight the point that the work of intercultural rhetoricians is far from complete. We still have much to learn about the rhetorical preferences of many cultures.

§ 10.2.4 Some Final Thoughts

The work of intercultural rhetoricians is far from complete. As a result, readers of this chapter may be somewhat disappointed that their country or culture is not represented in the examples or that the examples do not cover every point that they would like to see made. Admittedly, more work must be done before we have a complete picture of the rhetorical preferences of various cultures.

In the meantime, our hope is that by being more explicit about some of the preferences of the United States legal culture and comparing those preferences with those of some non-United States and non-legal cultures, ESL writers can more easily adapt to writing for the United States legal culture. After all, being explicit is one of the valued characteristics of legal writing in the United States!

Bibliography for ESL Law Students and Legal Writers

For more information on reader-responsible and writer-responsible languages

John Hinds, *Reader Versus Writer Responsibility: A New Typology,* in WRITING ACROSS LANGUAGES: ANALYSIS OF L2 TEXT (Ulla Connor & Robert B. Kaplan eds., 1987).

For an excellent synthesis of the difference between the rhetorical preferences in the United States and many other cultures

María Luisa Carrió-Pastor, *A Constrastive Study of the Variation of Sentence Connectors in Academic English,* J. ENG. ACAD. PURPOSES, Sept. 2013, at 192.

Karen Englander, WRITING AND PUBLISHING SCIENCE RESEARCH PAPERS IN ENGLISH: A GLOBAL PERSPECTIVE 57 (2014).

Ilona Leki, UNDERSTANDING ESL WRITERS: A GUIDE FOR TEACHERS (1992).

Gayle L. Nelson, HOW CULTURAL DIFFERENCES AFFECT WRITTEN AND ORAL COMMUNICATION: THE CASE OF PEER RESPONSE GROUPS (1997).

Richard E. Nisbett, THE GEOGRAPHY OF THOUGHT: HOW ASIANS AND WESTERNERS THINK DIFFERENTLY . . . AND WHY (2003).

Jill J. Ramsfield, *Is "Logic" Culturally Based? A Contrastive, International Approach to the U.S. Law Classroom*, 47 J. LEGAL EDUC. 157 (1997).

Jill J. Ramsfield, CULTURE TO CULTURE: A GUIDE TO U.S. LEGAL WRITING (2005).

Julie M. Spanbauer, *Lost in Translation in the Law School Classroom: Assessing Required Coursework* in *LL.M. Programs for International Students*, 35 INT'L J. LEGAL INFO. 396 (Winter 2007).

Marcus Taft, Denisse Kacanas, Winnie Huen & Ramony Chan, *An Empirical Demonstration of Contrastive Rhetoric: Preference for Rhetorical Structure Depends on One's First Language,* 8 INTERCULTURAL PRAGMATICS 503 (2011).

Jiang Xueqin, *Thinking Right*, CHRON. HIGHER EDUC. (July 19, 2011).

For other common problem areas that appear in ESL students' writing

Diane Hacker, *ESL Trouble Spots*, in A Writer's Reference (2d ed. 1992).
Raymond C. Clark et al., The ESL Miscellany: A Treasury of Cultural & Linguistic Information (2d ed. 1981).

The remaining sources are grouped by country or language.

Arabic:

Shirley E. Ostler, *English in Parallels: A Comparison of English & Arabic Prose,* in Writing Across Languages: Analysis of 2L Text (Ulla Connor & Robert B. Kaplan eds., 1987). (Note that Ostler's research has subsequently been criticized by John Swales because Ostler compared student essays written in Arabic with published texts in English. Swales believes that contrastive rhetoricians must compare writing in the same genre.)

Terry Prothro, *Arab-American Differences in the Judgment of Written Messages*, 42 J. Soc. Psychol. 3-11 (1955).

English for Specific Purposes in the Arab World (John Swales & Hassan Mustafa eds., 1984).

Richard Yorkey, *Practical EFL Techniques for Teaching Arabic-Speaking Students,* in The Human Factors in ESL (J. Alatis & R. Crymes eds., 1977).

Japan:

John Hinds, *Japanese Expository Prose*, 13 Papers in Linguistics: Int'l J. Human Comm. 158 (1980).

John Hinds, *Linguistics & Written Discourse in Particular Languages: Contrastive Studies: English & Japanese*, in Ann. Rev. Applied Linguistics (Robert B. Kaplan et al. eds., 1979).

Keiko Hirose, *Comparing L1 and L2 Organizational Patterns in the Argumentative Writing of Japanese EFL Students,* 12 J. Second Language Writing 181 (2003).

H. Kobayashi, *Rhetorical Patterns in English and Japanese*, Dissertation Abstracts Int'l 45(8):2425A.

Hebrew:

Michael Zellermayer, *An Analysis of Oral & Literate Texts: Two Types of Reader-Writer Relationships in Hebrew & English,* in The Social Construction of Written Communication (Bennett A. Rafoth & Donald L. Rubin eds., 1988).

China:

Zhongshe Lu, Lan Li & Karen Ottewell, *Rhetorical Diversity and the Implications for Teaching Academic English,* 3 Asian J. Applied Linguistics 101 (2016).

Carolyn Matalene, *Contrastive Rhetoric: An American Writing Teacher in China*, 47 Coll. Eng. 789 (1985).

Patricia Ross McCubbin, Malinda L. Seymore, Andrea Curcio, & Llewellyn Joseph Gibbons, *China's Future Lawyers: Some Differences in Education and Outlook*, 7 Asper Rev. Int'l Bus. & Trade L. 293 (2007).

B.A. Mohan & A.Y. Lo, *Academic Writing & Chinese Students: Transfer & Developmental Factors*, TESOL Q. 19:515-534.

Robert T. Oliver, Communication & Culture in Ancient India & China (1971).
Shelley D. Wong, *Contrastive Rhetoric: An Exploration of Proverbial References in Chinese Student L1 & L2 Writing*, 6 J. Intensive Eng. Stud. 71 (1992).

India:
Robert T. Oliver, Communication & Culture in Ancient India & China (1971).

Korea:
William G. Eggington, *Written Academic Discourse in Korean: Implications for Effective Communication,* in Writing Across Languages: Analysis of L2 Text (Ulla Connor & Robert B. Kaplan eds., 1987).
Jennifer Yusun Kang, *Written Narratives as an Index of L2 Competence in Korean EFL Learners,* 14 J. Second Language Writing 259 (2005).

Thai:
Indrasuta Chantanee, *Narrative Styles in the Writing of Thai & American Students*, in Writing Across Languages & Cultures: Issues in Contrastive Rhetoric 06 (Alan C. Purves ed., 1988).

In addition to this bibliography, which was designed for writers who may wish to read the source material relevant to a particular language or culture, *The Teaching Notes for Just Writing* (4th ed.), at the end of the teaching notes for Chapter 10, contains a bibliography of other source material for legal writing professors.

Glossary of Usage

In grammar, "usage" simply means what word or phrase a native speaker of the language would use in certain situations. In legal writing, appropriate usage will typically be that of the educated professional. Choices usually reflect a conservative, more traditional view of language.

Even in law, though, usage is not static. The language of law may be traditional and formal, but it is still living and changing. As a consequence, "correct" usage varies from time to time.

In addition, all usage errors are not created equal. Some are egregious; others more forgivable. The usage questions in the following glossary marked with an asterisk (*) are important to learn first, either because they appear frequently in legal writing or because they represent an error that would distract most legal readers.

*A/An. Use "a" before words that begin with a consonant sound, and use "an" before words that begin with a vowel sound. Notice that some words begin with a vowel but still use "a" because the initial sound in the word is a consonant sound ("a university," "a one-hour delay"). A few words (usually silent "h" words) begin with a consonant but still use "an."

*Adverse/Averse. "Adverse" means "unfavorable," "opposed," or "hostile." One can get an "adverse verdict" or "adverse criticism." "Averse" means "disinclined" or "reluctant." Use "averse" to show a distaste for something or a tendency to avoid something. One may be averse to representing certain types of clients.

Advice/Advise. "Advice" is the noun; "advise" is the verb. One can "advise a client," or one can "give advice to a client."

Affect/Effect. Generally, "affect" is used as a verb meaning "to influence, impress, or sway": "The jury did not seem to be affected by the defendant's emotional appeal for mercy." "Affect" may also be used as a verb meaning "to pretend or feign": "The witness affected surprise when she was told that the signature was forged." Less common is "affect" used as a noun in psychology meaning "emotion."

The most common use of "effect" is as a noun meaning "the result, consequence, or outcome." "Effect" is also used to mean "goods," as in "one's personal effects," and "impression" as in "done for effect."

"Effect" is used as a verb meaning "to bring about or accomplish": "The mediator successfully effected an agreement between labor and management." Had the preceding example been "the mediator affected an agreement between labor and management" the meaning would have been significantly different. "Effected an agreement" means the agreement was reached; "affected an agreement" means the mediator had some influence on the agreement.

A lot. "A lot" is always spelled as two words. "Alot" as one word is never correct. Notice also that "a lot" tends to sound rather informal and may also be imprecise. For these reasons, "a lot" is often not the best choice in legal writing.

Among/Between. Use "among" when discussing three or more objects or people; use "between" when discussing two objects or people: "The members of the Board of Directors could not agree among themselves." "Attorney-client privilege refers to those confidential communications that occur between a client and her attorney."

Amount/Number. Use "amount" with nouns that cannot be counted and "number" with nouns that can be counted: "The amount of grief this mother has suffered cannot be measured by the number of dollars a jury awards her."

And/Or. Many authorities consider this usage cumbersome; others point out that it can be ambiguous, unless you use "and/or" to show that three possibilities exist (for example, husband and/or wife can mean (1) husband, (2) wife, or (3) both). Consequently, because the reader has to stop and sort through the three possibilities, it is easier on the reader to present each of the three possibilities separately (for example, "husband or wife or both").

As/Because/Since. Because "since" has at least two meanings—"from some time in the past" and "because"—some sentences that begin with "since" may be ambiguous: "Since you have made these improvements, you have used the property almost daily during the summer months." The example sentence may mean that you have used the property almost daily since you made the improvements, or it may mean that you have used the property almost daily because you made the improvements. For this reason, it is better to use "since" only for time references and "because" for cause-and-effect references. Similarly, avoid using "as" in cause-and-effect sentences because it may also be ambiguous and misunderstood to mean "while."

As/Like. "Like" can be used as a preposition, not just as a conjunction. Consequently, if a full clause follows, use "as" or "as if": "The defendant looked as if she were lying."

A while/Awhile. "A while" is an article plus a noun; "awhile" is an adverb. Use "awhile" only when it modifies a verb, not as an object of a preposition: "The shopkeeper waited awhile before answering the officer's question; then he paused for a while before showing the officer the safe."

Bad/Badly. "Bad" is an adjective; "badly" is an adverb. When the verb "feel" is used as a linking verb (a state of being, a state of mind), it must be followed by an adjective. Consequently, one "feels bad": "Olsen claims that he felt bad when he fired Baxter."

But however/But yet. These phrases are redundant; avoid them. Use just "but" or just "however" or just "yet" alone.

Can not/Cannot. Generally, they are interchangeable. "Cannot" works for almost all situations. Reserve "can not" for when permission is forbidden.

Compare to/Compare with/Contrast. Use "compare to" when pointing out only similarities; use "compare with" when pointing out similarities and differences; use "contrast" when pointing out only differences.

Complement/Compliment. A complement completes something: "Ajax, Inc. considered Smith to be the perfect complement to its sales department." A compliment is a flattering remark.

Comprise/Compose/Include. "Comprise" means "to contain": The panel comprises three judges. Notice that "is composed of" can substitute for "comprise." For precision's sake, do not substitute "include" for "comprise." "Comprise" denotes a complete listing; "include" may mean a partial listing.

Continual/Continuous. "Continual" means "frequently repeated"; "continuous" means "unceasing": "His clients' continual complaint was that he never returned telephone calls." "Continuous water flow cools the reactor."

Convince/Persuade. To convince someone means to change that person's mind; to persuade someone means to move that person to action: "Ms. O'Brien's goal was to convince Mr. Taylor that she was hardworking and then persuade him to give her a raise."

Study Aid

Use "convince of" or "convince that" but "persuade (object) to."

Criteria/Criterion. "Criteria" is the plural form; "criterion" is the singular form. "Acme published the following criteria for the new position: a four-year college degree, experience in sales, and willingness to travel.

It waived the first criterion for applicants who had completed Acme's own in-house training program."

Different from/Different than. Use "different from" unless the resulting sentence would be awkward.

Disinterested/Uninterested. "Disinterested" means "neutral, unbiased"; "uninterested" means "bored": "We want judges to be disinterested, not uninterested, in the cases before them."

Eminent/Imminent. "Eminent" means "distinguished," "prominent," or "high ranking." An expert witness may be an "eminent scholar." "Imminent" means "about to happen" or "impending." "Imminent" is often used with danger or misfortune as in the phrases "imminent attack," "imminent disaster," or "imminent harm."

Etc. Avoid using "etc." in legal writing. Whenever possible, replace "etc." with specifics, or use the appropriate English equivalent ("and so forth" or "and others") instead. Never use "and etc." This phrase is redundant; it means "and and so forth."

Every day/Everyday. If something happens each day, use "every day." If something is commonplace or routine, use "everyday."

Farther/Further. Use "farther" for geographical distances and "further" for showing other additions: "The placement of the fence suggested that the property line was farther north." "We can discuss this matter further after we have more facts."

Fewer/Less. Use "fewer" for objects that can be counted; use "less" for generalized quantities or sums that cannot be counted: "Elaine used fewer sick days than any other employee. She also had less work."

***Good/Well.** Use "good" as an adjective and "well" as an adverb, except when referring to health: "The prosecutor is a good lawyer who prepares well for trial. Will the witness be well enough to testify in court?"

Hanged/Hung. Use "hung" as the past tense for "hang" in all situations except executions: "The counterfeit bill was framed and hung in the lobby." "The whistleblower was hanged by the members as a warning to others."

***Have/Of.** "Have," not "of," should be used after the auxiliary verbs "could," "should," and "would": "The plaintiff could have offered a compromise before initiating the lawsuit."

***Imply/Infer.** "To imply" means "to indicate, suggest, or express indirectly": "At the show-up, the police officer implied that the defendant was the assailant when he asked, 'Don't you think that's him?'" "To infer" means "to deduce, conclude, or gather": "The jury may infer that the defendant is guilty if it hears about her prior convictions." Use "infer" when the actors in the sentence are drawing inferences *from* something.

Is when/Is where. Do not use these constructions in sentences that are definitions. A well-crafted definition should have a noun following "is": "An endowment is the transfer of money or property to an institution." Not: "An endowment is when someone transfers money or property to an institution."

*Its/It's. "Its" is the possessive form of "it." Like many other pronouns, "it" forms the possessive by simply adding "s," not "'s" (hers, yours, ours). "It's" is a contraction for "it is" or sometimes "it has." Because contractions are generally avoided in legal writing, "its" or spelling out the words "it is" will be the correct choices in most legal writing.

Lay/Lie. "Lay" is a transitive verb, which means it must have an object. "Lay" means to "put, place, or set down": "Just lay the file on my desk." "Lie" is an intransitive verb, which means it does not have an object. "To lie" means "to recline or remain": "The file will lie unopened on my desk until the bill is paid."

Literally. "Literally" is not an all-purpose intensifier. It has a specific meaning: "exactly what the words say." The improbable sentence "The defendant was literally on pins and needles waiting to hear the verdict" means that somehow the defendant was positioned atop pins and needles.

*Lose/Loose. "Lose" is the opposite of "win": "I am afraid you will lose in court." It can also mean "to mislay." "Loose" is the opposite of "tight": "The victim described his attacker as wearing loose clothing."

On/Upon. In almost every instance, "upon" is just a more stilted way of saying "on." Some writers still prefer "upon" when they want to convey an upward motion, but in most other circumstances, "on" is preferable.

*Principal/Principle. "Principle" is a noun meaning a "rule, truth, or doctrine": "The principle of negligence per se may make the plaintiff's evidentiary burden easier." "Principal" can be a noun meaning "the head person or official." In finance, "principal" also means "the capital sum," as distinguished from interest: "The principal of Lincoln High School authorized an investment that earned less than one percent on the principal." In criminal law, a principal is the chief actor or perpetrator or aider and abettor present at the commission of the crime. In real estate, a principal is a person who empowers another to act as his or her representative: "The broker owes his principal, the seller, loyalty and good faith."

"Principal" as an adjective means "main" or "chief": "The principal question before the jury is whether the eyewitness is credible."

The reason is because. Do not use this construction. Replace with "the reason is that."

Supposed to/Used to. Be sure to include the final "d" in both expressions.
Sure and/Sure to. Always use "be sure to."

*Than/Then. Use "than" for comparisons, such as "taller than," "greater than," "more than," and "rather than." Use "then" to denote a time.

That. (When it cannot be omitted).Do not omit the subordinate conjunction "that" when it will prevent a possible misreading. This problem occurs when a noun clause is used as the direct object. In such cases, the subject of the noun clause alone can be misread as the direct object. *Incorrect:* "Florida courts found a woman who had attempted three suicides and had been committed to a state mental hospital was an unfit and improper person." *Corrected:* "Florida courts found that a woman who had attempted three suicides and had been committed to a state mental hospital was an unfit and improper person."

That/Which/Who. Use "that" and "which" for things; use "who" for people. Use "that" for restrictive clauses and "which" for nonrestrictive clauses: "The defendant's truck, which does not have oversized tires, was identified by the victim as the vehicle that hit him." The clause "which does not have oversized tires" is nonrestrictive because it does not restrict or limit the meaning of "defendant's truck." Unless the defendant has more than one truck and the reader needs the clause to determine which truck is meant, the phrase "defendant's truck" is already clearly identified. The clause "that hit him," on the other hand, restricts or limits the meaning of the noun "vehicle."

   Exception: "Which" is used in restrictive clauses that use the constructions "that which," "of which," or "in which."

*Their/There/They're. "Their" is the possessive form of "they." "There" denotes a place ("stay there"), or it can be used as an expletive ("There is one last point I want to make"). "They're" is a contraction for "they are."

Through/Thru. Always use "through."

Thus/Thusly. Always use "thus."

*To/Too/Two. "To" is a preposition with a great number of functional and idiomatic uses: "The defendant drove back to the city. To his surprise, the police had set up a roadblock. Ultimately, he was sentenced to death." "Too" is an adverb meaning "also," "very," or "excessively": "His story was too implausible." "Two" is the number.

Toward/Towards. Both are acceptable; "toward" is preferred in the United States because it is shorter.

Try and/Try to. Always use "try to."

Use/Utilize. Whenever possible, use "use."

When/Where. "When" denotes a time; "where" denotes a place. When indicating a particular situation, choose "when" or "in which," not "where." Avoid the expression "a case where . . . ." A case is not a place. Replace with "a case in which . . . ." Common practice, however, seems to be to use "where" in parentheticals after citations.

Which/Who. "Which" should not be used to refer to people.

Who/Whom. Use "who" in most subject positions and "whom" in most object positions. (See below for the exception.)

This rule of thumb means, however, that you will have to analyze a sentence before you can determine whether "who" or "whom" is correct. One easy way to analyze question sentences is to answer the question. If in the answer you use the subjective form ("I," "we," "he," "she," or "they"), then use "who" in the question. If in the answer you use the objective form ("me," "us," "him," "her," or "them"), then use "whom" in the question.

Who is calling? *(He is calling.)*
(subject)

To whom does the clerk report? *(The clerk reports to her.)*
  (object)

For some questions, you may find it easier to determine whether to use "who" or "whom" if you recast the sentence in normal subject/verb/object order.

Whom should I pay?
(object)

I should pay whom? *(I should pay them.)*

The greatest confusion concerning "who/whom" occurs in sentences in which the same pronoun appears to be the object of one part of the sentence and the subject of another part of the sentence.

> The police questioned a woman who they thought matched the victim's description.

The sentence above is correct. Although "who" may appear to be the object of "they thought," it is actually the subject of "matched the victim's description." A simple way to determine which form of the pronoun is correct in such situations is to mentally delete the subject/verb immediately after the "who" or "whom." If the sentence still makes sense, use "who"; if not, use "whom."

> The police questioned a woman who ~~they thought~~ matched the victim's description.

Use the same method to determine that "whom" is the correct choice in the following example.

> The man whom the police questioned matched the victim's description of her assailant.

> The man whom ~~the police questioned~~ matched the victim's description of her assailant.

When the subject and verb following the "who/whom" slot are deleted, the second sentence no longer makes sense. Notice too that you can isolate the clause "whom the police questioned," put it in normal order, "the police questioned whom," and answer the question ("the police questioned him") to determine that "whom" is the correct form.

Exception: The one exception to the rule is that "whom" is used for subjects of infinitives.

Whom does our client want to represent him?

Our client wants whom to represent him? *(normal word order)*

Our client wants her to represent him. *(Answer the question or substitute another pronoun.)*

Your/You're. "Your" is the possessive form of "you." "You're" is the contraction for "you are."

Index